GEARS AND GOD

TECHNOCRATIC FICTION, FAITH, AND EMPIRE IN MARK TWAIN'S AMERICA

NATHANIEL WILLIAMS

The University of Alabama Press
Tuscaloosa

The University of Alabama Press
Tuscaloosa, Alabama 35487-0380
uapress.ua.edu

Inquiries about reproducing material from this work should be addressed to the
University of Alabama Press.

Typeface: Minion and Futura

Cover image: From the cover of the dime novel "Over the Andes with Frank
Reade, Jr., in His New Airship, or Wild Adventures in Peru," *Frank Reade Weekly
Magazine*, no. 28; (New York: Frank Tousey, May 8, 1903); courtesy of Digital
Collections, University of South Florida
Cover design: David Nees

Cataloging-in-Publication data is available from the Library of Congress.
ISBN: 978-0-8173-1984-7
E-ISBN: 978-0-8173-9186-7

GEARS
AND
GOD

For my family
with love and gratitude

Contents

Illustrations

Acknowledgments

When I began searching for articulations of religious faith in proto-science-fiction series, I knew I would need help doing two things: accessing many of the rare (and not-yet-available-online) texts and developing a methodology for analyzing the connections between at least one series of texts that numbered in the hundreds. Whatever original contributions this book makes came about because many people pointed me in the right directions.

I must thank a number of librarians who have preserved rare nineteenth-century texts and made them accessible to scholars. Thanks to Lynne M. Thomas and the staff at Northern Illinois University Libraries for helping me utilize the LeBlanc dime novel collection and securing funding for trips through a Horatio Alger Fellowship. Thanks to Eric Frazier at the Library of Congress, Elspeth Healy at the University of Kansas Libraries, Matthew Knight at University of South Florida Libraries, Meredith Mann at the New York Public Library, and Robert Hirst, Ben Griffin, and Neda Salem at the Mark Twain Papers at University of California, Berkeley, all of whom provided access to material at key junctures. Finally, thanks to Roberto Delgadillo from the University of California, Davis, whose ongoing support has been invaluable.

I want to thank colleagues and mentors who viewed the earliest versions of some of these chapters and offered suggestions for their development: Philip Barnard, Susan K. Harris, Laura Mielke, Philip Baringer, and James E. Gunn. Priscilla Wald and Amy Devitt provided early advice. Chris McKitterick, Kij Johnson, and the staff of the Gunn Center for the Study of Science Fiction provided support along the way. Many thanks to Hsuan Hsu,

Bruce Michelson, and Elizabeth Miller, who read drafted portions and offered insights. Pamela Bedore, J. Randolph Cox, Brooks Landon, Benedict Jones, and Jess Nevins generously shared ideas at conferences and by e-mails. Reverend Eric Laverentz helped contextualize Presbyterian church history. Colleagues and friends in the Mark Twain Circle of America offered encouragement. I also want to thank the speculative fiction writers who have taken time to discuss their work crafting stories set in (or inspired by) the nineteenth century, particularly Bradley Denton, Tim Powers, and Howard Waldrop. Their imaginative work often preserves public interest in the *real* C19 as much as academic scholarship.

The Academic Federation at the University of California, Davis, helped make this book possible by providing a Non-Senate Faculty Professional Development Award. The Horatio Alger Society supported my library fellowship at NIU. Additional thanks to sponsors of AboutSF at the Gunn Center for the Study of Science Fiction, including Tor Books, the Science Fiction and Fantasy Writers of America (SFWA), and the Science Fiction Research Association (SFRA).

Material from chapter 3 appeared in *American Literature* and material from chapters 1 and 6 appeared in *Nineteenth-Century Contexts*. I am grateful to Dan Waterman and the staff at the University of Alabama Press, as well as the two anonymous peer reviewers for their help in shaping the final version of this book.

Finally, thanks to my colleagues in the University Writing Program at UC Davis, who are an inspiration to me daily.

GEARS
AND
GOD

Introduction

"This is Religious, and Totally Different"

Early in Mark Twain's *Tom Sawyer Abroad* (1894), Tom explains his view of international relations to Huck Finn. Tom is bored after his adventures recounted in Twain's previous books, and he has decided that he wants to go on a crusade to liberate the Holy Land. Huck, as Tom's commonsensical and humane foil, points out that this notion doesn't sit right with him. After all, Tom admits that the Holy Land doesn't belong to them, and that people living there have "always" lived there.[1] Huck reasonably states that it seems unjust to run someone out of the home where they have always lived. If someone owned a farm, he asks, wouldn't it be unfair for someone else to take it from him? Tom replies:

> Oh, shucks! You don't know enough to come in when it rains, Huck Finn. It ain't a farm, it's entirely different. You see, it's like this. They own the land, just the mere land, and that's all they *do* own; but it was our folks, our Jews and Christians, that made it holy, so they haven't any business to be there defiling it. It's a shame, and we ought not to stand it a minute. We ought to march against them and take it away from them. . . .
>
> Farming is just business, just common low-down business: that's all it is, it's all you can say for it, but this is higher, this is religious, and totally different. (21–22)

Tom's education, drawn from the Bible and books about chivalric knights, has limited his ability to empathize with the Holy Land's non-Christian inhabitants and encouraged his desires for international conquest. While Huck avoids this trap by immediately considering the situation from the Middle Eastern Arabs' point of view, Tom relies on the narrative for justification of his hypothetical crusade. By the novel's end, Tom gets his longed-for trip to the Holy Land, but not the way he expects. Tom, Huck, and their friend, the former slave Jim, become stowaways in a fantastic, winged aerial "balloon" that is prematurely launched on its maiden voyage; Tom inadvertently guides the ship across the Atlantic and into Egypt and the Middle East after the craft's inventor/pilot disappears overboard. Tom, Huck, and Jim never "liberate" the Holy Land, but they see the Sahara, the Pyramids, and Mount Sinai, and Tom finds the excitement for which he longed.

In Tom's adventure, we find a comingling of American obsessions: exploration of faraway locations, appeals to biblical or established Christian narratives, and adoration of new, mobile technology. Stories featuring this combination were ubiquitous in Twain's era; Tom's balloon was far from the only giant airship in American fiction of the late 1800s. In fact, he wasn't the first fictional boy to pilot an airship across the globe accompanied by an older African American man and a boisterous friend with an Irish surname. That honor goes to Frank Reade Jr., whose dime-novel exploits sent him traveling in submarines and airships with his partners, an Irishman named Barney O'Shea and an African American named Pomp. By 1894, the year *Tom Sawyer Abroad* was published, over fifty tales featuring Frank, Barney, and Pomp had been released, many in a weekly series bearing the main character's name, *The Frank Reade Library*. And Reade Jr. was only the tip of the "boy inventor" iceberg. There were recurring characters like Tom Edison Jr., "Electric Bob," and others who built airships, submarines, and other fanciful modes of transportation. Reade Jr. and his ilk appeared at least as cocksure and intelligent as Tom Sawyer, but their adventures were presented un-ironically, never beckoning readers to question their young, white protagonists' authority as Twain did. Twain appropriated elements of the "boy inventor" story to sardonically show Tom's naiveté, a trait his character shared with many real-life Americans who agreed with the sort of Christian exceptionalism Tom embraced. Naïve or not, by melding travel and technology with appeals to a religiously grounded American nationalism, the dime novel stories accomplished essentially the same cultural work as *Tom Sawyer Abroad*. The sheer number of such texts—over three hundred published in roughly ten years—suggests Americans were drawn to this material.

While their heyday occurred in the late 1800s, these technocratic adventure novels inspired later fiction about science and technology, and they have been periodically rediscovered by writers and editors. In these moments of historical reevaluation, the narrative's legacy becomes most apparent. One significant moment, for example, came in the 1920s when publisher Hugo Gernsback profiled these nineteenth-century, proto-science fiction novels in his magazine *Science and Invention*. Gernsback was trying to define the kind of fiction he would eventually publish a few years later when he founded *Amazing Stories*, the first modern magazine devoted exclusively to science fiction and the one that shaped—for good or ill—the twentieth-century American public's view of that genre in all its silver-rocket and bug-eyed-monster glory.[2] Gernsback's interest in "boy inventor" stories, along with his love of Edgar Allan Poe, Jules Verne, and H. G. Wells, led to the inception of science-fiction periodical publishing. But within Gernsback's burgeoning definition of genre boundaries was an appeal to the same religious status quo that Tom Sawyer embodied a generation earlier. The October 1920 issue of *Science and Invention* magazine—the same issue with an article profiling the Frank Reade Jr. series—features a cover stating "Science Explains the Great Flood." A full-color painting adorns the cover, with an enormous tidal wave about to crash down on tiny, silhouetted people in the bottom, left corner. The article, "What Caused the Great Flood?" is sandwiched between the magazine's standard assortment of write-ups about new inventions and advertisements for correspondence courses in engineering and drafting. It offers an explanation for the flood described in the book of Genesis, noting fossil evidence of a worldwide flood and mentioning professors who assert the biblical story of the deluge was founded in fact. The story culminates by presenting a "plausible reason" that posits as follows:

> If some celestial body in its wanderings thru the heavens past [*sic*] sufficiently close to the earth, that is within ten or twelve thousand miles, there is no question of a doubt that such an encounter would have caused havoc on earth. . . . The mutual gravitational influences would then raise tremendous tidal waves. . . .
>
> Now if Noah had been, as he presumably was, a wise man, he no doubt would have been able to foresee what was coming, just as any astronomer can foretell the return of a comet years in advance.[3]

This article, approved and likely written by Gernsback, suggests much about the conceptualization of science and religion by the magazine's audience. Gernsback's *Science and Invention* catered to an American readership drawn to "how to" engineering projects, scientific fiction, and new technology articles.[4] While the article begins with a caveat that the flood is "not taken seriously" by most scientists, it nevertheless portrays the Bible as an authoritative historical source, featuring the biblical Noah as a real, historical figure. Not a literalist interpretation of the book of Genesis, it is instead a "between the lines" reading that imagines Noah as a science-savvy astronomer without deviating from the original story's details. The imagined scenario allows science to take a prominent role in the story, while supporting the Bible's place as factual history and cornerstone of American consciousness. *Science and Invention*'s explanation, of course, is pure conjecture; the hypothesis simply provides a *possible* explanation of the flood rather than a scientific verification of the event. For my purposes, the article is less important for the theory presented by Gernsback the would-be scientist than for what it demonstrates about Gernsback the publisher. Clearly, he sensed that an article offering an allegedly scientific explanation of the biblical flood, presented as a factual, historical occurrence, would sell magazines, not merely as an article but as the month's cover story. Like Twain, the editor knew the bulk of his American audience were technophiles and pious Christians, the Tom Sawyers of the early twentieth century. Gernsback understood that American audiences—including his magazine's target market of technology enthusiasts, basement tinkerers, and would-be engineers— were receptive to narratives in which science and mainstream Christianity were made to blend harmoniously.

Gears and God. Faith and technology. This book examines connections between these two American obsessions by charting the development of a cultural narrative about technology, expansion, and religion that made discussions such as the 1920 flood article possible. Faith in both God and technology drove expansionist fervor in the United States, and technophilic fiction sprang from these circumstances. Their appeal continues in our current era of iPhones and intelligent-design textbooks. We rely upon discussions of religious faith and technology to inform our national consciousness, and we trot out their respective iconographies and nomenclatures to distinguish one type of American from another: creationists from evolutionists, technophobes from bleeding-edge power users, true believers from agnostics. The late nineteenth century's proliferation of fiction featuring technologists traveling to remote parts of the globe was, on the surface, a celebration of progress and novelty, envisioning technologists as powerful, independent heroes on uncharted frontiers. On a deeper level, these tales provoked consideration of what the era's audience saw as core American values: pro-technology, pro-expansion, and pro-Christianity. This narrative ultimately reinforced prevailing views toward science and religion. By the time of Gernsback's article, its conceptual cornerstone—the notion that applied science and technology could help "prove" biblical stories—had been repeated in decades of popular nineteenth-century fictions.

Despite their influential narrative, most of these novels rarely have been studied beyond science-fiction genre histories or collections where they are often (somewhat reluctantly) relegated to the amorphous "proto-science fiction" sideline, while studies of post-Gernsback publishing of the 1930s and beyond dominate the contents.[5] In a 2009 roundtable sponsored by the journal *Science Fiction Studies*, Brooks Landon noted the need for an "overdue culturally-oriented exploration of dime novels we have thought of as early sf but have not so far considered outside the narrow formal context of genre history."[6] Similarly, Carter Hanson ended a study of nineteenth-century British proto-SF by emphasizing the need for "a more complete study of . . . the American dime novel invention story [to] not only shed light on a neglected genre of American fiction but also bring into sharper relief the anxiety" found in British variants of the same texts.[7] To that end, I want to accomplish two things: a reevaluation of the portrayal of empire that has pervaded earlier, genre-exclusive studies of these texts, and a consideration of their role in larger nineteenth-century conversations about science and technology's impact on religious faith. The latter aspect is overdue for consideration, particularly in light of other studies of nineteenth-century literature from postsecular American literary studies. Witness, for example, Dawn Coleman's work on nineteenth-century sermons, which uncovers the profound influence religious oratory had on nineteenth-century American life.[8] Her work challenges the "implicit secularism of the humanities" by recovering moments when the language and rhetoric of the sermon is deployed by nineteenth-century writers such as Melville and Stowe. Similarly, Tracy Fessenden reads popular religious writing, such as *The New England Primer*, alongside figures such as Twain and James. Subsequently, Fessenden has reminded Americanists studying sacred texts to avoid treating literature itself as a sacred category and to resist categorizing the religious concepts in literature into a false good/bad dichotomy.[9] Clearly, dime-novel stories about flying boats or "electric alligators" have little risk of being interpreted in some Matthew Arnold–like reading that grants them spiritual insight in a godless modernity, certainly not compared to, say, Walt Whitman's poetry of the same era. Nevertheless, the fiction covered herein was conversant with Americans' religious preoccupations and fears during the end of the nineteenth century. It hides in plain sight, part of a neglected, apparently secular, scientific genre aimed at popular audiences. While many of these novels and short stories are forgotten today, they influenced Americans like Gernsback who were already enamored with technology. Their ideas filtered into twentieth-century science fiction, and are still with us. This, then, is the story of how that exploration narrative became part of America's cultural consciousness and how it persists.

The first chapter defines the technocratic exploration narrative and contextualizes it within the debates regarding science and faith during its era. The narrative became formalized over multiple retellings, primarily during the last three decades of the nineteenth century. Each story features a core structure in which a protagonist uses advanced technology to access a distant location and/or engage in adventures at that destination. Through their reiteration, particularly in hundreds of dime novels aimed at young audiences, these novels facilitate the American audience's burgeoning faith in technology. This technophilia grows at a time when skepticism about science, particularly Darwinian evolutionary theory, is also on the rise. While they contribute to the public's conceptualization of technology and science as separate spheres, they also begin to incorporate appeals to religious authority. By the end of the century, technocratic exploration stories often include encounters with evidence that validates the Bible's portrayal of history. Their assertion that technological travel can potentially reestablish the Bible as an authority on historical matters found a receptive audience in turn-of-the-twentieth-century America.

The second chapter examines the first major dime-novel articulation of the form: Edward S. Ellis's *The Steam Man of the Prairies* (1868). The story of a disabled boy and his anthropomorphized machine, it is the first novel-length science-fiction work produced in the United States, and it established the template for subsequent technocratic exploration tales. The story's protagonist, genius adolescent inventor Johnny Brainerd, builds a steam-driven automaton to enable him to travel to the frontier despite physical disabilities that would prevent him from making the journey otherwise. This dime novel conceptualizes technology as prosthetic and anthropomorphized, and it wholeheartedly embraces an expansionist agenda as Johnny attacks opponents who would prevent him from succeeding in the West. To clarify its central importance to the technocratic exploration tale, I contrast it with earlier variants of imaginative US fiction dealing with expansion and technology. Washington Irving's nightmarish portrayal of a lunar invasion in *A History of New York* shows an early national writer willing to use a proto-science fiction narrative to challenge American technocratic thought, including religion's integral place in that conceptualization. Furthermore, no story better demonstrates the pervasiveness of US expansionism in tales of technology than Edgar Allan Poe's short "The Man That Was Used-Up," now understood as the earliest portrayal of a cyborg in American letters. Like Johnny Brainerd, Poe's titular hero is an expansionist adventurer who uses technology to augment a disabled body. Poe's own ambivalence about technology gives his tale a satirical edge that *Steam Man* lacks, but it essentially demonstrates science fiction's push to yoke its imaginary inventions to exploration.

The third chapter argues that the technocratic exploration tale was capable of articulating multiple, contradictory understandings of empire—even in the same dime-novel series. To do this, I consider a technocratic dime novel series that developed over two decades and featured well over 100 separate novels. Taken collectively, these stories—featuring the exploits of globe-trotting boy inventor Frank Reade Jr.—clearly outline an imperial allegory in which technology enables individuals to travel to remote locations and justifies their autocratic interference with events in those regions. In each novel, Reade Jr. builds a device that helps him reach an exotic locale and have adventures there. While the series shares the militaristic bent of the *Steam Man* novel that inspired it, it contains nuances that subvert its own apparent imperialistic core. The series' primary writer, Cuban American author Luis Philip Senarens, develops a narrative formula that avoids considering technology's transformative impact on society, and the stories consistently stop short of considering the kind of long-term implications of empire. Although they have been derided for being racist and imperialist, the Reade novels contain oddly inconsistent treatments of race and empire. Nowhere is this more prevalent than in the stories written and edited by Senarens between 1895 and 1898. Evidence shows that Senarens used his editorship at Tousey to counter pro-imperialist attitudes toward Cuba during that country's revolution against Spain. To this end, he wrote three stories using the two most popular inventor heroes of his era—Frank Reade Jr. and his doppelganger, Jack Wright—to promote Cuban sovereignty.

The fourth chapter returns to Senarens's Frank Reade series to uncover its engagement with biblical literalism. If dime-novel technocratic exploration could not fully function as imperialist allegory, it could affect the American imperial consciousness by reinforcing its Judeo-Christian underpinnings. Foreshadowing Twain's *A Connecticut Yankee in King Arthur's Court* (1889), the series' technocratic hero occasionally exploits "superstitious" religious people by passing off his inventions as divine powers. Despite this element, the novels consistently treat the Bible's portrayal of history with a good deal of reverence and precision. During the 1890s, the same period when the Reade series took an overtly anti-imperialist turn, multiple storylines presented scenarios in which the protagonist discovered evidence of Old Testament history in his journeys to remote destinations. These tales treat traditional Scripture as "fact" from which plausible stories may be drawn. In doing so, they promote a worldview where technology discovers these links to the past, reasserting the Bible's historical authority. They favor technocratic expansion not for the power or wealth it can grant young imperialists, but for its potential to reconcile the split between science and religion.

How did technocratic exploration novels' use of religious tropes shape

America's imperialist identity? The fifth chapter answers this question by looking at the work of two men who willfully injected religious commentary into the form. One was a failed politician from the Midwest whose battles with spiritual doubt and mental illness were destroying him; the other was his younger brother, who was becoming the most famous American author on the planet. In 1878, Orion Clemens wrote a technocratic exploration manuscript and mailed it to his sibling, Samuel, for critique. The manuscript uses a scientific expedition to the center of the earth to mock Protestant notions of hell and the afterlife. While the complete manuscript is lost, portions survive along with Sam Clemens's biting and sarcastic response, replies that include some of his frankest statements of his own views regarding technology and religion. Their conversation about religion, exploration, and the technocratic novels of Jules Verne clearly had a profound impact on both men. While Orion attempted to wrestle with religious doubt explicitly by using the form, his brother discouraged this approach. Of course, Samuel Clemens's fascination with technology, religion, and empire would inform his subsequent works as Mark Twain, most notably *A Connecticut Yankee in King Arthur's Court* and *Tom Sawyer Abroad* (1894). His well-known, late-life stance against US imperialism is prefigured by these satirical novels. Moreover, they show a major American author toying with the idea that Protestant Christianity would facilitate and drive technocratic exploration. Twain's technocratic exploration novels present characters with seemingly unreflective pro-expansionist stances, but they undermine this by suggesting that their protagonists' religious presumptions cause their downfalls.

The sixth chapter examines later technocratic exploration novels that articulated assertions of the Protestant Christian status quo in the face of evolutionary science's growing erosion of this view of history. Some works, such as Anna Adolph's independently published *Arqtiq* (1899), share Orion Clemens's idiosyncratic interpretations of travel and religion. Others, such as the early polar exploration novel of Twain's biographer, Albert Bigelow Paine, mock their explorers' secularism. But such articulations are also found in better-known, widely published fiction of their day. Garrett P. Serviss's *Edison's Conquest of Mars* (1898) and Pauline Hopkins's *Of One Blood* (1903), for example, use technocratic exploration tropes to consider scenarios in which discoveries made by scientists in remote locations would reaffirm the Bible's portrayal of history. Hopkins asserts an Africa-centric view of Christian history, while Serviss presents a conceptualization of whiteness that goes back to the Garden of Eden. Despite their radically different assertions about race, both stories demonstrate a longing to provide a narrative in which biblical history and science coexist amicably in a way that reaffirms an earlier American identity. All these tales connect exploration and discovery to religious tradition and biblical history.

In a brief conclusion, I examine the long-term influence of the technocratic exploration narrative. Twenty-first-century Americans live in a world where these stories' concepts are entrenched in common ways of thinking about expansion and identity. The recurring debate about evolutionary science in school textbooks provides one prominent example, but the prevalence of these concepts runs deeper. While debates about what kind of science will be taught explicitly to students in the classroom continue, ostensibly educational television networks continue to present the kinds of narratives found in lost-race technocratic exploration novels. For example, oft-rerun cable TV series such as *Decoding the Past* or *Mysteries of the Bible* promise that scientific research in Africa and the Middle East will find evidence validating biblical narratives. Using the same type of language Gernsback did in 1920, they conflate historical evidence and religious tradition. In such cases, exploration of remote or romanticized historical sites is encouraged, while new technology is used to access and accumulate evidence from these areas. Technology and exploration rise again as tools to reconcile apparent contradictions between scientific and Bible-based views of history. While such programs may not feature giant, anthropomorphic steam-men or cynical gunsmiths intent on overthrowing monarchy, their ideological core grows from the nineteenth-century narrative.

The story of technocratic exploration fiction is more significant than a footnote in a literary genre's history. Today, postsecular scholars reexamine nineteenth-century Americans' portrayal of their religious practices, their spiritual desires and needs. Scholars in Science and Technology Studies (STS) weigh the accuracy of the public and practitioners' understanding of technology's role in society, and investigate the historic roots of these understandings. Literary scholars become further acquainted with the sheer depth and number of ephemeral texts generated during the long nineteenth century. Contemporary Americans continue to debate the merits of colonial and imperial endeavors past and present. For all these audiences, the story of the technocratic exploration narrative's development holds consequence. What follows will chart that development. If it is not already apparent, this will not be an account of early science fiction focused on which author came up with what idea first—who wrote the first moon rocket story, the first robot story, and the like. Nor will it be history of scientific case studies, filled with digressions about when a technology was invented and who was involved. Instead, it is the tale of how one type of story became formularized, and how that formula was subverted and compounded as it appeared more and more frequently. Gradually, the technocratic exploration narrative shone a light not just on Americans' increasing faith in technology but on their wilting faith in traditional Christianity, and their initial conceptualization that the former might be used to help regain the latter.

PART I
GEARS

1

Inventing the Technocratic
Exploration Tale

God, Gears, and Empire

The "boy inventor" dime novel subgenre that flourished in late-nineteenth-century best demonstrates the connection between technological stories from the postbellum United States and the larger sociopolitical transformations of that era. Such tales appeared in weeklies with names like *The Boys Star Library*, *Happy Days*, and *New York Five Cent Library*, printed on cheap paper and treated as disposable reading material for young men, bearing a kinship to the British "Penny Dreadful" and the later, twentieth-century American comic book in that respect. They featured protagonists who invented steam-driven automatons and multi-propellered airships. Their stories had titles like *The Steam Man of the Plains; or, The Terror of the West*, *Frank Reade, Jr., and His Electric Air Yacht; or, The Great Inventor among the Aztecs*, and *Tom Edison Jr's Electric Sea Spider; or, The Wizard of the Submarine World*. While most studies have tended to scrutinize them exclusively in context of the development of the science-fiction genre, American dime-novel invention stories performed significant cultural work in the United States. They established a narrative in which independent young men could make a difference in the world through applied science, presenting their youthful, predominantly male audience with stories of technological empowerment. Science-fiction scholar John Clute dubbed such works "Edisonades," evoking the spirit of inventor Thomas Alva Edison, who came to prominence during roughly the same timeframe.[1] The first such dime novel, Edward S. Ellis's *The Steam Man of the Prairies* (1868), was published two years before Thomas Alva Edison founded American Telegraph Works in 1870 and over a decade before Edison found widespread fame for inventing the phonograph in 1877. Thus, the Edisonade subgenre predates even the rise of Edison himself.[2] Clute describes the components of the story, defining an Edisonade as "any story which features a young US male inventor hero who uses his ingenuity to extricate himself from tight spots. . . . The invention by which he typically accomplishes this feat is not, however, simply a weapon, though it will almost certainly prove to be invincible against the foe and may also make the hero's fortune; it is also a means of transportation—for the edisonade is not only about saving the country (or planet) through personal spunk and native wit, it is also about lighting out for the Territory."[3] Clute's nod to the final lines of *Adventures of Huckleberry Finn* further emphasizes the optimistic wish fulfillment offered by Edisonades; as Twain understood, Huck's desire to "light out for the Territory" was shared with multitudes of American boys.

The narrative also has problematic elements. Edisonades portray an idealized version of independent technology creation that results in traveling to a distant location and engaging in combative adventures. In the standard dime-novel variant, the invention—be it aircraft, land rover, submarine, or other—offers protection from violent attack and serves as a staging ground for other advanced weapons, such as bombs or machine guns, that often far exceed the armaments of the traveling protagonist's opponents. Typically, those opponents are the native population of the new land the protagonist is exploring, who resent his appearance for one reason or another. Early SF historian Everett Bleiler finds these texts filled with "aggressive, exploitative capitalism, particularly at the expense of 'primitive' peoples" and the frontier mentality, with slaughter of 'primitives'" as its natural outcome.[4] Similarly, Bill Brown notes that "The inventor fantasy . . . not only satisfied the adolescent longing for autonomy and fabulous individualistic achievement; it also expressed the jingoistic and racist longing for imperial conquest."[5] Brown succinctly relates the concepts expressed in the tales to the larger cultural movement toward US empire that coincided with these tales' proliferation. Because of their promise that spirited individuals will create inventions to aid both mobility and martial capability, Edisonades are by their nature pro-expansionist, militaristic, and technocratic. Clute underscores this fact, taking it even further by noting that the Edisonades' "basic story has been an essential shaper of US realpolitik for more than a century."[6] As Clute suggests, the Edisonades' legacy is part of an ongoing, broader concept of American identity that blends rugged individualism and technophilia to justify expansion of power and influence around the globe.

I refer to such nineteenth-century fictions as *technocratic exploration tales*. By this term, I generally mean stories in which a protagonist travels to a re-

mote location, either utilizing imagined technology to travel there or de-
ploying imagined technology once the destination is reached. The characters
are either traditional explorers who strike out with the intent of reaching a
far-off destination or lay persons, like Tom Sawyer, who are pushed into the
travel adventure by circumstances outside of their control. Whether they appeared in novels by respected authors or en masse in all-you-can-read-for-
a-nickel weeklies, each tale's plot is driven by the exploration of new frontier
territory and a positive view of technology. As such, the definition includes
the Edisonades along with other popular literature of the time. It encompasses tales of exploration for scientific purposes, such as *A Journey to the
Center of the Earth* and similar novels of Jules Verne, whose work was being
badly translated, bowdlerized, and devoured by American audiences during this timeframe. Many technocratic exploration stories, moreover, have
characters who are not inventors, but who certainly embrace a technocratic
worldview, such as Pauline Hopkins's scientist protagonist Reuel Briggs in
Of One Blood. From this perspective, Twain's *A Connecticut Yankee in King
Arthur's Court*, which focuses on an American using his mechanical skills
to usurp power after being transported to sixth-century England, is a technocratic exploration novel, while a portal fantasy such as L. Frank Baum's
The Wizard of Oz (1900) is not; although it is built on the same convention
of a modern American magically sent to an archaic world, the latter book's
protagonist, Dorothy Gale, does not presume the right to control Oz simply
due to her understanding of advanced technology.[7] Additionally, the definition does not encompass the entirety of technological fiction being published during the latter half of the nineteenth century. Because technophilia
is one of their defining components, these tales differ dramatically from the
era's more ambiguous portrayals of technology. They are in stark contrast
with the works covered by Leo Marx in his landmark work *The Machine in
the Garden*, which points out that nineteenth-century American literature
is filled with tales where machine technology is an "intruder" on an idyllic, pastoral environment, where the machine "invariably is associated with
crude, masculine aggressiveness in contrast with . . . the landscape."[8] Similarly, tales of science that do not involve geographical expansion, such as
Hawthorne's "The Artist of the Beautiful" or "The Birth-mark," cannot be
considered part of this subgenre, nor could the wide array of lost-world
travel narratives in which a modern protagonist discovers a utopian community in some remote corner of the globe.[9] As scholars such as Thomas
Clareson and Nadia Khouri have noted, these latter stories offered readers
escape from modernity and technology by featuring modern protagonists
who encounter a secluded, pastoral, often prehistoric community that was
explicitly or implicitly found superior to modern Western society.[10] True

technocratic exploration tales favor their own era, and they primarily occur in an imagined present. This injection of extraordinary, fictional technology into the audience's contemporary society is a hallmark of the form, setting it apart from other science fiction that uses the future as its setting.[11] While fantastic technology appears, these stories feature nineteenth-century protagonists who use that technological advantage to expand their influence for good or ill against a population deemed inferior. Still, I acknowledge technocratic exploration novels' place in the larger body of nineteenth-century science fiction by referring to them as a subgenre, part of a larger whole of utopian novels, pseudoscientific sketches, and scientific romances that make up the whole of "proto-science fiction."[12]

Technocracy, for my purposes, simply means the use of technology to justify control, where the right to lead and the ability to create and utilize advanced technology are viewed as roughly analogous and mutually reinforcing. In the twentieth century, the term took on more pointed political meaning, and it became further complicated in the wake of Science and Technology Studies' (STS) challenge to simplistic conceptualizations of technology creation and deployment.[13] The technocracy described here should not be mistaken for the more political movement of the 1920s, or for the term's more recent use to describe the unelected, educated leaders of (often transitional) European governments who tackle economic problems of a global scale without concern for local consent.[14] It also differs from the technocracy discussed when STS reconsiders technology's place in the production of scientific knowledge production or contemplates alternative modes of science in which existing influences such as funding, corporate interest, or desire for tenure do not come into play.[15] In many ways, technocracy as conceptualized in nineteenth-century popular literature is one of the ideas that modern STS dismantles and complicates; it embraced the same central idea that STS scholar Sally Wyatt finds contingent in modern technological determinism: "the notion that technological progress equals social progress" (168).[16] Technocracy's allure during the period covered by this book should not be underestimated. The concept, as it appeared in nineteenth-century America, proved one of the building blocks—along with Anglo-Protestant views of racial and religious superiority and the concerns of market-driven capitalism—of US empire.

Indeed, it would be easy to see the repeated variants of the technocratic exploration narrative as a sort of primer for US global imperialism. These stories flourished in the 1880s and 1890s. By 1898, as the United States defeated Spain and seized control of Puerto Rico, Guam, and the Philippines, such dime novels had been providing young audiences with a recurring narrative of techno-expansionism for over two decades. While they certainly contributed to Americans' conceptualization of empire and foreign territories, their wider influence came in contributing to Americans' conceptualization of themselves. I argue that technocratic exploration tales offered a narrative template that allowed fantasies of technological empowerment, but without a consistent endorsement of empire. In fact, once it became established in the US consciousness, the narrative was frequently used to *oppose* imperialist undertakings, even by the authors who wrote early dime-novel variants of the form. Instead, the American identity articulated time and again by these texts is one that is progressive technologically, but oddly conservative socially. It is an identity smitten with technology but skeptical of theoretical science, that challenges the social status quo by imagining new inventions but longs to retain a theological status quo by reiterating an earlier era's view of science and religion's compatibility. Technocratic exploration narratives often imagine resolutions for the controversies surrounding science, technology, and religion in the United States. They contemplate the socioreligious underpinnings of America's imperialist identity. Technocratic exploration novels' real legacy comes in their espousal of a narrative that presents Americans as both pious, traditional Christians and as resourceful, scientific innovators—two identities that seemed less and less compatible during the period covered herein. The frontier technocrats envisioned by them use technology to preserve an existential American status quo.

As we will see, the technocratic exploration narrative grows exponentially from its earliest articulations shortly after the Civil War to the start of the twentieth century. The subgenre features an unwieldy number of separate fictions, including a series of over one hundred issues featuring a single protagonist who invents a different machine each adventure. In their heyday during the 1880s, such stories appeared several times a week. Thus, while part of the narrative's thrust came from its constant repetition, its broader significance comes as larger shifts as the narrative occurs over decades. With this in mind, it may be helpful to outline the major developments of the technocratic exploration tale:

• It is immediately associated, even in its earliest articulations, with violent expansion on the frontier, indicative of an expansionist urge inherent in US culture.
• It is grounded in a hypothetical present, imagining fanciful technology injected into the day-to-day world of its audience. That is, it does not rely on a futuristic setting to naturalize the appearance of extraordinary technology.
• It views technology positively, and celebrates the individual technocrat's ability to use his invention(s) to achieve power and/or wealth, generally

without consideration of the broader influence of technology on contemporary society.

- It participates in the continuing disassociation of technology and science in the minds of Americans during the last half of the nineteenth-century.
- It becomes increasingly used to consider scenarios in which technology can reinforce prevailing understandings of mainstream religious faith.

The transformations in Americans' feelings toward science and religion occurred simultaneously with a change in reading habits and publishing capabilities. Technocratic exploration narratives flourished, I contend, not merely because outlets such as dime novels were available, but also because they offered a version of technology palatable to US audiences of the time. In sum, what began as cut-and-dried frontier adventure tales articulating America's already prevalent expansionist urges became a venue to showcase a broader American identity, particularly by considering the all-important roles that technology and Christianity—gears and God—played in that identity.

The Pervasiveness of US Imperialism

My claim that technocratic exploration novels articulated a conflicted view that simultaneously justified and undermined US imperial desires is based upon current understandings of empire in the United States. When a nation extends its territory through imperial conquest, it necessarily understands and justifies this action though appeals to its prevailing values and identities. Edward Said famously defined imperialism as "the practice, the theory, and the attitudes of a dominating metropolitan center ruling a distant territory . . . supported and perhaps even impelled by impressive ideological formations that include notions that certain territories and people *require* and beseech domination."[17] The nineteenth-century US imperialism addressed here contains some idiosyncrasies that require elaboration beyond Said's foundational definition. In general, US imperialism deals with westward expansion on the North American continent—the well-known era of Manifest Destiny—by which new territories are brought into control and made part of the Union. The closing of the frontier in the 1890s coincides with stirrings to expand internationally, culminating with the Spanish-American War in 1898 and the acquisition of protectorates that followed. Shelley Streeby and Jesse Alemán have cautioned scholars of nineteenth-century literature against focusing studies of US imperialism on the key date of 1898, noting that such an approach ignores the string of territorial acquisitions that occurred throughout the nineteenth century, punctuated by military excursions such as the

Seminole Wars, the Mexican-American War, and others.[18] Such territorial expansion was predicated, in no small part, on the formulation that Said mentions, with First Nation and Mexican societies presented as inferior to Anglo-Protestant America and therefore fair game for usurpation. In *Habits of Empire*, Walter Nugent addresses US imperialism in such a context, emphasizing continuities between nineteenth-century expansion and the earliest European colonization of the New World: "The frontier experience, ever since Plymouth and Jamestown, taught Americans . . . that they should expand the area of civilization and shrink the area of savagery, first on the North American continent, then across the Pacific and around the Caribbean, and then around the world."[19] While the post-1898 phase of US empire obviously conforms to Said's description, it is merely a continuation of an already-established series of actions that were, essentially, imperialism.

Heeding Streeby and Alemán's warning, I view the writings examined here not merely as primers for an imperialist mindset unleashed by the Spanish-American War, but as articulations in conversation with an ongoing US policy of acquisition and management of new territory in North America that existed well before Edgar Allan Poe and Washington Irving began dramatizing fanciful technology in the service of conquest and domination. My use of the term "US imperialism" is not limited to the era of international expansion that occurred in the wake of the Spanish-American War, although that is clearly one significant moment in the growth of American empire. From this perspective, we can see the technocratic exploration narratives as reiterations of a preexisting expansionist impulse. Poe's pre–Civil War portrayals of Indian wars and Ellis's post–Civil War portrayals of frontier gold-mining present the same expansionist desires that led Americans to retain Spanish colonies after the Spanish-American War. Later fictions that consider global US expansion more overtly and critically, including works by Mark Twain and Pauline Hopkins, must reiterate such impulses in order to intervene against them. Regardless of their approach toward empire, technocratic exploration stories always imagine variants of this kind of expansionism whether the action occurs in the American Southwest or Northern Africa, in Camelot or on the planet Mars.

Of course, empire involves more than simple territorial control; it requires the "ideological formations" mentioned by Said—new narratives, ideas, and norms concerned with the imperial practices, the controlled Other, and the imperialists themselves. When I discuss America's "imperial imagination," I mean to signify the full spectrum of those ideological formations: not merely the expansionist actions, but also the assumptions of technological, ethnic, and spiritual superiority that were used to justify them. Much of the era's literature, including technocratic exploration tales, appeals to the prevailing definitions of "American," its Anglo-Protestant doctrines of nationalism, ethno-racial categories of citizenship, market-based definitions of freedom, and its idea that this worldview can and should be adopted by the territory's original inhabitants, by force if needed.[20] Benedict Anderson's definition of the nation as an "imagined political community [that is] both inherently limited and sovereign" is helpful here.[21] Anderson has shown that popular literature plays a role in developing the nation, reinforcing ways individuals see themselves as joined with others by race, religion, social class, and other factors that construct national consciousness. He famously ties novels and newspapers to the development of national consciousness, including even the type of dime novels that published Edisonades. For Anderson, *all* novels, including "the masterpieces of Balzac but also any contemporary dollar-dreadful . . . [are] clearly a device for the presentation of simultaneity in 'homogeneous, empty time.'"[22] Novels and newspapers gave each reader a perception that his or her reading was "being replicated simultaneously by thousands (or millions) of others of whose existence he is confident, yet of whose identity he has not the slightest notion."[23] Technocratic exploration novels play a key role in this identity construction, and their publishing history makes them uniquely well suited for understanding the changing landscape of US identity during this era. They were published, popularized, and serialized for generations of postbellum Americans. Their narrative's constant repetition occurs over the course of several decades, during a period that saw the end of Reconstruction, the celebration of a Centennial of nationhood, the "closing of the frontier," and the beginnings of Pacific empire. As they narratively hypothesize ways that technology could enable territorial expansion and military power (and which dominant American values and viewpoints would benefit from that expansion), all of the fictions examined in this study reveal aspects of these new formations participate in the kind of nation-building Anderson considers. Simply put, technocratic exploration novels weren't exclusively pro-imperialist, but they shaped the US imperial personality by developing Americans' perceptions of themselves. While the stories do not all articulate precisely the same viewpoint on these subjects, nevertheless they utilize the same narrative template of technology, invention, and expansion.[24]

The Malleable Boundaries of Science and Religion

What larger cultural forces surrounded technocratic exploration narratives, and how did they speak to those concerns? If the imperial impulse was pervasive in the era of the technocratic exploration tale, it is one of the few constants in the subgenre's protean tale. The nineteenth-century public's perception of science and technology was changing from an eighteenth-century model of educated, independent investigation—exemplified by renaissance men such as Benjamin Franklin, who could be readily seen as both scientist and technologist—to a professionalized mode in which scientists and technologists were seen as two different types of people doing different kinds of work. This perception occurs simultaneously as the impact of Darwinian evolutionary theory on religious faith became obvious to scientific and public communities. The growing disconnect between technology and science was acutely felt by an American society increasingly hostile to science's undermining of its spiritual identity while enormously receptive to technology's benefits. The growing tension between science's post-Darwinian worldview and an earlier Judeo-Christian perspective shaped plotlines in the nineteenth century, much the same way that it continues to shape politics today.

First, technocratic exploration tales served to separate science and technology in the minds of American readers, presenting plots that simultaneously underscored science's mutability and technology's creation of opportunity. By doing this, the texts simplify the conceptualization of both fields, becoming part of a broader, longer debate regarding where, how, and *if* science and technology overlap philosophically and structurally. STS has reinvigorated debates over differences between science and technology, and Bruno Latour has deployed the term *technoscience* to call attention to the shared assumptions and methodologies encompassed by them.[25] While a hard, fast distinction between "science" and "technology" may be problematic for such twenty-first-century readers, it is important to consider the major role such a distinction played in the development of science in America, and how the boundaries could be sharpened or blurred to suit participants' needs. As historian of science Robert Bruce points out, during the nineteenth century, science moved out of the realm of the "self-financed amateur" and into two differing professional roles.[26] Pure or applied "science" became the domain of a professional class of scientists whose research was supported by academic posts and grants from government. "Technology," in contrast, developed from the work of middle-class engineers and inventors who "carried on no experimental research to derive new principles or generalizations" but "used well-known mechanical principles" to create tangible (and patentable, and *lucrative*) benefits.[27] Technology denoted the use of existing scientific knowledge to create concrete results, including the invented object, its impact on the real world, and its economic power as a financial boon for its creator and potential investors. Science was theoretical and distant, done by people paid to think; technology was practical and beneficial, made by ingenious people who hoped to earn a buck from their invention.[28]

This is not to say that Americans saw no connection between science and technology. In fact, the connection they saw partly enabled these texts' valorization of the technocrat hero. As Bruce notes, many nineteenth-century American scientists who hoped to vindicate their theoretical work "heartily endorsed the delusion" that all theoretical science would result in some practical application—a trait that, as Bruce points out, continues in the sciences today.[29] This notion developed into what STS scholars call the "linear model," in which technology is an accumulating application of existing science, built using trial and error, frequently during attempts to improve existing technology, but ultimately reliant on scientific research to open new possibilities and innovations.[30] Modern STS's examination of the sociohistorical factors behind science suggests that the old understanding of technology as "applied science" is flawed or incomplete.[31] By 1994, Nathan Rosenberg confidently stated, "Everyone knows that the linear model of innovation is dead."[32] In nineteenth-century America, however, the linear model took root at the same time that a cult of the independent technologist grew in Western society. Christine MacLeod, in her study of British nineteenth-century patent law, notes the proliferation of inventor biographies in the late nineteenth century, as the culture began to downplay the collaborative nature of knowledge creation in favor of idolizing single inventors.[33] Implicit in this worldview was the notion that science was only as good as the application a technologist discovered for it. American technophilia became even more pronounced, leading to what Bruce calls a "swelling current of American faith in the unalloyed beneficence of technology."[34] Technology flourished, creating labor-saving devices and quickening communication processes, opening new areas to economic expansion, and creating new, technologically based employment (railroads, telegraphs, munitions, etc.), and the independent technologist—Edison, Fulton, and others—became one of the era's avatars.[35]

The US technocratic exploration novel mirrors these cultural trends. In their pages, a fictional protagonist could be a technologist without necessarily being concerned with theory or larger implications of ideas beyond their practical application and economic value. The stories overwhelmingly focus on technology rather than theoretical science. Edisonades, for example, most obviously deal with the weapon and/or transportation mechanisms created and assembled by their characters. The protagonists are *technologists*, essentially middle-class, independent-minded inventors who build machines and weapons through hard work and ingenuity. In some cases, such as Twain's inventor in *Tom Sawyer Abroad*, they resemble what STS scholar Derek de Solla Price calls "little science," in which the scientist is "the lone, long-haired genius, moldering in an attic or basement workshop, despised by society as a nonconformist, existing in a state of near poverty, motivated by the flame burning within him."[36] They are not, however, Victor Frankenstein–like scientists, seeking to plumb the wonders of nature and apply that knowledge. Rarely are they Charles Darwin–like explorers, visiting the remote reaches of the globe to find evidence that will ultimately support a grand theory. Rather, technocratic exploration novels portrayed the simplistic notion that technology is produced by single individuals, whose engineering feats are the result of hard work that utilizes theoretical science's principles (particularly physics) without contributing to the body of knowledge. In its admiring portrayal of technologists, the subgenre highlights the role of the independent inventor, even as it further defines a distinction between "technology" and the more purely theoretical "science" that was already occurring in the minds of late nineteenth-century American readers.

The period produced narratives in which characters enjoyed technology's benefits without accepting the implications of science. Science was becoming problematic. From 1870 to 1900, the Western world saw multiple views on evolution and its compatibility with Protestant Christianity. Historian E. J. Hobsbawm notes that, during this era, scientific discoveries countered religious belief, and that secularism's "militant attack on religion" resulted in counter-attacks by the faithful.[37] Scientists of an earlier generation had accommodated Christian biblical traditions in their interpretation of geology and evolution, but ministers and collegiate administrators became less and less satisfied with such approaches as the century closed. As the seeds for modern fundamentalist Christianity were sown by some of the era's ministers, pro-Darwinian educators became more strident as well.

Technocratic exploration tales, then, are part of an ongoing national narrative asserting the Bible's centrality in American life. As such, they are part of a longer, ongoing struggle for public-sphere authority that generally frames science and religion as oppositional forces. In 2015, Timothy O'Brien and Shiri Noy received a good deal of press for an *American Sociological Review* article suggesting that this debate of "science versus religion in America" has been misunderstood and misportrayed. Building from such studies, O'Brien and Noy found that 21 percent of the US population represent a group that is both pro-religion and pro-science.[38] Borrowing a phrase already popularized by scholars such as Jürgen Habermas and Talal Asad, they dub this group "post-seculars," made up of individuals who view "conflict between science and religion as limited to a narrow but important set of issues" such as the evolution of humanity.[39] Post-seculars are highly educated, and have a "distinctive worldview that reconciles science and religion in all but a few ways."[40] Scholars in the humanities have heeded Asad's call to "unpack the various assumptions on which secularism . . . is based," to scrutinize its assertions of rationalism and egalitarianism and to uncover ways secularism facilitates the very acts of intolerance that it claims to oppose.[41] Studies like O'Brien and Noy's remind us we must do so without oversimplifying the apparent antagonism between secular science and religious faith. In fact, there has always been a sizable segment of Americans who are simultaneously pro-science and pro-religion, and who desire narratives where both coexist harmoniously. Nineteenth-century writers who injected biblical commentary into technocratic exploration novels understood this.

The established tradition for American scientists in the early to mid-nineteenth century involved explaining how scientific findings influenced readings of the Bible without undermining biblical authority. An 1852 study that found about "one half of the Christian public" believed that the creation described in Genesis was literal fact.[42] Ronald Numbers asserts that literalists made up "a minority voice" in America during the nineteenth century.[43] Instead, the nonliteralist reading was prevalent in investigations of the creation of the earth, where participants from both science and theology frequently acknowledged "long epochs" of development. Scientists espoused a view similar to the one found in early science fiction of the era, perhaps best articulated by Professor Arronax in Jules Verne's *20,000 Leagues under the Sea* (1870), who explains that "the 'days' of the Bible represent epochs and not an interval between sunrise to sunrise."[44] Works such as Robert Chambers's anonymously published 1844 work, *Vestiges*, provided a proto-Darwinian view of evolution tempered with faith in a Divinity and the kind of progressivist, human-centric language Darwin ultimately eschewed.[45] While later scientists and theologians eventually rejected Chambers's ideas, uncomfortable with both its scientific flaws and its theological implications, thinkers such as Ralph Waldo Emerson found his ideas compelling.[46] One idea, the nebular hypothesis of Laplace, fared better at bridging the gap between evolutionary thought and conservative Christianity by explaining how celestial bodies formed over long periods of time. Such an idea could be accepted only if one read Genesis as a metaphor. Yale geologist James Dana argued in favor of the nebular viewpoint.[47] Even Tayler Lewis, the author of 1855's *The Six Days of Creation* and one of Dana's chief foils in the creation debate, essentially agreed that the "days" mentioned in the Genesis creation story were not literally days but "long epochs."[48] Such examples underscore the fact that, while biblical literalism existed, it was not the key criticism of Darwin's early opponents. The "long epochs" viewpoint already had a stronghold in US scientific circles before *On the Origin of Species* was printed in 1859.

This is not to say that all of Protestant America embraced these concepts, or that the conflicts between evolutionary science and Christian traditionalism weren't foreseeable. Still, theologians' positions on the issue were complex. The preeminent minister Henry Ward Beecher expressed acceptance for evolution in an 1882 essay in the *North Atlantic Review*: "The debate is not about the reality of evolution, but, of the influences which produce or direct it. That the stellar world was not created instantly by the Divine will, but gradual through uncountable ages; that this inorganic globe was the product of slowly unfolding changes; . . . that the human race has been subject to the same great law and method of creation—may be said to be undisputed among scientific men, whether Christian or not Christian."[49] Beecher's work ends with an acceptance of evolution as an idea not incompatible with theism. Similarly, Presbyterian minister James McCosh, then-president of Princeton University, went so far as to send Princeton students to study evolution with "Darwin's Bulldog," Thomas Henry Huxley, in Britain.[50] Clearly, some of the nation's prominent theologians felt evolutionary teaching could be embraced by American Christians.

The Reverend Charles Hodge at Princeton Theological Seminary provides a good example of the conflicted case against Darwinism frequently found during the era. Hodge famously condemns evolutionary thought in his 1874 text *What Is Darwinism?*, and scholarship on the reception of Darwin's theory often repeats Hodge's response to the titular question, namely that Darwinism is "atheism."[51] He does so, however, while approvingly mentioning Laplace's nebular hypothesis, and thus accepting a nonliteral reading of Genesis.[52] Hodge actually praises Darwin as "a naturalist, a careful and laborious observer . . . [who] explicitly and repeatedly" refers to a creator.[53] Like Beecher, his frustration with evolutionary science came not from its challenge to the story told in Genesis, but because it diminished the importance of a creator. Close analysis of the text shows that Hodge strained to make his case, relying not only on scriptural evidence but from appeals to scientific authority of Darwin's doubters such as Louis Agassiz and the Duke of Argyll. While he finally declares "What is Darwinism? It is Atheism," he immediately adds, "This does not mean, as before said, that Mr. Darwin himself and all who adopt his views are atheists."[54] Hodge frames this comment around the example of Harvard's Asa Gray, who promoted evolutionary theory in works like 1876's *Darwiniana* while asserting that they could be held while maintaining teleology and theism.[55] In using an evolutionist's own words to support an anti-Darwinian stance, Hodge condemns Darwin's ideas while validating their use by avowed theists such as Gray.[56] Hodge's text illustrates an important point: even some of Darwin's American critics approved of the blending evolutionary science and Christianity.

During the same period in the 1880s, however, evangelical movements laid the seeds for modern fundamentalism's outright rejection of evolutionary thought. Preacher Dwight Lyman Moody condemned evolution—

without naming it outright—as one of many "False Doctrines" in his oft-quoted "Temptations" sermon.[57] Moody also promoted the concept of biblical infallibility, a view that gained popularity during the era. From 1876 to 1895, Moody's views influenced groups such as the Niagara Bible Conference, which made "scriptural inerrancy" one of the five central tenants of its members' Christian faith.[58] The growth of these views—both hostile to evolution and devout in their belief that the Bible revealed factual, literal truth in all matters—established a template for the kind of Christian fundamentalism that followed.[59] Biblical literalism, which asserted that early history occurred just as it was portrayed in Genesis, began to form. While the views of Christian leaders such as Moody and Hodge did not fully embody what most Americans today would recognize as "fundamentalist Christianity," their concepts demonstrated the growing contentious relationship between Protestant Christianity and pure, theory-based science.[60]

As the doctrine of scriptural inerrancy grew, so did intolerance of evolutionary thought in religious teaching institutions. James Woodrow, Presbyterian minister and science professor at the Columbia Theological Seminary, was dismissed by the Synod of South Carolina from his teaching job because of his pro-evolutionist views.[61] Vanderbilt University, a Methodist school, fired geologist Alexander Winchell in 1878 after he suggested that the biblical "Adam" was a product of evolutionary development, at least in part to facilitate the white supremacist view that blacks weren't evolved from this Adamic line.[62] The Ohio Episcopal Church initiated its first heresy trial in 1890, targeting Ohio Episcopalian Reverend Thomas Howard MacQuery for writing an evolution-friendly book entitled *The Evolution of Man and Christianity*.[63] At the same time, scholars began to push back. German author Albert Dodel wrote *Moses or Darwin?* in 1890, protesting that only those lucky few who went to universities were exposed to the scientific facts of evolution while European primary schools—often religious in nature—ignored this aspect of science. The translator of the American edition of *Moses or Darwin?* pointedly declared that the same problem existed in America despite alleged separation of church and state in public education. This criticism demonstrates the growing frustration among American educators that religion was trumping science in its portrayal of history.[64]

Is it any wonder, under these circumstances, that popular literature dealing with science and technology would begin focusing on tales that valorized preexisting views of history? This book hopes to demonstrate that technocratic exploration tales provided one outlet for the articulation and reconciliation of these conflicting worldviews that faced nineteenth-century Americans. I agree with Clute's suggestion that the narrative of Edisonades has been an "essential shaper" of American identity, but not solely for the reasons he and others have suggested. Their template for techno-expansionism prefigured the US's foray into global imperialism, but it developed in a complex and sometimes contradictory manner that undermines overt imperialist themes. The writers covered here showcase the ideological and cultural contradictions found in nineteenth-century scientific debates, and as they utilize and develop the narrative, they necessarily touch upon (not always consciously) factors of race, national sovereignty, and religion that were used to support the idea that Americans had a destiny, or a mission, or a right, to spread their influence outside their country's borders. Rather, this straightforward adventure story gradually becomes fixed on Western empire's religious underpinnings—concerned as much with preserving a fraught, preexisting Anglo-Protestant American identity as with spreading that identity across the globe.

2
Building Imperialists

The Steam Man, "Used Up" Man, and Man in the Moon

This chapter considers the early development of technocratic fiction in the United States, culminating in its first, major novel-length articulation. The technocratic exploration tale was not always an avenue for religious speculation, but it was *always* tied to American expansionism and empire. In some ways, this is unsurprising. The subgenre presents Americans taking machines to strange locations, and it is logical to assume that this blend of technology and travel comes with imperialist overtones, at least in some passing, unreflective way. But the development comes with an ironic twist: the earliest American fiction of this kind actually considers empire more overtly than the subgenre that follows. From its onset, the technocratic exploration tale dealt with America's imperial desires explicitly, voicing criticisms that later variants avoid.

These first considerations of technocratic exploration culminate in 1868, when Edward S. Ellis's *The Steam Man of the Prairies* established the narrative template for the hundreds of dime novel tales that followed. Now hailed as the first American science-fiction novel, it sold poorly at first, but dime-novel publishing juggernaut Beadle and Adams ultimately reprinted it at least six times under varying titles—most notably, *The Huge Hunter* —over the next two decades, demonstrating American audiences' receptiveness to this type of narrative.[1] Moreover, Gregory Pfitzer has suggested that it influenced Mark Twain as he wrote *A Connecticut Yankee*, indicative of its broader literary impact.[2] The novel's uniqueness comes from its choice of protagonist and its absolute reliance on imagined technology for its plot, portraying repeated scenarios where technological skill provides a direct link to mobility (physical *and* economic), sociopolitical influence, and problem solving. In it, Johnny Brainerd, a boy from St. Louis, builds an enormous steam-driven automaton shaped like a giant metal man wearing a literal stovepipe top hat. Brainerd hitches a wagon to his steam man and sets out for the American West, where he helps a group of miners protect their claim from outlaws and Native Americans who periodically confront them, using the steam man as a device to frighten would-be assailants and to quickly evade any attack. Ellis's work does more than simply recount a boy inventor's exploits. Brainerd's tale contains a further element of techno-logical empowerment because the steam man serves as a prosthetic device designed to compensate for the inventor's physical form. Johnny is described as a hunchbacked "dwarf" with a brilliant mind for engineering."[3] The steam man enables Johnny—who is portrayed as intellectually, but not physically, fit for life on the frontier—to participate in expansion, particularly violent confrontations that require physical rigor. Part of the story's thrust comes from its suggestion that an ingenious contraption such as the steam man could overcome physical deformity. This approach offers a promise of bet-ter living through technology at a key moment in US history. *The Steam Man of the Prairies* is a post–Civil War novel that deals with, as Bill Brown points out, technology's ability to heal the "loss of slave labor [and] the no-torious loss of limbs" resulting from that conflict in a manner that "legiti-mizes prosthetic technology."[4] As Brown notes, this celebration of technol-ogy's potential leads the narrative to a problematic outcome: Ellis showcases Brainerd's prosthetic empowerment by emphasizing the steam man's ability to frighten and fight off the native population.[5] One of the novel's legacies to the subgenre it spawned, then, is an unabashedly pro-expansionist ideology in which control and domination of civilizations is justified by the protago-nists' technological achievement.

Despite *The Steam Man of the Prairies'* pivotal role in the publishing his-tory of technocratic exploration tales, it was not the first US speculative fic-tion to connect technology, disability, and genocidal violence. It wasn't even the first work of US fiction to use imaginary technology as a lens for ex-amining imperial expansion. The latter honor goes to Washington Irving's *A History of New York* (1809), which contains, embedded in its fifth chap-ter "A Mighty Question," a hypothetical description of Earth's invasion by the moon. Irving's *History* is famously written in the meandering academic voice of historian Diedrich Knickerbocker, and much of the book's humor comes from Irving's ability to use that voice to send up the conventions of more standard, hero-worshipping histories. The science-fiction scenario he presents is somewhat atypical of the book's larger content, but it features the same iconoclastic underpinnings: it is pointed satire. Moreover, in Irving's work, we find an approach to expansion very dissimilar from the one found in *The Steam Man of the Prairies*, and this difference illustrates technocratic exploration fiction's capacity for criticism of expansionist policies.

Near the end of the book's first section, Knickerbocker rhetorically asks, "What right had the first discoverers of America to land, and take possession of a country, without asking the consent of its inhabitants, or yielding them an adequate compensation for their territory?"[6] After running through a list of "rights" that includes cultivation of the land and the introduction of the Christian faith, Knickerbocker concludes that a final right has validated the European expansion: "the RIGHT BY EXTERMINATION, or in other words, the RIGHT BY GUNPOWDER" (419). Because Knickerbocker allegedly fears that readers need a closer example to understand this justification of Europe's right to conquest, Irving begins a lengthy digression supposing "that the inhabitants of the moon, by astonishing advancement in science . . . had arrived at such a command of their *energies*, such an enviable state of *perfectibility*, as to controul the elements, and navigate the boundless regions of space" (420). These technologically advanced lunar explorers come to Earth, where they engage in their own colonial adventures. The moon men are

> possessed of vastly superior knowledge in the art of extermination— riding on Hypogriffs, defended with impenetrable armour—armed with concentrated sun beams, and provided with vast engines, to hurl enormous moon stones: in short, let us suppose them, if our vanity will permit the supposition, as superior to us in knowledge, and consequently in power, as the Europeans were to the Indians, when they first discovered them. . . .
>
> Let us suppose, moreover, that the aerial voyagers, finding this planet to be nothing but a howling wilderness, inhabited by us, poor savages and wild beasts, shall take formal possession of it, in the name of his most gracious and philosophic excellency, the man in the moon (421)

What follows is a tale of Earth's subjugation, in which the moon people's presumption to cultural superiority justifies their destruction of cities, forced conversion of Earth's Christians to a lunar religion, and compulsory relocation of the remaining Earthlings to the least desirable corners of the planet while their new conquerors enjoy the Earth's full resources (421–24). In content and complexity, Irving's 1809 lunar invasion prefigures H. G. Wells's 1898 classic *The War of the Worlds*, a work that on several levels mocks empire-building by imagining a better armed, but similarly technocratic, foe attacking the imperial West.[7] Irving and Wells provoke their audiences by posing the central question behind imperialist anxiety: What if someone from *out there* were to do the same thing to *us*? The entire sequence foregrounds the obvious hypocrisy of a young America that would justly protest outsiders doing to them the very things their forefathers did to North America's original inhabitants, and that they continued up to that very moment. Like Huck Finn questioning Tom Sawyer's crusade by assuming the perspective of a Middle Eastern Arab, Irving and Wells force unreflective imperial audiences to imagine themselves as the subjugated other.

Irving's mention that the moon men are "as superior to us . . . as the Europeans were to the Indians" initiates a direct analogy that he continues throughout the tale. The moon men's aerial ships surpass his modern age's balloons, a disparity "greater than that between the bark canoes of the savages and the mighty ships of their discoverers" (421). His haughty lunar conquerors deride Earthling conventions of marriage and monotheism. They note that they have attempted to help earthlings—"particularly the females"—by providing large helpings of their favored intoxicant, nitrous oxide (422). The moon men embody cultural traditions of polygamy and polytheism. These are, of course, the same institutions that many Western colonists pointed to among the Native American population when they sought to label them "savages." While their culture is Indian-like, they practice the same types of subjugation that Europeans used, from introduction of intoxicants to outright forced migration. The escapade ends when, Knickerbocker hypothesizes, "our philosophic benefactors . . . seize upon our fertile territories, scourge us from our rightful possession, relieve us from our wives, and when we are unreasonable enough to complain, they will turn upon us and say—miserable barbarians! ungrateful wretches!" (423). In such details, the story simply mirrors European colonization under the "right by gunpowder." The relocations and forced religious conversions faced by his besieged Earthlings are the contemporary reality of the Native American population.

Irving's inclusion of religion in this imaginative scenario is telling and significant. He has an understanding of religion's place in the imperial undertaking. In fact, Knickerbocker's preamble to his lunar invasion story features some of the clearest, pointed satire of Westerners in his *A History of New York*. Explaining the first European settlers' influence, he states, "The Indians improved daily and wonderfully by their intercourse with the whites. They took to drinking rum . . . learned to cheat, to lie, to swear, to gamble, to quarrel, to cut each others throats, in short to excel in all the accomplishments that had originally marked the superiority of their Christian visitors" (418). Irving's sarcastic use of the term Christian is hard to miss. The lunar representative notes, "We have insisted upon [the Earthlings] renouncing the contemptible shackles of religion and common sense," asking the man in the moon's permission that all lunar colonists be "authorized and commanded to use every means to convert these infidel savages from the darkness of Christianity" (423). The notion that technocracy would be augmented by an evangelizing impulse—one that desires, and ultimately uses the advanced technology's power to enforce, the conversion of the colonized—is treated by Irving as the natural order of things because it is the narrative they observe and are living. For Irving to omit conversion of infidels from his imperial satire would be to overlook something obvious to him and his readers. In this, Irving anticipates later developments in the technocratic exploration narrative, which will imagine configurations of technocracy and religion.

The explicitness of Irving's analogies between the lunar invaders and America's European colonists may be at odds with the book's narrative voice. By this point of the narrative, Knickerbocker has been firmly established as a charming, idiosyncratic mess, and putting these damning statements in his mouth potentially obscures their power. A reader would reasonably ask, "Why take Knickerbocker's opinions seriously?" Indeed, this may have been the case. The book was not devoid of other contemporary political commentary, all of which seems to have reached audiences easily. Irving famously satirized then-president Thomas Jefferson by making the Dutch New Netherlands leader, William "the Testy" Kieft, a mirror of Jefferson's policies, personal habits, and problems.[8] Despite this, audiences have historically gravitated toward reading *A History of New York* as a work of gentle humor. One anonymous 1810 reviewer praises Irving as a writer who "laughs at what makes others groan. . . . The people of New England are the subject of many humorous remarks, but we are glad to observe, made with so much good-nature and mingled compliment and satire, that they themselves must laugh."[9] Like Mark Twain after him, Irving's pointed criticism of America's expansionist policies was diminished by an audience who viewed him primarily as a genial humorist.[10]

Poe's Prosthetic War Stories

If Irving proves that American writers were perfectly capable of imagining technocratic expansion *and* criticizing the colonial impulse at the same time, then Edgar Allan Poe's work demonstrates something different. Poe considers ways technology could surreptitiously minimize the costs of expansion. He anticipates *The Steam Man of the Prairies* by addressing technology's ability to facilitate frontier advancement by prosthetically improving disabled bodies. Poe's short story "The Man That Was Used Up" (1839), however, avoids Irving's explicitly critical approach to colonialism's unfairness. Instead, Poe approaches the material much more ambivalently, mocking the same tropes that Edisonades later embrace. He roots his story in the Jacksonian era's Indian wars, presenting a tale in which the title character is a celebrated military general who has lost the majority of his body during battles against Native Americans and uses prosthetic devices to recapture his pre-conflict bodily form. While Poe and Ellis address similar concepts about disability, expansionism, and technology in very different ways, they ultimately suggest that the inevitable end of technology is expansionist, with warfare against the native population anticipated as the natural outcome. Both texts articulate an understanding of American culture that embraces prosthetic technology, at least in part, because it enhances expansionist warfare and material gain.

Poe's role as godfather to the science-fiction genre is well established.[11] Even before Hugo Gernsback named him as a progenitor, a 1905 essay in *The Saturday Review* criticizing scientific romances called Poe "probably the father" of the genre.[12] Poe's fascination with the American culture of science and technology informed many of his tales, serving as one arrow in a narrative quiver that contained the gothic, the political/satirical, and other established nineteenth-century literary forms. "The Man That Was Used Up" contains one essential element found the technocratic exploration stories that followed it: the story is rooted in a hypothetical present that places imagined technology side-by-side with contemporary realities, such as removal of native peoples and the political candidacies of former military officers.[13] The story's ultimate implication is that technology *already* exists that could allow the events in the story to happen, that the life of the characters has already been transformed by technology, the same approach subsequently used by Verne and the American Edisonade dime novelists. Subtitled "A Tale of the Late Bugaboo and Kickapoo Campaign," the story's key inventive device involves the titular character, General John A. B. C. Smith, an American military man who uses a variety of technologically marvelous prosthetic devices to conceal the brutal dismemberment that resulted from his battles against two Native American tribes. He is, as many recent studies concur, a nineteenth-century cyborg—completely reliant on machine technology for his mobility and presentability.[14]

The extent of Poe's engagement with the rhetoric of empire becomes clearer when we consider Donna Haraway's work. Taking human-machine hybridity as the current cultural norm—a given for nearly anyone in contemporary society—Haraway sees the image of the cyborg as an "ironic political myth" for "mapping our social and bodily reality" that can overcome "the tradition of racist, male-dominant capitalism; the tradition of progress; the tradition of the appropriation of nature as a resource for the productions

of culture."[15] The disruption caused by a move away from nature is, to Haraway's eyes, a positive force that can break up existing systems of domination.
Cyborgian hybridity indicates a broader movement "from an organic, indus-
trial society to a polymorphous, information system."[16] As Haraway notes:
"The main trouble with cyborgs, of course, is that they are the illegitimate
offspring of militarism and patriarchal capitalism, not to mention state so-
cialism. But illegitimate offspring are often exceedingly unfaithful to their
origins."[17] The cyborg, then, is a disruptive figure, capable of challenging
and transforming traditional Western views of gender, race, and economics.
While Haraway presents the cyborg as an image that promotes wider societal
change and ironically counters existing systems, the earlier Edisonades further a myth of American expansion, one that embraces rather than resists
the "tradition of appropriation" that Haraway opposes. The utopian promises that she uncovers in the cyborg are nowhere to be found in the human-
machine combinations of Poe and Ellis. In fact, Poe's "The Man That Was
Used Up" suggests that Americans will accept prosthetic technology precisely *because* it facilitates military expansion and genocide.

"The Man That Was Used Up" relies on a twist ending, and technology's
pivotal role in the plot is not revealed until the conclusion. The first-person
narrator meets General Smith at a party. The narrator wants to know more
about Smith, but each individual he questions is interrupted before he or
she can recount the general's story. The frustrated narrator resolves to ask
the general himself, calling on him at home where he makes the shocking
discovery that gives the story its title: the general has been so mutilated in
wars against Native Americans that he is an assembly of prosthetic devices.
When he enters the house, the narrator mistakes the general for an "odd-
looking bundle of something" on the floor, and then is shocked when the
bundle speaks to him.[18] He is further astounded when a slave enters and as-
sembles the general before his eyes, using cork legs, false teeth, wig, prosthetic palate, and more (387–89). The narrator relates this discovery to the
reader with horror.

How one reads "The Man That Was Used Up" depends greatly on the
reader's perception of this problematic, unnamed narrator who seems hor-
rified by Smith's prosthetics and frames the story as if he's revealing the hidden truth about the general. Poe's short fiction, particularly his proto-SF,
often uses this type of "debunking" approach where a hoax is perpetrated
and revealed.[19] Jonathan Elmer, for example, notes that Poe selected "The
Man That Was Used Up" to be published alongside "Murders in the Rue
Morgue" in a two-story collection, a sign that Poe felt it was quality material and perhaps an indication that he saw a connection between the ratio-
cination in both tales, as their main characters gather facts and intuit con-

nections to solve a riddle.[20] Unlike Dupin, the hero of "Murders in the Rue Morgue" who consistently displays flourishes of genius, the narrator of "The Man That Was Used Up" seems ill informed. The narrator believes he has set himself above the masses because of the special knowledge he has discovered, but the narrator is connected to the mob in many ways.[21] He exemplifies an American "type" who is obsessed with appearances and power, but distrusts his fellow citizens when he sees them doing the very same thing.

But why is the narrator so fascinated with Smith, and is he right to think others don't know about the general's prosthetics? The introduction establishes the normalized physical grandeur of Smith in two long paragraphs:

> There was something, as it were, remarkable— . . . about the entire individuality of the personage in question. He was, perhaps, six feet in height, and of a presence singularly commanding. . . . His head of hair would have done honor to a Brutus;—nothing could be more richly flowing, or possess a brighter gloss. . . . [He had] the most entirely even, and the most brilliantly white of all conceivable teeth. From between them, upon every proper occasion, issued a voice of surpassing clearness, melody, and strength.
>
> The bust of the General was unquestionably the finest bust I ever saw. . . . The arms altogether were admirably modelled. Nor were the lower limbs less superb. These were, indeed, the ne plus ultra of good legs. (379)

Certainly, this enthusiastic description could give readers the illusion that the story's underlying theme is the male gaze, with our narrator obsessed by the beauty and seeming perfection of Smith to the point of becoming something of an antebellum celebrity stalker. Scholars who consider Smith a cyborg have frequently pointed to these initial voyeuristic elements as a suggestion that the narrator suspects something wrong with Smith and/or is enamored with him physically.[22] However, the vividness of his description serves as precise contrast to the tale's ending in which all the things the narrator mentions—legs, shoulders, hair, even the general's bold voice—are revealed to be constructions of prosthetic assembly.

He may embody the US public's tendency to find manliness and elegance in military heroes, but the narrator's primary motivation is *not* Smith's physique. He notes, "I could not bring myself to believe that *the remarkable* something to which I alluded just now—that the odd air of *je ne sais quoi* which hung about my new acquaintance—lay altogether, or indeed at all, in the supreme excellence of his bodily endowments" (380). Already, the narrator begins to contemplate the wider mystery of his character. Smith's physique, however, is *not* the cause for the narrator's interest. Rather, the narrator's friend mentions Smith's "high reputation for courage," and describes him: "A downright fire-eater, and *no* mistake. Showed *that*, I should say, to some purpose, in the late tremendous swamp-fight away down South, with the Bugaboo and Kickapoo Indians . . . Bless my soul!—blood and thunder, and all that!—*prodigies* of valor!—heard of him of course?—you know he's the man—" (380). Smith then abruptly steps in and introduces himself, preventing the speaker from finishing his statement.

While talking with Smith, the narrator makes it plain where his interest lies, stating explicitly that the "theme I had just then most at heart [was] the mysterious circumstances attending the Bugaboo war," and he does not bring up the subject himself out of a "sense of delicacy" although he states that "in truth, I was exceedingly tempted to do so" (381). After their meeting, the narrator reasserts that his primary reason for quizzing his friends about Smith is "particularly respecting the tremendous events . . . during the Bugaboo and Kickapoo campaign" (382). The narrator is not obsessed by Smith's body, but by Smith's mysterious *past*. His voyeurism is of a distinctly imperialist variety. A recounting of the bloody events of Indian combat—not Smith's physical appearance—is the true object of his quest. Simply put, he wants to hear war stories.

From this perspective, the entire tale is a contemplation of technology's ties to expansionist warfare in the antebellum United States. The narrator is disappointed when the general steers the topic of conversation away from his courageous battles and begins discussing his favored topic of conversation—"the rapid march of mechanical invention"—unaware that the two are intimately connected for the general. Smith speaks exuberantly about the "wonderful age" (381) filled with "*useful* mechanical contrivances" (382). The story implies that Smith's technophilia comes from his culture's ability to reconstruct his body after the war.

Poe assumes that the American public at large shares the narrator's thirst for stories of brutal combat, and he mocks them on several levels. Tellingly, in "The Man That Was Used Up," Poe deliberately thwarts his narrator's (and presumably this audience's) wishes by never revealing details of the Kickapoo/Bugaboo war.[23] Promising the goods and then never delivering them can be seen as textbook Poe, part of what Terrance Whalen calls Poe's "barely repressed enmity toward the reading public" as a writer trying to survive by appealing to popular tastes he doesn't respect himself.[24] Additionally, Poe's characters are types. The individuals questioned by the narrator suggest an audience accustomed to a steady diet of harrowing tales of Indian removal and frontier violence, who are able to speak of such horrors in trite language filled with mock refinements. As several scholars note, the interviewees' meaningless clichés are always interrupted before they are finished.[25] These fragments clue us in to which elements of Smith's story are prioritized by the individuals. When he asks "Miss Tabitha T." in church, she replies, "Bless me, I thought you *knew* all about *him*! This is a wonderfully inventive age! Horrid affair that!—a bloody set of wretches, those Kickapoos!—fought like a hero—prodigies of valor—immortal renown" (382). Every subsequent person recounts the story in the same fragmented way. Dashes come in abundance in their speech, a narrative approach that, according to Stuart and Susan Levine, Poe uses to signify insincerity or frivolity.[26] Key clichés reappear. In fact, "prodigies of valor" repeats a phrase from the narrator's friend's introduction of Smith, while "wonderfully inventive age" repeats Smith's own phrase used during their first encounter. Both phrases reappear in some form during the narrator's subsequent interviews along with reference to "immortal renown." Repeated in equal measure is the ferocity of Smith's Native American foes, who are consistently referred to as "wretches" or "creatures." The names of the tribes are used interchangeably, but each of the interviewee's short narratives address the horrifying nature of the Indian other: "a bloody set of wretches, those Kickapoos!" (382); "—great wretches, those Bugaboos—" (383); "—terrible wretches those Kickapoos!—" (384); "Dreadful business that of the Bugaboos, wasn't it?—terrible creatures, those Indians!—" (385); "Savage affair that with the Kickapo-o-o-os, wasn't it?" (385). Poe's public describes genocide in breathless overgeneralizations.

More importantly, the speakers' comments suggest they already understand that much of Smith's body is prosthetic. Their repetition of the phrase "wonderfully inventive age" as they speak of Smith indicates that they already connect the General with invention and technology. Moreover, Smith is genuinely shocked at the narrator's reaction to seeing him in his unassembled, "bundle" form: "Strange you shouldn't know me though isn't it?" he asks the narrator at a point in which he is "a single leg" (387). Smith expects recognition, even in his mutilated, nonprosthetically enhanced form. All this suggests that the public actually knows the truth about Smith.[27] If the posturing narrator thinks he has revealed some secret, the joke is on him. Smith's public understands him, and his acceptance is rooted in the successfulness—rather than the secrecy—of his prosthetics.

Just as significantly, Smith accepts his new body with zeal, and does so because he perceives it as one more in a series of steps that apply the wonder of technology to the problems of war. When he speaks approvingly of the "wonderful age," he enthusiastically lists items related to colonial expansion and military conquest: "Parachutes and railroads—man-traps and spring-guns. Our steam-boats are upon every sea" (381). Boats and railroads, along with the reference to parachutes used in hot-air balloon travel, suggest an interest in new modes of transport, while the other items are more obviously martial in nature. Indeed, Smith later shows no reluctance to share specifics of his prosthetic body, listing each part as its assembled and recommending manufacturers: "Thomas . . . is decidedly the best hand at a cork leg; but if you should ever want an arm, my dear fellow, you must really let me recommend you to Bishop. . . . Pettitt makes the best shoulders, but for a bosom you will have to go to Ducrow"(388). As Thomas Olive Mabbott notes, "Most of the tradesmen mentioned [in "The Man That Was Used Up"] apparently were real people" who advertised their wares in Philadelphia papers in the late 1830s.[28] Poe did not have to look far to make his cyborgian technology seem darkly plausible in a city filled with wooden-limb makers and dental surgeons. Smith seems equally pleased with all these items, and his love of new military tools and new modes of transportation as well as prosthetics show that Smith conceptualizes technology as a force for expansion. In the end, we find Smith unaware of his unnatural appearance before he is "assembled" and enthused about not only his own prosthetic possibilities, but those of the nation as well.

"The Man That Was Used Up" offers a vision of a contemporary society where the human/machine hybrid is a welcome member. While it satirizes the public's desire for tales of Indian combat removed from the ugly realities of violence and laments the public's willingness to grant fame and authority to a veteran of such affairs, "The Man That Was Used Up" presumes that the US public could readily accept Smith's hybridity if it were related to his military service, to his expeditions fighting Native Americans and engaging in violent—and undoubtedly unevenly matched—combat. Poe's story understands that technology, expansion, and warfare are intimately connected in American minds, so much so that they will accept and glorify an individual who physically embodies those concerns.

From Prosthetic Technology to Edisonade: Enter Steam Man

Ellis's *The Steam Man of the Prairies* delivers what Poe's story withholds. We get the kind of detailed account of violent frontier conflict that Poe's narrator sought. Although it appears nearly thirty years after "The Man That Was Used Up," it utilizes the same notions of cyborgian possibilities, warfare, and expansion as Poe's short story. It takes the same scenarios Poe wrote about in the 1830s and 1840s and plays them out un-ironically, without Irving's sarcasm or Poe's skepticism about the masses and their motivations. Despite this difference, Ellis comes to similar conclusions about the inevitability of human-machine interconnectedness and its acceptance as a force serving

American identity and empire. If Poe's story hints that prosthetic technology can be accepted by the masses primarily for its ability to influence military expansion, *The Steam Man of the Prairies* embraces this concept and plays it out on a wider, imperialist scale, shifting the focus from prosthetic technology that indirectly enables expansion by repairing the damage caused by violence to prosthetic-expansionist technology that directly facilitates westward expansion and exploitation.

Like Poe, Ellis wrote for the popular marketplace, and his literary career was shaped by changes in the publishing realm. In 1860, he penned the bestselling dime novel *Seth Jones, or The Captives of the Frontier* for publishers Beadle and Adams, and subsequently authored serialized fiction for a number of major publishers under both his own name and a variety of pseudonyms.[29] *Seth Jones, or The Captives of the Frontier*, first published as *Dime Novel* no. 8 by Beadle, was written while he worked as a school teacher in New Jersey; it was heavily advertised before release and sold between 40,000 and 60,000 copies during its immediate release in October 1860.[30] Ellis's success with *Seth Jones* helped prove the marketability of the dime novel format, and he accepted Beadle and Adams's offer to write "no fewer than four novels a year."[31] These novels primarily were frontier tales, built on plot and setting formulas derived from James Fenimore Cooper's oeuvre; *The Steam Man of the Prairies* is no exception in this regard.

Just as Poe referenced real prosthetic vendors for verisimilitude, Ellis took inspiration from actual technology. He allegedly based his story on a real steam engine, the Newark Steam Man, designed to look like a seven-foot-tall human with a smoke stack shaped like a top hat on its head and a torso that encased an engine and boiler. Reports of the steam man were made in local papers around Newark.[32] Like the litany of real-life prosthetic suppliers tallied by General Smith at the end of "The Man That Was Used Up," the steam man's technology is grounded by a reference to the contemporary world. The real steam man's ability to move was never confirmed, suggesting that he was possibly a hoax, more sculpture than automaton. For a hoax to work, however, it must have a receptive audience. Articles about the Newark Steam Man in post–Civil War newspapers suggest that reporters saw the appeal of such a tale, confirmed or not. The public's enthusiasm for such technology would explain why *The Steam Man of the Prairies* became enormously popular after it was reprinted by Beadle and influenced subsequent proto-SF dime novels.

The Steam Man of the Prairies begins in medias res, with two western prospectors named Mickey McSquiggle and Ethan Hopkins, shocked by the appearance of the steam man: "Several miles to the north, something like a gigantic man could be seen approaching, apparently at a rapid gait. . . . Occasionally, it changed its course, so that it went nearly at right angles. At such times, its colossal proportions were brought out in full relief, looking like some Titan as it took its giant strides over the prairie" (9). Shortly after Mickey and Ethan determine that it is a "human contrivance" rather than some supernatural phantasm, they are shocked to find that the steam man pulls a carriage holding their friend, "Baldy" Bicknell, and a strange young boy who turns out to be the steam man's creator and manufacturer, Johnny Brainerd. After establishing the steam man's astounding appearance, the narrative tells how Baldy left the trio's claim and reached St. Louis, where he met the automaton's young inventor and brought him back to help them defend their mine.

In Johnny and Baldy, Ellis creates characters that encompass many of the same promises of prosthetic technology as Poe's Smith. Like Smith, "Baldy" is a victim of frontier violence; he received his nickname because he was scalped by Sioux Indians and hides his bald pate under a hat; he is also the group's outdoorsman and embodies the normalized physique, a "strong, hardy, bronze trapper, powerful in all that goes to make up the physical man" (24). Johnny Brainerd, in contrast, is a non-normalized body, clearly portrayed as exceptional and problematic. The book's presentation of Johnny's physical form melds his body's deformity with his technical inventiveness. He is

> hump-backed, dwarfed, but with an amiable disposition that made him a favorite with all whom he came in contact.
>
> If nature afflicts in one direction, she frequently makes amends in another direction, and this dwarf, small and mis-shapen as he was, was gifted with a most wonderful mind. His mechanical ingenuity bordered on the marvelous. (18)

If Baldy is a Smith-like frontier survivor/hero, Johnny is the "bundle" variant of Smith, the disabled body. Yet, like Smith, prosthetic technology normalizes Johnny Brainerd in a way that facilitates public acceptance and physical achievement. Technological advances enable him to participate in frontier activities, including violent adventure and the search for fortune.

The steam man becomes a completion of Johnny's body. Moreover, Johnny's identification with the steam man is complex and complete. Johnny is always physically himself; he never attempts to disguise or hide his "mis-shapen" physical attributes, but he also fully identifies with the external technology of the steam man that makes his adventure possible. For example, when Indians encounter the steam man while Johnny hides from them in a tree, one of the men swings a tomahawk into the steam man's stomach.

We are told, "This blow hurt the boy far more than it did the iron man, and he could hardly repress a cry of pain" (63). Johnny perceives his creation as a supplemental body, at once less intimate and more essential than General Smith's prosthetics are to him. The steam man provides a fearsome and powerful tool that is actually an improvement over the human body. After all, as Brown points out, Johnny Brainerd and his steam man—not the physically idealized Baldy—ultimately solve the miners' problems.[33]

In this application of Brainerd's invention, *The Steam Man of the Prairies* cuts to the heart of expansionist technology. The steam man is a massive improvement in transportation—moving at "railroad speed" without the confinement rails (10), and its value as prosthetic device providing mobility to Johnny is already clear. These enormous benefits, however, quickly become secondary to the steam man's ability to provoke fear and awe in Native Americans who threaten the miners. The two hardiest frontiersmen in the book have identical reactions upon seeing the steam man. Baldy Bicknell, knowing his friends are defending their claim, offers to purchase the steam man when he first encounters Johnny. Johnny questions how he would use it, and Baldy replies, "Thar's three of us goin' out to hunt fur gold, and that's jist the thing to keep the Injins back and scart. I've been out thar afore, and know what's the matter with the darned skunks. So tell me how much money will buy it" (25). Baldy's impulse to use the steam man for scare tactics comes into even fuller focus past the novel's midpoint in chapter 14, with the appearance of a character called the "Huge Hunter."[34] Left alone to guard his machine, Johnny finds himself confronted by a "white man, in the garb of a hunter" who is "fully six feet and a half high" (69). This imposing figure further exaggerates the ideal of Western manliness found in Baldy. Unlike Baldy, the hunter is less scrupulous in dealing with young Brainerd; he quickly announces his intent to steal the steam man from Johnny. The Huge Hunter's immediate plan for the giant automaton's use, however, is precisely the same as Baldy's upon hearing Johnny's description of how it works: "I'm goin' to take it myself to chase redskins in," he exclaims (71). Johnny barely escapes the Huge Hunter and keeps his steam man. This episode seems to have no other purpose in the grand narrative of *The Steam Man of the Prairies* than to highlight an additional white frontiersman's reaction to Johnny's creation, solidifying the book's central conceit. The two most physically imposing characters in the novel—Baldy and the Huge Hunter—immediately perceive the steam man as a device for terrorizing Native Americans. Ellis seems to take this for granted, suggesting that technology and expansion are already so melded together in an existing American cultural narrative that the story's characters could not see the invention as anything but a potential frontier weapon, one whose time has come.

Indeed, Johnny's fellow miner Ethan Hopkins first voices the idea that the steam man's invention is inevitable, a logical outcome of applied technology. Hopkins is consistently portrayed as the realist of Johnny's band of new friends, described from the onset as a level-headed, unsuperstitious "Yankee," in ways that have invoked comparisons to Twain's later creation Hank Morgan.[35] As such, Hopkins is impressed, but unsurprised, by the steam man. Upon seeing it, he states, "Do you know I've been thinking of that thing for ten years, ever since I went through Colt's pistol factory in Hartford, when I was a youngster" (14). While Twain's more famous Connecticut Yankee character actually *works* at the Hartford factory, Hopkins has merely been exposed to Colt's operation at some earlier point in his youth. This experience alone, the book suggests, was enough to capture his imagination. Hopkins's exposure to nineteenth-century American military technology has planted an intellectual seed, one whose logical outgrowth is the conceptualization of a large steam-driven humanoid. Johnny's mother has a similar insight. Johnny gets the idea for his invention from her, when he asks her to suggest an endeavor for his mechanical talents. "Yes there is something I have often thought of," she replies, "and wonder why it was not made long ago. . . . *It is a man that shall go by steam*" (20). Johnny Brainerd's achievement is a feat of engineering, not of imagination. Ellis's novel consistently gives plausibility to its central SF motif by portraying it as a concept that would be easily conceived in the face of technological progress and that will easily find applicable use, an idea that simply waits for a clever engineer to bring it into reality.

The novel's ending emphasizes the advantages of such a cyborgian body, even as it portrays the destruction of the device that makes it possible. Johnny falls asleep at his post as night watchmen—dreaming up some "improvement" to his steam creation—while the group is camped in a canyon on their trip home with their gold (92–93). Confronted by Native American adversaries who barricade their escape route with boulders, Johnny increases the fire in the steam man to enable it to become a hybrid battering ram/bomb:

> The steam man was turned directly toward the wall, and a full head of steam let on. It started away with a bound, instantly reaching a speed of forty miles an hour.
>
> The next moment it struck the boulders with a terrific crash . . . and the instant of touching ground upon the opposite side directly among the thunderstruck Indians, it exploded its boiler! The shock of the explosion was terrible . . . the steam man being blown into thousands of fragments, that scattered death and destruction in every direction. (99)

Ellis recounts this mayhem approvingly, reveling in the steam man's facilitation of frontier violence against unevenly matched foes. The explosion of the steam man represents a way for Johnny to make up for his delinquency as a watchman; he gives up his prosthetic body for the protection of his friends. Even in the destruction of the steam man, the novel maintains an unremitting optimism.[36] Cyborgian bodies, after all, can be modified and reproduced. The book ends with a promise that Johnny, now wealthy from the gold mine, "is educating himself at one of the best schools in the country," and, upon completing his formal education, "it is his intention to construct another steam man, capable of more wonderful performances than the first" (100). Johnny's loss of his prosthetic body is traumatic but ultimately *temporary* because of the inherently replaceable nature of his prosthetic mechanism. Such a re-creation, it should be noted, is implicitly possible because of the enormous wealth Johnny is able to gain because of his Western adventure enabled by the steam man. The same money used to pay for "one of the best schools in the country" can be applied to rebuild his mechanical counterpart body when the time comes.

Ellis shows prosthetic technology as a tool that enables conflict on a military scale by individuals whose physicality might otherwise not permit them to engage in such adventures. Poe, in contrast, shows the cyborg as a method for concealing the physical damage sustained by bodies during war. Whether it is found in Smith's adoring, gossiping public or Brainerd's physically inclined comrades, the American culture presented by both authors embraces prosthetic technology, at least in part, because it enhances expansionist warfare and material gain. In both cases, bodies can be rebuilt in a way that may indeed be an improvement over the natural body, similar to the manner Haraway suggests but with extremely different goals and consequences. The interplay between human and machine in most technocratic exploration novels may be "the illegitimate offspring of militarism and patriarchal capitalism," as Haraway notes, but they are quite faithful to existing military and expansionist urges that form them. In a nineteenth-century society where genocide and territory acquisition have become normalized, these cyborgs fit right in.

The critical satire found in Irving's tale from sixty years earlier is nonexistent in Ellis's novel. Even the ambivalence toward the bloodthirsty American public that informed Poe's work is missing. Ultimately, *The Steam Man of the Prairies'* uncritical and pro-expansionist take on prosthetically enabled travel grew in influence. While its original 1868 printing seems to have come and gone with little fanfare, despite its grounding in the then-contemporary news reports on the Newark Steam Man, its contents were recycled as per dime novel publishing standard. When the book was reprinted in 1876 under the title *The Huge Hunter, or, The Steam Man of the Prairies*, it found an audience, one that included one or more members of a rival publishing firm owned by Frank Tousey. Within the year, Tousey's press issued their own take on the same tale, *The Steam Man of the Plains* by Harry Enton.[37] That dime novel featured a boy inventor named Frank Reade, whose normalized physicality robs the narrative of the prosthetic enablement found in Johnny Brainerd's tale. Instead, the "steam man" boy inventor trope becomes a story of technocracy grounded in the non-disabled US population, essentially an extended contemplation on how a huge automaton could facilitate expansion for the kinds of Americans who had already been doing the expanding for the past fifty years and more. The first Frank Reade novel's motif—technocratic expansion as a tool for the non-disabled proto-imperialist American—was disseminated rapidly, as Tousey Press's *The Steam Man of the Plains* became the first of a series that would extend until the end of the nineteenth century and define the formula of the technocratic exploration tale.

3
Imagining Inventors

Frank Reade and Dime-Novel Technocratic Exploration

The dime novels featuring boy inventor Frank Reade Jr. make up the Edison-ade subgenre's backbone, with each novel reiterating its narrative formula: the hero invents a fantastic, technologically enhanced form of transportation and uses it to travel to some remote destination where he has a series of adventures. The Reade series, printed by Frank Tousey's publishing company, began in 1876 and proved so popular that it went into weekly publication during its heyday in the early 1890s, ultimately producing between 179 and 192 different novels.[1] While these novels began as serialized tales running concurrently with other adventures in monthly periodicals, the Frank Reade Jr. dime novels have a particular significance because in September 1892 they went into weekly publication devoted exclusively to the character and bearing his name—*The Frank Reade Library*. Thus, they achieved significance to science-fiction historians by becoming the first SF series in regular publication.[2] In 1889, when Mark Twain sent his technocratic industrialist gunsmith Hank Morgan back in time to wage war against medieval Britain's woefully primitive forces in *A Connecticut Yankee in King Arthur's Court*, technocrat Frank Reade and his son, Frank Reade Jr., had been fighting equally lopsided battles against various enemies for over a decade.

As covered previously, most scholars agree that these works provided a predominantly young, white, male, working-class readership with fantasies of colonial power enabled by technology, ultimately performing the cultural work of preparing US readers for their country's subsequent forays into imperial conquest.[3] The portrayal of imperialism in the Frank Reade novels, however, is complicated by their authorship and publishing history.

Tousey's company attributed all the Frank Reade novels to "Noname," a house pseudonym used by a variety of authors, following a common dime-novel publishing technique meant to ensure that readers could associate a series with a particular author, even if the individual texts were produced by a stable of writers. The majority of the Frank Reade Jr. novels, however, were actually written by a single author—Luis Philip Senarens, a Cuban American writer who began composing dime novels while in his teens.[4] The Frank Reade Jr. tales make up only a fraction of the approximately 1,500 dime novels that Senarens wrote under various pseudonyms, an achievement that makes him one of the most prolific writers of late nineteenth-century America.[5] And, in fact, Senarens authored the exploits of another boy technocrat—Jack Wright—for Tousey, making him the author of both the first and second most ubiquitous "boy inventor" characters in post-bellum literature. Because he rapidly produced texts for mass consumption under a pseudonym, Senarens's success is rarely acknowledged outside a few comprehensive studies of early science fiction.[6] By 1920, Senarens's identity had become known enough for some early science-fiction fans to dub him "The American Jules Verne."[7] Such accolades were given credence by the oft-repeated but unsubstantiated claim that Verne himself wrote at least one complimentary letter to "Noname" praising his inventiveness.[8] Senarens's career paints an intriguing picture of nineteenth-century publishing, American empire, and the first-generation citizen's experience. Simply put, a vast number of these technocratic tales of a young Anglo-American hero encountering (and frequently) exploiting native cultures around the globe were composed by a Cuban tobacco merchant's son who was born and rooted in metropolitan New York. As Senarens produced this body of work, he repeatedly touched on concepts of imperial expansion. Upon examining these texts, however, one fact becomes clear: the Reade novels deal with empire in complex, often contradictory, ways. Their stories' approach stems from the practices uniquely tied to dime novels, the research practices of their authors, and their constant reiteration of formula.

Dime Novel Mythology and Methodology

Close analysis of Senarens's Frank Reade Jr. stories challenges some of the notions about how Edisonade dime novels operated within their era. Earlier technocratic works addressed expansion and genocide, either with tacit approval in some cases—such as in Ellis's *Steam Man* novel—or with overt protest, as in Irving's writing. Unlike these works, the Reade novels present a somewhat conflicted portrayal of empire, one that is extremely technocratic but not fully jingoistic, and in which the categories of race and nationalism inherent in empire are more fluid than previous scholars have reckoned. Instead, they present an imperial imaginary that allows for individual technological empowerment without larger cultural implications.[9] Rather than portray the long-term, wider impact of each invention, the Frank Reade Jr. dime novels focus on serial adventure, setting up a strange, repeated formula where transformative technology is constructed, used on a personal scale, and then withdrawn from society with no real impact on the status quo. In this approach, the Reade stories are radically dissimilar to the type of science fiction that addresses what Raymond Williams calls "the technological transformation," where utopian possibilities are opened up by a new technology that changes the world around it.[10] The absence of this larger element from Senarens's novels actually facilitates their use as political commentary. They celebrate self-determination and a promise of technological empowerment that operates on a limited, independent level. When their narrative is applied to contemporary events directly related to US empire building, the Frank Reade novels' technocratic expansionist motifs ultimately undermine the very notions of race and nationalism that enable imperialism.

To see this in action, we must look at the earliest Frank Reade adventures that appeared in dime-novel weeklies such as *The Boys of New York* and *Happy Days*, viewing them as a case study in how series fiction played out themes over long timeframes. The first of the series, *The Steam Man of the Plains; or, The Terror of the West*, appeared in 1876 and was composed at publisher Frank Tousey's request after he saw a reprint of Edward S. Ellis's *The Steam Man of The Prairies* and determined that copying its formula might have lucrative results.[11] Everett F. Bleiler, J. Randolph Cox, and Edward T. LeBlanc, among others, have catalogued these novels over their many reprints, an exhaustive endeavor that allows historicization of the first appearance of concepts or tropes in the series. Unfortunately, additional background about the Reade novels is lost because they have suffered the same fate as other popular, cheaply printed, and ephemeral commercial literary forms. Business records and editorial correspondence—items essential to the literary historian's body of evidence—are non-extant for Tousey's press.[12] While a large body of collectors and fans-turned-scholars investigated such matters throughout the twentieth century, records are missing, and hard evidence for who wrote what story or why specific business or narrative decisions were made does not exist.

Despite the lack of historical artifacts from the publishing arena, scholars such as Michael Denning and Franco Moretti provide methods for assessing the relevance of mass-produced, serialized texts such as the Reade dime novels. Denning's *Mechanic Accents: Dime Novels and Working-Class Culture in America* counters earlier studies that presumed dime novels provided "escapist" leisure reading for working-class audiences.[13] Denning cautiously avoids any assumption that these readers used narrative reading practices identical to today's audiences. Instead, Denning asserts that these works were read by their working-class audiences *allegorically* rather than narratively. Denning explains the way working-class readers understood such texts: "Thus the households and families in dime novels that would be interpreted as typical households if read novelistically are interpreted as microcosms of the social world when read allegorically; individual characters are less individuals than figures for social groups."[14] Working class readers, then, understood that characters embodied specific social types and that they functioned less as representations of individuals than as representations of groups who shared their concerns. The elements of "longing for autonomy" and "individual achievement" that Bill Brown finds in inventor dime novels are read, from Denning's perspective, allegorically.[15] Indeed, Denning explains how this mode operates: "For an allegorical mode of reading to shape a system of reading, there is usually a master plot, or body of narratives, that are shared by a culture . . . Such a single tale, a master plot, existed in nineteenth-century working-class culture. . . . This plot was made up of nationalist, class-infected stories of the American Republic [and] sometimes contradictory tales of its origins and threats."[16] For Denning, these texts offered a single master plot of American idealism and individual justice that figured the "utopian longings" of a lower class.[17]

The earliest Reade novels play out exactly this sort of allegory, particularly the first four titles in the series, which appeared between 1878 and 1881 and were written by Harry Enton.[18] In these books, Frank Reade epitomizes all independent, hard-working individuals who achieve success through a blend of discipline, applied technological skill, and physical prowess.[19] Senarens sums up this element in *Frank Reade, Jr. and His Steam Wonder* (1882), his first work for the series, by reintroducing Reade, who had last appeared in a *Boys of New York* serial in 1881.

> No reader of the *Boys of New York* has forgotten Frank Reade. He well remembers the great genius that invented the world-renowned *Steam Man* of the plains, the *Steam Team*, and the *Steam Tally-Ho*.
>
> Well, Frank Reade, after making an ample fortune out of his invention, married the girl of his choice, brought a large tract of plain-land out west, [and] settled down to farming by steam. . . . He used one-fourth only the force his neighbors did, and thus made four times as much money.[20]

Reade's ability to transform technological know-how into income is highlighted, aligning the narrative of the early Reade dime novels with the kind of working-class allegory Denning studies.

When Senarens took over the writing, he shifted the focus to Frank Reade Jr., the son of the elder Reade. These novels flourish at the end of the nineteenth century, a transitional moment in which Denning finds an "eclipse of the plebian, producer narratives of the dime novel, and the ascendancy of stories of upper-class schoolboys and heroic all-American detectives."[21] Indeed, Reade Jr. is not a plebian producer, but the son of the successful inventor, essentially a privileged scion groomed to take over the family business of inventing and adventuring. The Reades can be read as fictional counterparts to what science historian Robert Bruce sees as a growing "middle-class" of professional technologists.[22] This is not to say the novels do not appeal to the same work ethic found in the rags-to-riches variant of dime novels; in fact, approving mentions of Reade Jr.'s hard work and dedication appear repeatedly in the series. Nevertheless, Reade Jr. begins with material resources available to him from the outset. *Frank Reade, Jr., and His Steam Wonder* tells the audience that Reade Jr. has constructed his new device "in the farm carpenter-shop" using "many of the tools and implements his father had used years ago" (2). When the son proudly exhibits his new invention, a steam-powered wagon that travels on land like a modern-day van or recreational vehicle, the elder Reade states, "I had no precedents, and you had" (2). Unlike his father, then, Frank Reade Jr. represents a different inventive class, one that already possesses accumulated capital and an established infrastructure that facilitates success.

The focal transition from Frank Reade to Frank Reade Jr. represents a move away from the master narrative recognized by Denning and toward a different kind of recurring plot. While the earlier stories can be discerned as empowerment fantasies that highlight the technological skill of an independent producer class, the Frank Reade Jr. stories focus instead on the hero's ability to use his technological creation to journey to ever-more distant locales and intervene in circumstances there as he sees fit. In these stories, we find a variant of the frontier myth studied by Richard Slotkin, where adventurous rugged individualism plays out the "contradictory attitudes of Americans" who are both "committed to equality but thirsting for distinction; ambitious for progress but lamenting the loss of that world of pure potential."[23] Reade Jr.'s goal is to challenge himself through frontier adventures, not explicitly to advance economically or socially. As such, he represents the burgeoning imperialist technocrat who has both inventive know-how and enormous financial resources at his disposal.

Instead of dwelling on financial opportunities afforded by technological skill, then, the Frank Reade Jr. stories focus instead on the hero's ability to use his technological creation to interfere in events and correct perceived injustices. Many of the Frank Reade Jr. novels begin with the hero at home, reading a newspaper or a letter that either requests help or issues a challenge. Often this coincides with a visit from an acquaintance. A good example comes from *Over the Andes with Frank Reade, Jr., in His New Air-Ship*, first published in 1894 as part of the *Frank Reade Library*. In this story, Reade Jr. publicly announces his intent "to build an air-ship which will be able to carry a dozen or more persons around the world if need be."[24] He receives thousands of letters from individuals hoping to accompany him on this flight. After a lengthy description of how the airship works, coincidence strikes: Reade Jr. discovers that his assistant Barney's cousin, Patrick De Frontenac, has explored the Andes and wants to return to an "unexplored region" that only the airship can reach, and Reade Jr. agrees to take him there (78). The hero's technological skill allows him an opportunity to be part of an adventure, enabling someone else (in this case, De Frontenac) to achieve some goal.

In each story, Reade Jr. uses technology to visit remote settings, where he becomes embroiled in problems that his invention helps him fix. As John Clute points out, each invention in an Edisonade story is both a "weapon" and a "means of transportation," and this is the case with the series of steam-driven and electric tricycles, airships, submarines, and boats created by Reade Jr.[25] Each invention allows him to interfere with events that would otherwise be wholly outside his sphere of control, often in foreign territories. In the first Senarens-authored tale, Reade Jr. helps a man rescue his sister who has been kidnapped by Indians. In the second, he helps stop Canadian bootleggers. In the fourth story, he saves a kidnapped woman and helps the Mexican army defeat bandits. Each story follows this trajectory of invention, travel, and subsequent violent conflict. These repeated elements reveal the Edisonade myth, acting as what Claude Lévi-Strauss calls "constituent units" that, through their repetition of story elements and in the multiple retellings and variants, work to "render the structure of the myth apparent."[26] Edisonade texts use repeated tropes of scientific exploration, adventure, and the consistent reward of inventiveness to articulate an American myth in the Lévi-Straussian sense.

To see how this master plot develops in Senarens's dime novels over decades of publication, it is helpful to consider Franco Moretti's insights into mass-produced literature. Moretti proposes "distant reading" that studies groups of texts, analyzing or quantifying significant elements (rather than closely reading isolated texts) in order to reveal long-term development of "devices, themes, or tropes."[27] This approach encourages scholars to look at "patterns as a whole" rather than individual texts.[28] Moretti's work lends itself to dime-novel research, demonstrating how conventional wisdom about genres can be challenged or confirmed by looking at texts *en masse*, observing key elements as they recur in many texts over long periods.

In the case of the Frank Reade Jr. stories, this method may be applied to observe the American imperial imaginary and the conjoined variants of technocracy and expansion that inform it. Each of the novels has a similar approach in terms of narrative, following the aforementioned pattern of invention, travel, and episodic adventure. Almost all feature damsels to rescue, outlaws to capture, and numerous recurring events that are encountered during the trip or when the heroes reach their remote destination.[29] The main differences between stories come from the *type of invention* and the *locale* of the action. Other studies have catalogued the series and established the order and manner in which the stories appeared.[30] To fully demonstrate how the Frank Reade Jr. tales operate, such chronologies must include information about the actual setting of each narrative. If they are indeed archetypal or allegorical portrayals of American techno-imperialism in action, then these two elements—locale and invention—should provide clues as to how technocratic imperial conquest was conceptualized by dime-novel writers and readers.

As table 1 shows, the first decade of Frank Reade novels consists of stories set in the American West. The first five (beginning in 1876 with the original Frank Reade stories and the first Frank Reade Jr. tale) deal with steam-driven prime movers. While no Frank Reade stories appeared in 1877 or 1878, the first two were reprinted in 1879. The series then grows exponentially: one story per year in 1880 and 1881, then two stories per year from 1882 to 1884, then four Frank Reade Jr. stories in 1885. The last story covered in this period ends serialization on April 3, 1886, three weeks shy of the tenth anniversary of the first Reade story's conclusion. Even when the series takes its first major leap in science—from steam to electrical power in 1882's *Frank Reade, Jr. and His Electric Boat*—the North American setting remains. Most of the action in that adventure occurs on Lake Michigan, where Reade Jr. fights US-Canadian bootlegging. Similarly, the series presents another major nautical invention in the submarine from 1884's *Frank Reade, Jr.'s Marvel*. In that story, the adventure takes place in Louisiana's Red River. Unlike the *Nautilus* of Verne's Captain Nemo in *20,000 Leagues under the Sea* (1869), Reade's *Marvel* does not circle the globe or even venture outside US waters. Only in 1884, with *Frank Reade, Jr. in the Clouds*, does the series leave North America. Within two months, that story is followed by *Frank Reade, Jr. with His Air-Ship in Africa*, the first of many African expeditions in the series; subsequently, three more North American adventures appear

Table 1. Locales and Dates of First Decade of Frank Reade Series (1876–1886)

Year	Title	Locations Visited	First Appearance	Serialization Dates	Issues
1876	The Steam Man of the Plains; or, The Terror of the West	U.S. West	Boys of New York	Feb. 28 to Apr. 24, 1876	28–36
	Frank Reade and His Steam Horse	U.S. West	Boys of New York	July 17 to Sep. 25, 1876	48–58
1877	—				
1878	—				
1879	Steam Man (reprint)			Jan. 13 to Mar. 31, 1879	178–89
	Steam Horse (reprint)			July 21 to Oct. 20, 1879	205–18
1880	Frank Reade and His Steam Team	U.S. West (Missouri, Kansas)	Boys of New York	Jan. 5 to Mar. 8, 1880	229–38
1881	Frank Reade and His Steam Tally-Ho	U.S. West (Wyandotte, Devil's Hole)	Boys of New York	Jan. 10 to Apr. 4 1881	282–94
1882	Frank Reade, Jr., and His Steam Wonder	U.S. West	Boys of New York	Feb. 4 to Apr. 29, 1882	338–50
	Frank Reade, Jr., and His Electric Boat	Great Lakes	Boys of New York	Aug. 12 to Oct. 21, 1882	365–75
1883	Frank Reade, Jr., and His Adventures with His Latest Invention	U.S. West	Boys of New York	Apr. 7 to June 23, 1883	399–410
	Frank Reade, Jr., and His Air-Ship	Mexico/U.S. West (Rocky Mts, California, Mexico)	Boys of New York	Dec. 1, 1883 to Mar. 1, 1884	433–46
1884	Frank Reade, Jr.'s Marvel; or, Above and Below Water	Red River (New Orleans)	Boys of New York	May 10 to July 19, 1884	456–66
	Frank Reade, Jr., in the Clouds	North Pole, Denmark	Boys of New York	Sept. 6 to Dec. 20, 1884	473–88

1885				
Frank Reade, Jr., with His Air-Ship in Africa	Africa (Egypt, Zululand)	Boys of New York	Feb. 14 to May 2, 1885	496–507
Frank Reade, Jr.'s Great Electric Tricycle, and What He Did for Charity	Central U.S. (Chicago to New Orleans)	Wide Awake Library	May 13, 1885	662
Across the Continent on Wings; or, Frank Reade, Jr.'s Greatest Flight	U.S. West Coast (Utah, California)	Boys of New York	July 25 to Oct. 3 1885	519–29
Frank Reade, Jr., Exploring Mexico in His New Air-Ship	Mexico	Boys of New York	Dec. 12 1885 to Apr. 3 1886	539–55

Sources: Data from Bleiler, "Chronological Note to the Reader"; LeBlanc, *Bibliographic Listing of the Boys of New York* and *Bibliographic Listing of Wide Awake Library*.

before the setting moves abroad again. Significantly, the adventures from 1876 to 1885 that occur outside the United States all feature airships. As the Reade novels shift from steam-driven prime movers to rapid, heavier-than-air craft, the scope for the stories expands into international territory. Imagined technology begets imagined imperialism.

By September 1892, when the series entered weekly publication, Reade Jr.'s exploits were truly international affairs. Table 2 lists all the stories that appeared in the *Frank Reade Library* during 1894, when the series was predominantly a bi-weekly affair of original material, providing a stark contrast to the American West–dominated tales of the 1870s and 1880s. Reprints of older material made up part of the first year's weekly issues, making it difficult to assess these changes because international adventures were interspersed with earlier tales. Of the 25 separate novels in 1894, North America narrowly dominates with five tales set in the western United States, two in Canada, and two in Mexico. Beyond those, three stories are set in Africa, three in South America, one in Australia, and one in India. Electrical vehicles—the Electric Prairie Schooner, the Electric Caravan—figure heavily. Airships appear in several stories where the action takes place outside the United States (Peru and Canada), but just as often Reade Jr.'s adventures in foreign locales feature land vehicles, such as the Electric Buckboard used in Australia, or the Electric Wagon used to combat ivory hunters in Africa. Several of the stories featuring submarines have no precise location other than the ocean, but in the one year covered here Reade Jr. has adventures in the Pacific and Atlantic Oceans, the Arctic and the Yellow (East China) Seas. Just as interesting are the four arctic tales of technologically enhanced polar expeditions. All this demonstrates that, on their surface, the Reade dime novels play out key elements of technocratic expansionism.

To fully illustrate the difference in the manner suggested by Moretti's "distant reading" methodology, maps 1 and 2 contrast the locales portrayed in the first ten years of the series to the bi-weekly publication in 1894. Areas mentioned by name in the text, either in titles of the novels or in the body of the story, are marked on the world map. The early Reade stories' reliance on North America is apparent; the material from 1894 encompasses most of the globe, with the exception of much of Northern Europe and Asia. Clearly, by 1894, Frank Reade Jr.'s canvas is the world.

Despite their portrayal of a US imperial imaginary, some tropes of the novels subvert the imperialist underpinnings of the Edisonade. To see this, we must shift from the quantitative body of evidence to textual particulars. The following examples, primarily from the first four portrayals of Frank Reade Jr., demonstrate how Senarens conceives and develops a Reade plot. By looking closely at these novels, it becomes clear that Senarens did not

Table 2. Locales and Dates of New *Frank Reade Library* Stories Published in 1894

Year	Title	Locations Visited	Pub. Date	Issue
1894	*The Black Range; or, Frank Reade, Jr., among the Cowboys with His New Electric Caravan*	New Mexico	Jan. 6, 1894	68
	From Zone to Zone; or, The Wonderful Trip of Frank Reade, Jr., with His Latest Air-Ship	North Pole	Jan. 13, 1894	69
	Frank Reade, Jr., and His Electric Prairie Schooner; or Fighting the Mexican Horse Thieves	Texas / Mexico	Jan. 20, 1894	70
	Frank Reade, Jr., and His Electric Cruiser of the Lakes; or A Journey through Africa by Water	Africa	Jan. 27, 1894	71
	Adrift in Africa; or Frank Reade, Jr., among the Ivory Hunters with His New Electric Wagon	Central Africa	Feb. 3, 1894	72
	Six Weeks in the Clouds; or Frank Reade, Jr.'s Air-Ship, the Thunderbolt of the Skies	Canada (Hudson Bay)	Feb. 10, 1894	73
	Frank Reade, Jr.'s Electric Air Racer; or Around the Globe in Thirty Days	San Francisco, Japan, Pekin, Azores	Feb. 24, 1894	74
	Frank Reade, Jr., and His Flying Ice Ship; or, Driven Adrift in the Frozen Sky	Arctic, Norway	Mar. 10, 1894	75
	Frank Reade, Jr., and His Electric Sea Engine; or, Hunting for a Sunken Diamond Mine	Indian Ocean	Mar. 24, 1894	76
	Frank Reade, Jr., Exploring a Submarine Mountain; or, Lost at the Bottom of the Sea	Cape Horn (undersea)	Apr. 7, 1894	77
	Frank Reade, Jr.'s Electric Buckboard; or, Thrilling Adventures in North Australia	Australia	Apr. 21, 1894	78
	Frank Reade, Jr.'s Search for the Sea Serpent; or, Six Thousand Miles under the Sea	Arctic Sea, Alentian Isles	May 4, 1894	79
	Frank Reade, Jr.'s Desert Explorer; or, The Underground City of the Sahara	Egypt / North Africa	May 18, 1894	80

Continued on the next page

Table 2. *Continued*

Year	Title	Locations Visited	Pub. Date	Issue
	Across the Frozen Sea, or, Frank Reade, Jr.'s Electric Snow Cutter	Arctic / North Pole	June 22, 1894	83
	Lost in the Great Atlantic Valley; or, Frank Reade, Jr., and His Submarine Wonder the "Dart"	Azores, Bermuda, Gulf Stream (undersea)	July 6, 1894	84
	Frank Reade, Jr.'s Clipper of the Prairie; or, Fighting the Apaches in the Far Southwest	Arizona	Aug. 19, 1894	87
	Under the Amazon for a Thousand Miles; or, Frank Reade, Jr.'s Wonderful Trip	Brazil	Aug.24, 1894	88
	Frank Reade, Jr.'s Search for the Silver Whale; or, Under the Ocean in the Electric "Dolphin"	North Pacific Ocean (San Francisco, Baffin Bay)	Sept. 7, 1894	89
	Frank Reade, Jr.'s Search for a Lost Man in His Latest Air Wonder	Saskatchewan, Canada	Oct. 5, 1894	91
	Frank Reade, Jr., in Central India; or, The Search for the Lost Savants	India	Oct. 12, 1894	92
	The Missing Island; or Frank Reade, Jr.'s Wonderful Trip under the Deep Sea	Aztec Islands / Baja California / Cape Horn	Nov. 2 1894	93
	Over the Andes with Frank Reade, Jr., in His New Air-Ship; or, Wild Adventures in Peru	Peru	Nov. 16 1894	94
	Frank Reade, Jr.'s Prairie Whirlwind; or, The Mystery of the Hidden Canyon	New Mexico	Nov. 30, 1894	95
	Under the Yellow Sea; or, Frank Reade, Jr.'s Search for the Cave of Pearls with His New Submarine Cruiser	Yellow Sea	Dec. 14, 1894	96
	Around the Horizon for Ten Thousand Miles; or, Frank Reade, Jr.'s Most Wonderful Trip with His Air-Ship	Over the USA	Dec. 28, 1894	97

Note: Issues 81–82, 85–86, and 90 are reprints of earlier material. All stories appeared complete in single issues of *The Frank Reade Library.*

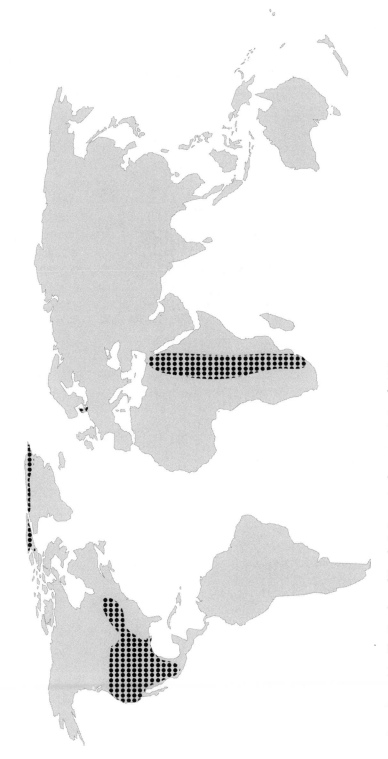

1. Locations visited by Reade and Reade Jr. in stories between 1876 and 1886.

2. Locations visited by Reade Jr. in stories from 1894.

approach technocratic expansion in an exclusively imperialistic or nationalistic way.

Reade Jr.'s interaction with other characters shows that the series' central allegory comes from its celebration of individual technological achievement without large-scale cultural impact, an element that obscures the logic of imperialism. The Senarens novels repeatedly demonstrate how technology empowers the individual to act as final arbiter. For the Frank Reade Jr. novels to work as allegories of such individual power, they must also constantly resist the temptation to display the larger cultural impact of Reade Jr.'s inventions. Technology provides opportunities for personal adventurism, but it has no tangible, long-term effects. A good example comes in *Steam Wonder* (1882) when Reade Jr.'s companion Jack notes that the Steam Wonder will "create a revolution in Western travel" (6). Shortly afterward, they encounter a wagon train and frighten its horses. The guide denounces Reade: "Git out!" he says. "That Union Pacific Railroad drove us guides away down hyer, and now *you* come snortin' erlong with that blasted ole steam machine to break us up. Git out, I say, or by the great prairie I'll fill yer skin chock full of lead" (6). Frank pilots the Steam Wonder away, noting to Jack that the guide is an "old crank" who has undoubtedly lost business to the railroad and thinks the Steam Wonder will "kill his business completely" (6). Reade Jr. later saves the same wagon train from Indian attack, and discussion of the Steam Wonder's potential to create social change is dropped completely. While the novels do not shirk from mentioning the potential disruption to the status quo that Reade's contraptions may create, they resist overt portrayal of such consequences and instead highlight technologically enabled acts of heroism.

Senarens also portrays individuals who immediately perceive the Steam Wonder's benefit and want to buy it, only to be rebuffed. Such rejected offers are a constituent element of the Reade myth.[31] In *Steam Wonder*, Reade turns down a postmaster who encourages him to use his device to deliver mail (19). He also rejects an offer from a wealthy stockbroker, Mr. Gregory, who asks to buy the Steam Wonder after their final attack on the Comanche village (23). In *Frank Reade, Jr. and His Electric Boat*, he turns down a government offer to buy his work for "millions."[32] As the wealthy son of an inventor, Reade Jr. does not need additional capital. He possesses knowledge and resources, so the construction of new technology serves primarily to enable his adventures without the interference from individuals or social bodies that could hamper his goals. A similar scene in 1883's *Frank Reade, Jr. and His Air-Ship* underscores this point. Reade Jr. aids a wealthy Mexican landowner who wants to buy the heavier-than-air craft. Frank replies, "Your offer is ten times greater than the cost of the air-ship. . . . But it's the only one in existence, and I am on a pleasure-trip. Some day I may either sell you this one or have one made for you" (14).

"Some day" never comes in the Frank Reade Jr. novels. His technology produces no repercussions and, while they frequently make lucrative discoveries of hidden mines or lost cities, Reade Jr. and his friends do not seek a fortune by patenting or selling technology. If the novels suggested that Reade Jr.'s inventions had repercussions beyond his "fun," they would need to address implications of the power inherent in his expansionist technologies. Reade Jr. would have to deal with consequences of his technology rather than taking pleasure in displaying its thrilling power. In the example of the wagon train, resistance to the (hypothetical) job loss caused by his invention is easily overcome by its martial utility in confronting sensationalized Indian violence, derailing any consideration of larger social ramifications. Such examples help explain why the dénouements of Reade novels frequently include his rejection of offers to buy his craft. If Reade Jr. commodifies his technologies, he relinquishes the autonomy so highly valued in the tales.

This allegorical turn contradicts claims that the stories are inherently nationalistic. A later Frank Reade Jr. story illustrates this point. In *Frank Reade, Jr., Exploring a Submarine Mountain* from April 7, 1894, Reade Jr. has this exchange with a government representative who wants to buy Reade's invention:

> "I do not approve of war or its horrible engines. I don't wish my invention to ever be turned to such a purpose. For that reason and the good of humanity at large I prefer to keep my secret."
> "But think of its value," protested the agent.
> "That may be. But money is no object to me at all. The government has enough to defend itself with now."
> "You are not patriotic!"
> "Just the same I am not lending myself to the invention of engines of destruction."[33]

By 1894, Reade Jr. disdains the use of his inventions as "engines of destruction" by government, after over a decade of stories in which he frequently chooses to use his inventions for this very end. The issue, then, is less about *how* the technology is used than about *who* controls it. Reade Jr.'s decisions throughout the series—to punish outlaws, to aid people in need, and to refuse to sell his items—all underscore the series' enthusiastic individualism. Technology enables not only travel but expansion of influence, not only military power but its judicious use on a personal level without recourse to a larger body (government, Church, etc.), even leading to accusations of being "unpatriotic" for not relinquishing his weapon to the US government.

Gunslinging Martí and Fighting Yankee Boys: Senarens and Cuba's Revolution

Broader evidence regarding the complex treatment of American expansionism can be found by examining Senarens's tenure at Tousey press during the War for Cuban Independence. In cataloguing Senarens's science-fiction writing, Bleiler notes that the author "might have been expected to be sympathetic with Latin Americans" due to his Cuban heritage, but instead used Mexicans and other Hispanic characters as stereotyped villains in many works.[34] Senarens, however, clearly had an interest in his Cuban heritage, and his involvement with the Cuban independence movement demonstrates the role literary works can play as wartime propaganda. In early 1895, Cuban insurgents declared war against Spain in the *Montecristi Manifesto* and invaded the island to liberate it. The war lasted until 1898, when US involvement after the explosion of the battleship *Maine* led to the Spanish-American War. During that three-year period, Senarens and the Tousey press became very involved in printing stories about the Cuban revolution, and the Edisonades that he wrote during that period are only fully understandable in this context.

Senarens's interest in Cuban independence is initially suggested in 1879. Prior to working for Tousey, when the author was only fourteen years old, he published *Ralph the Rover, or, The Cuban Patriots* in the Nickel Library. Its publication coincides with Cuba's short-lived revolution against Spain known as the *Guerra Chiquita*—or Little War—between 1879 and 1880. Although his name was misspelled as "Lu Senarnes" on the cover, the novel is one of a handful that appeared under his own name rather than a pseudonym. The hero is a young, adventurous Anglo-American, Ralph Seabright, who has no ethno-national ties to Cuba but nevertheless becomes embroiled in the war when he is kidnapped and sent abroad. From its tone, it is clear the readers' sympathies are meant to side with Cuba. The Cuban patriots, we are told, "fought for their country, with no pay—fought as heroes, suffering untold privations; starving at times, destitute of clothing at others; fought on, with no encouragement, no applause to their efforts, save that given to one another; their battle-cry, '*Vive la Cuba y libertad!*' (Cuba forever, and liberty)."[35] The story features a Spanish spy masquerading as a Cuban patriot who torments Ralph and his friends, and the story culminates

in a hair-breath rescue from a Spanish firing squad. While the Cubans ultimately lost the war to Spain's forces, the dime novel offered an optimistic
view of American involvement.

Sixteen years later, Senarens was a seasoned professional writer and Cuba
was about to begin a new fight for independence. In 1895, the same year Cubans began an organized resistance to Spain led by Jose Martí, Máximo Gómez, and others, Senarens became editor-in-chief of Tousey Press.[36] Senarens's
editorial work has received less scrutiny than his science-fiction writing, but
close examination of it suggests that the author used Tousey publications to
actively bring the Cuban cause—and the Cuban generals—to the attention
of young dime-novel readers and to advocate that North Americans should
respect Cuban sovereignty. Between 1895 and 1897, Tousey published at least
ten dime novels specifically about the war for independence in Cuba. Table 3
lists the titles, authors, and publication information for each of these texts.
These appeared in three different periodicals, and included both original
works set in Cuba and the incorporation of the war into storylines featuring popular, long-recurring characters such as the internationally famous
British schoolboy character Jack Harkaway and boy inventors Frank Reade
Jr. and Jack Wright. In many of these stories, actual Cuban leaders are portrayed, often encouraging US readers to admire the Cuban cause and to resist annexation in favor of a free, independent Cuba.

Such an approach, however, was not shared by other literary outlets. The
role of yellow journalism in fostering American support for a war against
Spain is well known.[37] Story papers of the era portrayed similar jingoistic
narratives. In April and June of 1896, for example, the *New York Ledger* ran
a serial by John H. Whitson titled "Fighting for Cuba's Freedom." Although
it appeared over a year after the Cuban resistance had begun their war, the
story was set during the *Guerra Chiquita* of 1879–1880. From the safety of
this historical distance, it presents the common, pro-annexation mentality,
right down to the idea that a war against Spain to win Cuba would help heal
the nation's lingering divisiveness over the Civil War. It featured two Civil
War veterans (one southerner, one northerner) on a filibustering trip where
their friendship grows as they fight to help Cuba. One character explicitly
states his reasons for participating: "I think that Cuba was intended to become a part of the United States, and that she will be!"[38] The *Ledger's* serial
mirrored ideas of American interests who thought the United States should
overthrow Spain and take control of Cuba itself.

The dime novels published by Tousey under Senarens's editorship con-
sistently offer a different perspective. The first of these stories appeared in
Happy Days, issues 43–50, beginning on August 10, 1895, five months after
Cuban rebels began fighting on February 24. *Two Yankee Boys in Cuba; or,*

Fighting with the Patriots is attributed to the house name P. T. Raymond, so it is uncertain who wrote it. What is certain is that it invokes a very specific approach to the Cuban perspective. As the title suggests, the heroes are Americans: two military cadets named Dick Royal and Ned Blake, who resemble Senarens's Frank Seabright in their youth, enthusiasm, and Anglo-American background. Dick falls in love with a beautiful Cuban girl named Fanita Peralto, whose father and brother are supporting the Cuban insurgents. After fighting alongside the Cubans in several skirmishes, they come to see the Cuban cause in no uncertain terms. In the September 7, 1895, issue, one Cuban officer tells Dick and Ned, "The Spaniards oppress the Cubans just as the English oppressed the American colonists."[39] After contemplating the similarities between the Cubans' cause and his country's history, Ned notes that the Cubans seem even more heroic in contrast:

> "In the American case the colonists had money, arms, men, and the aid of others; in the Cuban case, the patriots had but little money, arms or aid, and were placed at the disadvantage of being persecuted by foreign powers from whom they wished to purchase the means of war."
>
> "By thunder," said Dick, "it's an outrage for the Cubans to be ignored and harassed by other nations!"
>
> "I'm after wondering if the Americans would have had their independence to-day had they been suffering all the antagonism the poor Cubans now endure," said Ned sadly.[40]

The dime novel's rhetoric draws direct analogies between the Cuban cause and the US revolution against Britain, a method articulated in many outlets of the time. As Susan K. Harris notes, such analogies partially succeeded, and when the United States declared war against Spain in 1898, it did so in part because Americans "saw the Cuban situation through the lens of their own national history—as a colony in which patriots were fighting for freedom from an oppressive mother country."[41] The commonality between Cuban independence and US independence was promoted most notably by Cuban patriot José Martí in his response to a *New York Evening Post* article that argued against any US involvement because of the "helpless, idle" nature, and "defective morals" of Cubans in general. Martí's response, "A Vindication of Cuba," published in the *Post* on March 25, 1889, notes that the Cubans lost their first attempts at independence because "we had no Hessians and no Frenchmen, no Lafayette or Steuben, no monarchial rivals to help us. . . . We fell victim to the very passions which could have caused the downfall of the thirteen States."[42] As a writer and statesman, Martí understood the double-edged sword of US interest in Cuba. He wanted North

Americans to support their cause, but didn't want to simply exchange his country's status, from a Spanish colony to a US colony or state.

The similarity between Martí's letter and the views of the American characters in "Two Yankee Boys" is no coincidence: a few pages into the first issue of the serial, Martí himself appears as a character. He arrives at the Peralta plantation to receive a donation to his cause, described as "a careworn looking man with a dark mustache, clad in ragged clothing, and carrying a brace of revolvers and a machete, while a pair of spurs were on his heels."[43] Upon Martí's arrival, the group are confronted by Spanish collaborator (and Fanita Peralto's would-be seducer) Pedro Durango.

> "Halt!" roared Durango, sternly. "I'll shoot the first one who moves an inch."
> "Two can play at that game, senor!" hissed Marti, whipping out a revolver and aiming it at the captain. . . .
> Bang! Went the weapons of both at the same instant.
> Marti remained uninjured, but Durango gave a wild yell of pain and staggered back.
> "I'm shot, curse you!" he shrieked.[44]

Martí is portrayed not as the statesman or the thoughtful intellectual of his essays, but in the mode of a dime-novel cowboy, fast on the draw and capable of outgunning his opponent. However, Martí's presence in the novel serves a larger ideological purpose. The Cuban leader died fighting for Cuban independence very early in the war—on May 19, 1895, three months prior to the serialization of "Two Yankee Boys in Cuba." The writer incorporates this fact into the story, as Ned and Dick are given papers by another real-life Cuban General, Antonio Maceo, to deliver to Martí. The papers are stolen, and they learn from a soldier that Martí died because he lacked the lost information: They're informed "Marti has been killed at St. Jago. . . . May God help us now for our bravest leader is gone."[45] Thus, the story incorporates the leader's martyrdom to further emphasize the Cuban's cause. Similarly, a follow-up storyline, *Maceo's Boy Guerrillas* by Gaston Garne, features two young Americans who arrive in Cuba carrying letters of commission signed by Martí for them to aid the Cubans. When Maceo examines their letters, he sadly informs them that Martí "will never handle a pen again" and they mourn the loss of the Cuban leader.[46]

The use of real individuals—generals, police commissioners, politicians— was fairly common in dime novel writing, which often used newspaper articles for story ideas.[47] What is striking, however, is the number of stories published under Senarens's editorship at Tousey.

Table 3. Dime Novels about Cuban Revolution Published by Tousey (1895–1897)

	Date(s)	Series	Author	Title
1	Aug. 10 to Sept. 28, 1895	*Happy Days*, Issues 43–50	Raymond, P. T.	*Two Yankee Boys in Cuba; or, Fighting with the Patriots. A Story of the Cuban War*
2	Mar. 13, 1896	*The Boys' Star Library*, Issue 374	Noname [Lu Senarens]	*Running the Blockade; or, Jack Wright Helping the Cuban Filibusters*
3	Apr. 10, 1896	*The Boys' Star Library*, Issue 376	Noname [Lu Senarens]	*The Flying Avenger; or, Jack Wright Fighting for Cuba*
4	Apr. 18 to May 30, 1896	*Happy Days*, Issues 79–85	Garne, Gaston	*Maceo's Boy Guerillas; or Fighting to Free Cuba*
5	June 27 to Aug. 8, 1896	*Happy Days*, Issues 89–95	Noname [Lu Senarens]	*Frank Reade, Jr., in Cuba; or Helping the Patriots with His Latest Air-Ship*
6	Dec. 18, 1896	*Wide Awake Library*, Issue 1298	Hemyng, Bracebridge	*Young Jack Harkaway in Cuba*
7	Jan. 9 to Feb. 27, 1897	*Happy Days*, Issues 117–24	Garne, Gaston	*Maceo's Boys; or, Young America in the Cuban War*
8	Jan. 15, 1897	*Wide Awake Library*, Issue 1302	Hemyng, Bracebridge	*Young Jack Harkaway among the Cuban Insurgents*
9	Feb. 27 to Apr. 17, 1897	*Happy Days*, Issues 124–31	Garne, Gaston	*The 'Three Friends'; or, The Cuban Junta's Yankee Dead Shot. A Story of the Famous Blockade Runner*
10	Apr. 17 to June 5, 1897	*Happy Days*, Issues 131–38	Garne, Gaston	*Fighting with Gomez; or, Texas Cowboys in Cuba*

As table 3 shows, five of the ten stories printed during a two-year period from August 1895 to June 1897 were in *Happy Days*, the same publication that regularly printed Frank Reade Jr.'s exploits.[48] By February 1897, such tales were popular enough to appear on the cover of *Happy Days* with simply the words "Cuba!" to promote them. The February 20 issue highlights Gaston Garne's *The 'Three Friends'; or, The Cuban Junta's Yankee Dead Shot* as starting next week on its front page. The same issue features the penultimate chapter of *Maceo's Boys*, indicating that in the following issue—February 27, 1897—there were actually *two* stories of young Americans participating in the Cuban war running simultaneously. Notably, Bracebridge Hemyng's popular British schoolboy character, Jack Harkaway, appears in two *Five Cent Wide Awake Library* stories dealing with current events in Cuba. The globe-trotting Harkaway was already a popular dime-novel fixture when Tousey secured the rights to publish writing by Hemyng, a British author who had moved to the United States and previously had been under exclusive contract to Frank Leslie's dime novel publishing company.[49] Storylines presenting the famous character embroiled in events in Cuba would almost certainly reach a large audience, and the narrative capitalizes on this situation. Harkaway's adventures in Cuba follow a similar narrative to the other stories published under Senarens's editorship, with the notable difference that the English boy arrives with sympathies for Spain until he witnesses the Cuban fighters and meets General Máximo Gómez, whose bravery wins Harkaway's sympathies. We are told, "From what he had seen and heard Jack was convinced that their cause was just. His opinions had undergone a change."[50]

So what did Tousey's readership think of all this? Dime-novel columns responding to readers' mail provide clues. Following a nineteenth-century publishing convention, letter writers typically provided a pseudonym or description of themselves and the publishers printed responses directed at that identifying moniker without reprinting the original query. An 1896 response in *Happy Days'* "Answers to Correspondents" section is addressed to "Two Yankee Boys in Cuba," indicating that the story was popular enough for a letter writer to use it as a nom-de-plume (a typical convention for such letters).[51] On February 20, 1897, a correspondent calling himself "Diamond Dave" receives the reply: "General Maceo is undoubtedly dead," indicating that some readers were appealing to Tousey dime novels for actual reporting on the war, particularly about one of the generals they had immortalized in their serials.[52] More significantly, we find one response in the correspondence column of the July 4, 1896, issue of *Happy Days*—the same issue where the second installment of *Frank Reade, Jr. in Cuba* appears. It reads: "We cannot give you the required information. The headquarters of the Cuban insurgents in New York and Baltimore must necessarily be kept secret, as it is against the laws of neutrality between this country and Spain to allow the fitting out of bodies of men in the United States to aid the Cuban insurgents."[53] The response coyly tells the writer a great deal. They don't deny knowing the locations of the Baltimore and New York headquarters; they simply report that they cannot print it because it is secret. Instead, the reply calls attention to the same US "non-interventionist" policy criticized by Martí in his "Vindication of Cuba" letter and by Dick and Ned in "Two Yankee Boys." Thus, the response confirms that there *is* clandestine support of Cubans going on in New York and Baltimore and manages to call attention to the problem of the United States' official position on Cuba at the same time. All this indicates that, under Senarens editorship, Tousey dime novels expressed consistently pro-Cuban narratives that emphasized Cuban nationalism rather than annexation, and it suggests that readers were invested enough in the conflict to request more information via the outlet provided by dime novel publications.

The single most willfully anti-imperial Frank Reade Jr. story was constructed from real-life circumstances tied directly to Spanish colonialism and American empire building. *Frank Reade, Jr. in Cuba; or, Helping the Patriots with His Latest Air-Ship*, serialized in *Happy Days* from June 27 to August 8, 1896, takes the recurring myth established under Senarens's authorship and blends it with an exposé of international politics, revealing the possibilities and limits of its allegory. At this point in his career, the Cuban American writer had already written at least three dime novels incorporating his father's homeland and its struggle for independence from Spain, the first being *Ralph the Rover*. The other two featured Jack Wright, Tousey publishing's other main boy inventor who had been created after Frank Reade's success. *Running the Blockade; or, Jack Wright Helping the Cuban Filibusters*, for March 13, 1896, featured Wright using a submarine to provide Gomez and the Cuban insurgents with forty boxes of weapons.[54] It is virtually identical to *Frank Reade, Jr. in Cuba* in content and tone. He repeated the formula—this time with Wright piloting an airship—in *The Flying Avenger; or, Jack Wright Fighting for Cuba* from the April 10, 1896, *Boys' Star Library*. *Frank Reade, Jr. in Cuba*, then, was the culmination of four novels using the Cuban conflict, and it shows how Edisonades' treatment of imaginary imperialism narratively interacts with the realities of empire and US intervention. The story explores Reade Jr.'s participation in the war for Cuban independence, just over a year after Cubans began a war against their Spanish colonial rulers and two years before the United States declared war on Spain after the sinking of the battleship *Maine* in February 1898. In keeping with the Reade myth, Frank's invention—an airship called the Jupiter—has only limited effects and his actions are devoid of long-term social consequences. The relatively benign and altruistic nature of Reade Jr.'s interference underscores the text's appeals to Cuban patriotism: the Cubans are the heroes, while Reade Jr. assists their leaders with his technology. Appeals to Cuban sovereignty—the ostensible justification for US interference that ultimately occurred two years after the novel's first publication—occur frequently in the text. Several other key, contemporary debates involving US/Cuban relations and American international cultural and political expansion—potential annexation of Cuba or the establishment of a US protectorate—are never mentioned in the text.

Frank Reade, Jr. in Cuba presents numerous, discrete adventures that feature historical personages. Reade Jr. becomes a volunteer in the Cuban rebel's war against Spain, swayed by news reports of the Cuban patriots and their fight against General Weyler, who was sent from Spain in 1896 specifically to put down the most recent insurgency. The story begins with Reade Jr. perusing a newspaper and lamenting, "The savage brutality of Gen. Weyler's troops is becoming unbearable. Perhaps I may hasten the cessation of this cruel war" (2). Reade Jr. requests and receives permission to intervene in the conflict, presenting a "big letter from the Cuban junta in New York" to his cohorts: "See—it contains my commission to act for the army of liberation, and letters to Antonio Maceo, Gen. Maximo Gomez and Senor Betancourt, the first president of Cuba libre. . . . It is an acceptance of my recent offer to use my air-ship in behalf of the patriots."[55] Clearly, Senarens followed the events in Cuba closely and incorporated stories from the press into the novel when it was serialized in June 1896. He is critical of General Weyler's treatment of Cuban civilians, including acts denounced repeatedly in the US press in early 1896. His proclamation of many anti-democratic measures, which included extending the death penalty to anyone circulating news "favorable to the rebellion" or who would "belittle the prestige of Spain," were reported derisively in the February 17, 1896, *New York Times*.[56] On February 24, the *Times* quoted one unidentified "American planter" in Cuba who reported that Cubans were being "shot and no questions asked about internment the next morning."[57] Three days later, such policies hit home for Americans as the *Times* reported the liberation of an American reporter, Charles Michelson of the *New York Journal*, who had been held by Weyler under the new laws. The US Consul General appealed for the newsman and his interpreter's release.[58] Thus, the portrayal of Reade Jr.'s anger at such information seems typical of the times.

Another incident factors even more directly into *Frank Reade, Jr. in Cuba*'s plot. Reade Jr. tells his companions Barney and Pomp that, while he abhors Spain's "barbarous mode of warfare," his trip is also inspired by his desire to rescue his captive friend, Walter Dagmore. He explains: "Walter was a newspaper reporter, sent to Cuba by the journal he represented. For sending truthful reports of the war to his paper, and for exposing the real facts of a frightful massacre of non-combatants he was seized, thrown into prison, tried by a drum-head court-martial and sentenced to death. The US Consul General filed a vigorous protest . . . but no heed was paid to it, and poor Dagmore is to be shot" (2). While the narrative use of a captive newspaper reporter seems to reference the Michelson incident, the name "Walter Dagmore" alludes to Walter Dygert (reported variously as "Dygart" by the *New York Times* and "Dygatt" by the *Chicago Tribune*), an American who was imprisoned in Cuba in the months prior to the story's publication.[59] Dygert was arrested in Cuba after he moved there from Tampa. Allegedly, Spanish authorities mistook him for Alfredo Gold, an Englishman nicknamed "Inglesita" who was helping the revolutionaries. Spanish authorities reportedly beat Dygert during interrogation and imprisonment. According to one paper in Dygert's home state of Illinois, Spanish authorities were "evidently afraid to tell the truth for fear of the consequences" once the case of mistaken identity came to their attention.[60] The *Chicago Daily Tribune* reported that Dygert had been in Illinois during the same period when the acts of conspiracy he was accused of took place.[61] He was eventually released by Weyler after US Consulate appeals.[62] The Dygert case presented another example of Weyler's brutal methods, particularly directed at an American citizen rather than at Cuban insurgents. The entire text of *Frank Reade, Jr. in Cuba* ups its rhetorical ante by incorporating references to the Michelson and Dygert cases to build its case for Cuban independence.

To underscore this approach, Senarens continues the tradition of portraying Cuban leaders as characters, as established in the earlier Tousey dime novels he oversaw. Gómez, Maceo, and other leaders are portrayed heroically in Senarens's 1896 dime novel, but it is still perhaps Martí's spirit that looms largest. Although Martí was killed in battle a year before *Frank Reade, Jr. in Cuba* was published, his understanding of nationalism and the threat of US interference come to bear in the novel. He feared that Americans could justify interference in Cuba because their Anglo-Saxon conception of manifest destiny encouraged disdain for the ethnically diverse culture of Cuba.[63] Like "Two Yankee Boys," the Frank Reade story seems written in conversation with Martí's writing, particularly his landmark essay "Our America," which articulates the differences between the United States and the Latin American countries by valorizing the latter. As Martí emphasizes, "The disdain of our formidable neighbor [the United States] who does not know [Latin America] is our America's greatest danger."[64] As Laura Lomas has shown, Martí's writing counters pro-expansionist narratives, such as Frederick Jackson Turner's frontier essays, by highlighting the United States' history of lynchings, riots, and systematized racism in popular media, such as plays and Wild West shows.[65] Lomas has emphasized Martí's "strategy" for writing as an outsider within America, including his assertion that "one must be perennially inside the corpulent race, and convince it little by little."[66] This approach represents Martí's attempt to help the United States understand Latin America in general and Cuba in particular.

Frank Reade, Jr. in Cuba represents a strange blend of the techno-expansionist tale established by the earlier Frank Reade Jr. stories and the inflammatory, persuasive statement written "inside the corpulent race" that Martí suggested was needed for the United States to understand and respect Latin America. In light of the postwar limits placed on Cuba by the United States, Frank Reade Jr.'s affirmation of Cuban insurgency presents an optimistic view of Cuban-American relations and plays out the imperial imaginary in its most benign, altruistic sense. The Cuban insurgents embody the same independent spirit valorized by the Edisonades' master narrative. At one point, Reade Jr. observes:

> "Very few people make their way in the world by inactively waiting for good fortune to come their way and favor them. The Cubans are a good example. See all they have accomplished by their own exertions. Hard work, good judgment, plenty courage and a liberal amount of perseverance have made them practically masters of this island."
> "That's a fact," admitted Dagmore. (17)

To Reade Jr., the Cubans are kindred spirits who share his values of courage and hard work. The character explicitly connects the two peoples and delineates where US readers' sympathies should lie, matter-of-factly explaining to one insurgent, "As we are Americans, we are Cuban sympathizers" (11).

Moreover, Reade Jr. does not dominate the narrative's heroics. From above in the airship, Reade Jr. and his crew watch Cuban leader Máximo Gómez lead his troops in a thoroughly romanticized fashion: "With an ensign upon each side of him, bearing the colors of the new Cuban republic, Gómez brandished his sword, dug spurs into the flank of his horse, and dashed away" (7). Frank notes from the airship that he "never saw such noble courage and such grand generalship before" (5). Such descriptions idealize

Gómez, while the prominence of the Cuban flag underscores the country's sovereignty. The text's heroic presentation of Gómez secures the allegorical linking between Cuban and US patriotism. In the final showdown, Reade Jr. uses his airship not primarily as a weapon, but as a means of transportation to help Gómez infiltrate a pro-Spanish speech by Weyler, interrupt the proceedings, and proclaim Cuba's right to freedom (17). When Weyler's troops attempt to execute Gómez, Reade Jr. drops exploding bags of flash powder from the airship, blinding the Spanish troops and allowing Gómez's escape (17).[67] Gómez acknowledges the "sensation" that Frank has helped him create: "It showed my enemies that I had no fear of them . . . and it gained me many recruits" (17). *Frank Reade, Jr., in Cuba* emphasizes Cuban sovereignty and the heroism of Cuban rebels, asserting that the United States—embodied by Reade—could help the country gain freedom, but not assert its political or economic control over the country as Martí had feared.

Race and Empire in Frank Reade Jr. Novels

As we have seen, the US imperialism's inherent racial elements were dealt with explicitly in the science-fictional work of Irving, Poe, and Ellis, all of which portrayed expansion through the lens of violence against Native Americans. The Frank Reade Jr. books repeatedly deal with race and expansion, and an examination of this clarifies why they did not consistently operate as imperialist propaganda. As scholars such as Edward J. Blum and Walter Benn Michaels have shown, nineteenth-century Americans frequently promoted a notion of whiteness that aligned the concept of "American" with an exclusively Northern European–descended, Protestant construction of whiteness that, once established, facilitated the presumptions of superiority over other nations and races that, along with technocracy, drives imperialism.[68] Harris notes "the ability to cling to the fantasy of homogeneity required increasing rhetorical skill" for Americans at the turn of the twentieth century, faced with a history of slavery and Indian removal in North America and a future as imperial rulers abroad.[69] If the Reade series' approach to nation building is more complex than earlier studies have suggested, then the books' portrayal of race is equally complex in a manner that does not, ultimately, facilitate imperialism as it was constructed in the American minds during this era. True, the earliest Reade novels approximate Ellis's *Steam Man of the Prairies* in their treatment of Native American foes, and Bleiler notes "outrageous racial prejudice focused on blacks, Mexicans, and Jews" is typical of the series, particularly Senarens's writing.[70] Close examination of the story content demonstrates that the portrayal of race in the Frank Reade Jr. tales is anything but stable. Looking at Senarens's first four Frank Reade Jr. novels, it becomes clear that Senarens did not demonstrate the "outrageous racial prejudice" that Bleiler claims. Rather, the Frank Reade Jr. series features the same kind of conflicted portrayal of race found in other nineteenth-century popular works.

It helps to view the racial component from two perspectives: the treatment of the Native American characters who are frequently Reade Jr.'s foils in the early Western dime novels and the treatment of the African American characters who aid the hero in his adventures. In both cases, Senarens's writing addresses race more reflectively than *The Steam Man of the Prairies* or many of the "cowboys vs. Indians" variants of dime novel Westerns. In his discussion of American Western literature, Richard Slotkin has indicated that the "Myth of the Frontier" has always had racial underpinnings intermingled with its appeals "of Social Darwinism 'survival of the fittest' as a rationale for social order, and of 'Manifest Destiny' that have been the building blocks of our dominant historiographical tradition and political ideology."[71] Like Slotkin, Richard Drinnon traces these ideas back to colonial America and wars against Native American populations. He identifies this trend in the Americas as far back as 1638, in Philip Vincent's response to the Pequot War, which is an early articulation of a key concept in later imperialism: the "'one bloody good lesson' view of teaching natives how to behave."[72] From the earliest colonial history, indigenous populations were considered non-persons against whom violence was justified in the effort to control any unwanted actions toward the expanding European colonists.

The first four Frank Reade Jr. novels take place in the West, featuring multiple encounters between Frank and a variety of genericized, confrontational Native American groups. In its predecessors, Ellis's *Steam Man of the Prairies* and the Harry Enton-authored Frank Reade stories, violent battles with Indians occur frequently. Senarens's Frank Reade Jr. stories follow in this tradition. When Reade, his cousin Jack, and his black servant Pomp set out across the prairies in "an engine and car that doesn't need any track" in the *Frank Reade, Jr., and His Steam Wonder*, they quickly encounter Indians as they camp and sleep inside the vehicle (3). The narrator explains: "The reader will remember that Frank Reade, Jr., and his cousin, Jack Russell, were both under eighteen years of age, and had never seen hostile Indians in their lives. It is true that Frank had seen a great many red-skins, having been born in the West, yet he had never seen them in war-paint, nor heard their war-whoop. He and Jack . . . were, therefore, greatly excited when they were so unexpectedly awakened by the yells of the red demons outside their car" (4).

The Indians climb atop the Steam Wonder and try to get inside. The Steam Wonder, however, is portrayed as a bullet-proof, indestructible fortress, and the protagonists are never truly threatened. Frank temporarily frightens them by blowing the Steam Wonder's whistle. When they return, Frank fires up his vehicle and gives chase. "I'll give 'em a scare," he announces, before turning a hose on the Indians that pumps "a stream of boiling water upon them" (5). Such actions are typical of the treatment of Native Americans in the Frank Reade series: the heroes rarely face the threat of genuine harm, but use their technological marvel to humiliate and punish the Indians who encounter them.

Sadistic scenes such as this, however, frequently come with odd rhetorical flourishes. When Jack sees the Indians and suggests that they "give 'em a few bullets," Reade Jr. replies, "No—shed no blood unless compelled to. Father warned me against firing on Indians just because they were Indians. They are human beings as well as ourselves" (5). Jack is "astonished" by this reply, because he "had been reared in New York, where he had got the idea in his head that white men on the plains shot Indians as they did deer . . . every time they got the chance" (5). The line resonates with self-parody, potentially aimed at the young, urban audience of dime novels who were frequently titillated by portrayals of bloody frontier battles and gunfights. It may even be Senarens's self-deprecating acknowledgment of his own position writing such tales; he, too, was a New Yorker who had likely never been to the plains.

Such examples highlight the strange, pendulum-like swings between sadism and sympathy found in the Reade novels. Throughout *Frank Reade, Jr. and his Steam Wonder*, the protagonist struggles with such impulses. He humiliates one captured Indian by shearing off his hair, sending him back to his people with the admonition that "you Indians must let all wagons alone. . . . We are not your enemies. We cut off your hair to show you that we could cut off your head just as well. Tell your people to let us alone and we'll not bother them" (5). They perform a similar shearing on another captured Indian, but when one of the rescued girls claims she is "almost sorry you didn't take his scalp off with his hair," Reade replies: "I don't want to hurt them . . . unless compelled to in self-defense"(8). Frequently, however, Senarens's stories suggest that technology can provide the "one good lesson" approach that Drinnon sees as pervasive in American imperialism. After expressing with frustration that "the Indians have been receiving such lessons at the hands of whites for the last hundred years, and they don't seem to learn anything by it" (9), Reade Jr. and company help a man named Mr. Gregory attack the Comanche who burned his ranch and kidnapped his wife and daughters

(22). Because they are protected by the Steam Wonder's bullet-proof shell, they can attack without ever revealing themselves to danger; we are told that "twenty minutes passed, and the Comanches found that over one-half their number were down, and yet they had not seen a white-face" (22). In *Frank Reade, Jr., and His Adventures with His Latest Invention* (1883), Reade Jr. goes west in an electric tricycle that can travel at thirty miles an hour and is encased by a bulletproof mesh cage to protect the passengers.[73] When attacked by Indians, Reade Jr. runs an electric current through the wire cage around the tricycle, making it a brutally efficient killing device: "The six savages who had laid hands on the tricycle were instantly killed. They dropped to the ground in their tracks, and remained as motionless as only the dead can."[74] The deployment of this technology frequently comes with Reade Jr.'s appeal that he is using violence to teach his attackers that subsequent violence will not benefit them. *Frank Reade, Jr. and His Air-Ship* (1883), which famously portrays heavier-than-air flight for the first of many times in the series, features a scene where Reade captures an aggressive Indian chief, ties him by the heels to the airship, then takes flight, stating, "You know very well that the Indian is no match for the white man."[75]

Even these moments of frontier violence come with flourishes on Reade Jr.'s part that Indians should be treated with respect. *Latest Invention* points to this paradox. Reade Jr. provokes a fight with Chief Red Horse, explaining his method to his traveling companion, Jack, in the electric tricycle by stating, "Oh, I want a little fun out of them, and teach 'em a lesson that will have a tendency to let white people alone. Do you know, Jack, that while they are much sinned against, they are incorrigible thieves and murderers?" (5). The lines embody how Senarens's early Reade stories veer sharply—sometimes even within the same paragraph or sentence—into vague gestures of racial sympathy. Reade at once calls Indians "incorrigible" while in the same sentence explaining that they are "much sinned against." The Reade novels portray US expansionism as inevitable, while straining to show their hero's sympathy on some level with the individuals he is torturing and killing. What we find in the Frank Reade Jr. stories, then, is a continual alternation between sadistic action and empathy, a trope that reinforces the role of the technologically empowered individual as the final regulatory force on the frontier but that is tempered by these appeals to sympathy.

One brief interlude from *Electric Boat* (1882) demonstrates how far out of the way Senarens goes to address racial sympathy in the context of these technocratic, expansionist tales. *Electric Boat* features a strange episode between Reade Jr. and an "Indian maiden" he meets on the lake shore, in which she and Frank discuss the relative merits of each of their respective cultures. She says of her tribe, the Nipigons:

"They are very simple-minded people, and never say or do anything they do not mean."

"Ah! How I wish my people were *all* that way," said Frank.

"They would be better if they were," she remarked. "But the whites are a grand people, and no other race in the world can withstand them." (18)

In a series that thrives on such episodic, out-of-nowhere encounters that have no bearing on plot, this interchange stands out. Each respective party critiques his or her own people. The Nipigon woman expresses dissatisfaction with her own people, voicing the notion of her own people's inevitable decline because they cannot "withstand" white expansion. Frank, in contrast, expresses the wish that his people could be more like the Nipigons in terms of their forthrightness, specifically wishing whites were collectively more honest. Senarens's earliest Frank Reade stories struggle to portray the Indian as both adversary and object of pity, at times approaching what Laura L. Mielke calls the "moving encounter" that portrays contact between Native Americans and Whites in a way that "proposed the possibility of mutual sympathy . . . of community instead of division."[76] Senarens also occasionally critiques whites' understanding of their place in the world, as the exchange with the Nipigon maiden shows.

Much of the misconception that the Reade novels envision imperialism on racial terms, however, comes from Senarens's treatment of Pomp, Reade's African American assistant. Everett Bleiler calls Pomp "an embodied slur" whose traits include "stupidity, slyness, pompous illiteracy, superstition, laziness, and a razor in his footgear."[77] Examination of the first four Senarens-authored Frank Reade Jr. novels shows that, even from its onset, the Reade novels contain contradictory tones in their portrayal of the main, recurring African American character.[78] In the early Senarens-authored novels, Pomp is presented with the same disconcerting mixture of sadism and sympathy found in their treatment of Native Americans. This tone is established when Pomp is introduced on page three of *Steam Wonder* as a worker at Reade's farm who is a "privileged character" because he is the only African American in town. Pomp immediately runs into trouble as he guards the Reade household to prevent "red-shirt" cowboys from breaking into the workshop to see Reade Jr.'s invention. One red-shirt shows a revolver and threatens Pomp:

"I ain't killed er nigger in a month," he said, "an' I'm itchin' to shoot one. Ef that ar door ain't open in two minutes, thar'll be a funeral in Africa for sure.". . .

"I ant' got de key," said Pomp.

"Get it, then."

"Well, hole up dat pistol, den."

The red-shirt did "hole up" the pistol, and the next moment Pomp darted forward, like an old ram, and butted him in the stomach with such tremendous force as to lay him out as limber as a wet rag some twenty feet. (3)

The red-shirt voices a deliberately racialized threat, and Pomp responds with the same justified-when-threatened code of violence that Reade Jr. displays throughout the series. Pomp's head butt can easily be seen as degrading, an example of a black character acting like an animal when faced with trouble. It also, however, is the first of many incidents of Pomp enacting violence toward white lawbreakers throughout the series. Pomp shoots white men with astounding frequency. During the first three Frank Reade Jr. stories, he kills no fewer than four white ruffians, always to the approval of his companions.

In fact, Senarens frequently treats Pomp heroically in the early Frank Reade Jr. tales. Reade Jr. takes Pomp on his first journey west because "Pomp has forgotten more about such trips than I will learn in a year" (*Steam Wonder*, 4). Indeed, Pomp is able to predict Indian attacks because he carefully observes buffalo migration along the way (8–9). Rather than being portrayed exclusively as a comic stereotype, Pomp is more often than not portrayed as, in Reade Jr.'s words, "a man worth having around in a scrimmage" (*Electric Boat*, 8). One scene in *Steam Wonder* perhaps best demonstrates this tone. Two white outlaws attempt to steal the invention by capturing Reade at night, then leading him through the darkness to the door of the Steam Wonder. They make him call out to Pomp to open the door. Ever vigilant, Pomp has observed the proceedings and is more than prepared:

[Pomp] promptly opened the door of the car.

One of the outlaws sprang into the door, but Pomp planted his revolver against his head and pulled the trigger.

He fell into a heap at Pomp's feet.

"That settles the nigger," said the other outlaw, and even Frank himself thought Pomp was done for. . . .

The second outlaw put one foot on the step and was about to spring in, when a second shot broke his arm. His revolver dropped to the ground, and he sprang back with an oath.

"Who fired that shot?" he angrily demanded.

"De niggar did!" replied Pomp, leaping out and confronting him with his smoking revolver in his hand. (16)

It is difficult to read Pomp's use of racial epithet in this context as anything other than proud comic inversion. Pomp mockingly repeats the slur voiced earlier by his opponent, tossing the word back in the face of the white man he has just bested. Moreover, we are told that shooting these outlaws makes Pomp "a hero" to all the folks back in town (16). A similar scene plays out in *Frank Reade and his Latest Invention*, where Pomp shoots and kills a renegade white masquerading as an Indian chief who has attacked Reade's group. Frank looks approvingly on this: "By George that saves us a great deal of trouble," exclaimed Frank. "I could not shoot him down in cold blood. Bully for you, Pomp" (10). As an older male with frontier experiences, Pomp is capable of necessary violence in a way Reade Jr. is not.

This is not to say that Pomp is consistently portrayed with dignity. One incident in *Steam Wonder* involves him winning a barrel of whiskey in a head-butting contest with a "red-shirt" and becoming uproariously drunk. Even this scene eventually ends with Pomp appearing in a positive light. When Frank suggests he auction off the barrel of whiskey and give the proceeds to the two rescued Indian captives, Pomp immediately does so. As a result, "Black Pomp was recognized as a white man after that, and every red-shirt in town took him by the hand and asked him to drink it with him" (13).

The notion that a black man would be recognized as "white" by his white neighbors is, of course, reminiscent of the moment in Twain's *Adventures of Huckleberry Finn*—published two years after *Steam Wonder*'s first appearance—when Huck comes to the conclusion that his black companion, the escaped slave Jim, is "white inside" because of his unselfish behavior.[79] The comparison between *Huckleberry Finn* and the first Senarens Frank Reade Jr. story may be apt. *Huckleberry Finn* shares many elements with dime novels in terms of race and attitude, as scholars such as Steven Mailloux and Andrew Levy have shown. Mailloux argues that much of the public furor around *Huckleberry Finn* came from its relationship to the "bad boy boom" of dime novels.[80] He ties this to the lack of contemporary response to Twain's portrayal of race in the novel, intimating that "the contemporary readers of Huckleberry Finn were much more preoccupied by literature's effect on the 'Bad-Boy Boom' than they were on its relation to the 'Negro Problem.'"[81] Mailloux's observations are a response to long-running twentieth-century debates over race in *Huckleberry Finn*, particularly Leo Marx's assertion that Twain abandons his sympathetic portrayal of Jim in order to bring the story to its close, and Ralph Ellison's critique of Jim's minstrel-inflected behavior and its effect on the audience's perception of him as adult male in his 1958 essay, "Change the Joke and Slip the Yoke."[82]

The analogue to Twain serves as a reminder that conflicted portrayal of race is not limited to dime novels, nor was Twain the only nineteenth-century American writer attempting to create a black protagonist for a primarily white audience with problematic results. Critics of dime novels and Edisonades particularly tend to lament the books' racism without approaching them with the level of scrutiny or sympathy that a canonical author such as Twain receives. In the case of Pomp, the racism is both palpable and conflicted. Just as the text alternates between sympathy for and sadism toward Indians, it oscillates sharply between portraying Pomp as a noble figure and as a caricature used for comic purposes, not unlike Twain's Jim as read by Marx, Ellison, and others.

Senarens also portrayed another black character heroically: Antonio Maceo, the Cuban revolutionary who makes an appearance in *Frank Reade, Jr., in Cuba*'s chapter titled "The Great Mulatto." Maceo had already appeared in previous Tousey dime novels overseen by Senarens, and table 3 shows that two of those texts even used Maceo's name in their titles. In *Frank Reade, Jr., in Cuba*, Maceo attacks and disperses a Spanish force when Frank is injured, helping the American narrowly avoid capture. Maceo is first described as "a mulatto of military bearing" (8). Maceo's mixed-race status is not only mentioned, it is emphasized. The novel affirms Maceo's racial heritage and bravery, extending the approach found in the occasional heroic portrayals of Pomp in Senarens's early stories. When Reade Jr. provides Maceo secret letters informing him of "several filibustering expeditions" from the United States with "arms, ammunition, and medicines," the general declares, "We need all the aid we can get, for you must be aware that there are less than fifty thousand rebels pitted against nearly four times as many Spaniards. However, it is a common saying among my men that one Cuban is the equal to ten Spaniards" (8).[83] Maceo also does not conform to one major convention of the Reade myth. When Maceo sees Reade's airship, he notes that "it is a wonder. With several such machines we could drive every Spaniard from the island and win the war in a week" (8). He does not, however, subsequently make a plea for such machines, nor does he make the monetary offer that appears so frequently in the Reade novels. This disruption of a repeated motif in the Reade novels emphasizes the Cuban patriots' independent spirit and Maceo's leadership.[84]

From this perspective, the Frank Reade Jr. novels do not portray an American imperial imaginary that finds central authority in state, nationalism, or race. Just as their celebration of individual agency enabled by invention undermines overt nationalism or jingoism, their treatment of race situates them somewhat outside the overtly Anglo-Protestant nation-building rhetoric of their time. While they certainly contribute to an imperial mind-set by vindicating a technocracy in which the right to lead is a function of science and force, they also subvert that mindset by periodically calling into question these other elements of the American imperialist identity.

1. Beadle's 1885 reprinting of Ellis's *The Steam Man of the Prairies*, retitled *The Huge Hunter*. Courtesy of Albert Johannsen Collection, Rare Books and Special Collections, Northern Illinois University, The Nickels and Dime Project.

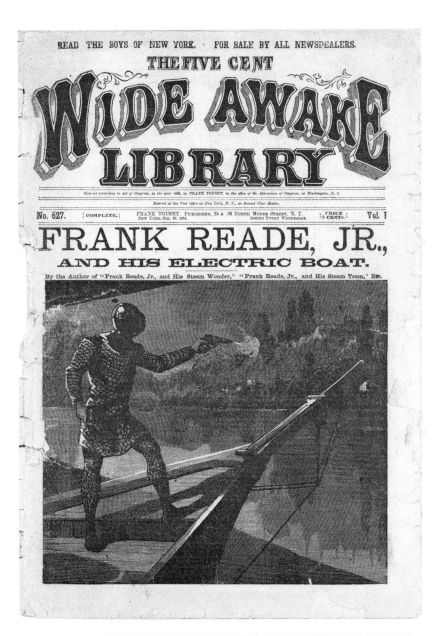

2. The hero dons bulletproof armor for a pistol shootout on Lake Michigan in one of Senarens's earliest Frank Reade Jr. stories, 1884. Collection of the author.

THE FIVE CENT
WIDE AWAKE
LIBRARY

Entered at the Post Office at New York, N. Y., as Second Class Matter.

No. 1096. {COMPLETE.}   FRANK TOUSEY, Publisher, 34 & 36 North Moore St., N. Y.   {PRICE 5 CENTS.}   Vol. II
New York, December 26, 1891.   Issued Semi-Weekly.

Entered according to Act of Congress, in the year 1891, by FRANK TOUSEY, in the office of the Librarian of Congress, at Washington, D. C.

FRANK READE, JR.,
AND HIS ELECTRIC COACH;
OR,
The Search for the Isle of Diamonds.

PART II.   By "Noname."

The coach was upset for the first time! A thrill of dismay shot through Frank, and he shut off the power. He scrambled out through a window and reached the ground.

3. Cover featuring Reade Jr.'s electric coach—part railroad car, part tank—in one of several storylines featuring an Israelite lost city, 1891. Courtesy of Edward T. LeBlanc Collection, Rare Books and Special Collections, Northern Illinois University, The Nickels and Dime Project.

4. One of many Frank Reade Jr. stories featuring a steam man or steam horse, 1892. Collection of the author.

5. Reade Jr.'s airship confronts a Spanish firing squad on the cover of *Frank Reade, Jr., in Cuba*'s original serialization, 1896. Courtesy of Edward T. LeBlanc Collection, Rare Books and Special Collections, Northern Illinois University, The Nickels and Dime Project.

PART II
GOD

4
Discovering Biblical Literalism
Frank Reade Redux

No novels better illustrate the technocratic exploration narrative's shift in emphasis from overt imperialistic concerns into religious matters than the Frank Reade Jr. dime-novel series. The stories entered print and proliferated between 1876 and 1898, as American obsessions with biblical history and global conquest reached fever pitch. As we have seen, the Reade novels reiterated an expansionist narrative—one that was unfailingly technocratic but also dramatically nonstatic in its presentation of imperial authority and the racial presumptions behind imperialism. If their portrayal of race and empire are ambiguous, then it might seem logical to presume that their portrayal of religious faith might be similarly inconsistent. After all, appeals to popular Christianity fueled many appeals for empire building, most famously culminating in 1899, when President William McKinley justified the US annexation of the Philippines partly by assuming it was America's duty to "uplift and civilize and Christianize" the Filipino people.[1] US policymakers and newspapers frequently linked territorial expansion and control to a larger Christian missionary impulse, a tendency that writers like Walter Nugent assert has been with us since the earliest European colonization.[2] Because the technocratic exploration narrative always explicitly touches these issues of cultural superiority, control, and vindication, it would seem likely that the Reade novels would wrestle with this component of imperial desire.

When the Reade stories deal with religion, particularly their era's popular Christianity, however, they do so in a remarkably *consistent* way. Many of the Frank Reade Jr. texts perform an oddly theological cultural work; on multiple occasions, their globe-trotting heroes make discoveries with religious implications. They demonstrate the dominance of Christian appeals, supported by the assumption that their audience would view the Bible as an authoritative source. More importantly, they combine these appeals to their technocratic template in a way that presents them as mutually reinforcing. They go beyond merely assuming the truth of Christianity in general, and ultimately suggest that technocratic explorers can uncover biblical truths. It is this element—the assertion that technocrats will vindicate literal readings of the Bible by making historical discoveries during their journeys— that gives the technocratic Frank Reade stories their cultural power.

Much of the discussion of "science vs. religion" in the United States stems from the moment when nineteenth-century science undermined literal readings of the Book of Genesis. As such, the Reade novels operate concurrently with other late nineteenth-century fiction that wrestled with Darwinian science. The popular view of Darwin's influence on literature tends to emphasize realist literature's attempts to wrestle with evolutionism's implications. Donald Pizer notes that the majority of these studies examine either how Darwinist concepts play out in specific novels or a single writer's body of work, or how evolutionary thought influenced in the conceptualization of realism. For such studies, Pizer states "the shift from a plot of extraordinary behavior and the frequent operation of chance to one of slow, fully explainable, and progressive change (in other words, from the romantic to the realist plot) is attributable to the absorption of a Darwinian mind-set by post Darwinian novelists."[3] More recently, Kimberly Hamlin has noted another trend by examining evolution's influence on utopian fiction such as Bellamy's *Looking Backward* (1888) and Gilman's *Herland* (1915), noting ways Americans tied evolution to a larger progressive, positive narrative of an ever-improving humanity.[4] Understandably, technocratic exploration novels fall outside of such distinctions, neither realist nor canonical in most cases. And, despite sharing utopian fiction's positivist outlook regarding science and technology, the Frank Reade dime novels seem in conversation with much different literary trends. Their narratives are grounded in the era's scientific debates, but their ultimate approach is neither progressive nor realistic.

Instead, the Reade novels construct narratives that meld biblical history and scientific adventure. In approach, they bear little resemblance to other contemporary literature wrestling with evolution's implications. Frequently, nineteenth-century American Christian leaders conceptualized evolution by asserting a kind of evolutionarily informed theism that emphasized the creator's agency in a world developed through a process uncovered by science. This was the view found in Jules Verne's novels, which promoted a nonliteral reading of Genesis, and the view embraced by figures as diverse as Asa Gray,

Henry Ward Beecher, and James McCosh.[5] In contrast, the Frank Reade series' story arcs that engage with biblical history present an early articulation of the kind of "post-secular" views sociologists O'Brien and Noy find in the twenty-first century. They envision an audience who will be both technocratic and religiously conservative, like the 21 percent of modern Americans who see themselves as both pro-religion and pro-science, differing with science only on rare occasions when it counters their reading of Scripture.[6] The religious narratives in Frank Reade Jr.'s adventures portray a fictionalized variant of this outlook, demonstrating Americans' longing for narratives that comingle adoration of science and technology with appeals to biblical literalism.

Overt use of biblical narrative devices does not happen immediately in the series. Also, there is no hard evidence of Senarens's own religious faith or practices. The author's *New York Times* obituary from 1939 does not mention a church affiliation, only a funeral service at Walter B. Cooke Funeral Home.[7] SF historian Sam Moskowitz indicates that Senarens belonged to the Protestant Dutch Reformed Church (his mother's faith) as a youth; however, like Moskowitz's claims that Jules Verne wrote to "Noname," such facts are unsubstantiated.[8] Senarens's early work contains passing references to religion, such as when a technophobic character fears Reade's steam-driven marvel is the work of the devil.[9] Similarly, in *Frank Reade, Jr., and His Air-Ship*, Pomp is mocked for his superstition, a hallmark of the era's African American caricature, because he expects to see or hear angels as they approach the clouds (13). While teased by his compatriots, Pomp processes this new knowledge quickly, holding out the possibility that superstition can be overcome through the type of technocratic exploration that Reade, Pomp, and O'Shea undertake.

Another emblematic scene occurs later in *Air-Ship*. Reade Jr. invents a heavier-than-air craft, the *Meteor*, and embarks on an aerial voyage. He discovers an ancient, sunken city—with an intact silver mine—under a lake in remote Mexican mountains. Along with his companions, Frank attempts to find a way to access the silver, a feat made easier because of their aerial transportation. Searching for information, he lands his airship in a Mexican village where the craft frightens everyone until Frank spots a priest and orders Barney to make the sign of the cross. To get answers, he implies that he is some kind of ghostly or angelic visitor, stating "'Come here father . . . and answer my questions as you value your soul" (17). Frank gets the information he needs from the priest and returns to the *Meteor*. As they rise into the air, he describes these events to Barney and Pomp: "'That old fellow thinks he had been talking to one of the people of the sunken city,' said Frank, 'and he will always tell his people so. They will hereafter regard him as a wonderful man. It may be that he will tell them a cock-and-bull story about visitors from heaven, and what they said to him'" (17).

In this episode, religious superstition is manipulated to get the hero what he wants—a practice that Mark Twain fully investigates over the course of *A Connecticut Yankee* five years later. Religious faith has mostly utilitarian value in Senarens's early Edisonades. Frank is not above pretending to be pious or impersonating a spiritual being in order to find the gold. He also somewhat wryly understands that his own "cock-and-bull" story of allowing the priest to think he is a supernatural visitor from heaven may result in further misrepresentation of the events in question. Regardless, he has the information he needs, and goes on with his expedition. Similarly, *Across the Continent on Wings; or, Frank Reade, Jr.'s Greatest Flight* features Reade Jr., his father, Pomp, and Barney using individual, motorized flying suits to navigate North America. When they reach Utah, they fly above Mormon settlers who initially mistake them for heavenly visitors and bow before them. Frank announces a plan to "have some fun with them," then acts as if he truly is a messenger, demanding the "faithful" bring him an abundance of food and wine.[10] The settlers comply, and Reade's father laughs at "the deception practiced on the superstitious Mormons," commending Frank's actions as "the best joke I've seen in many a day."[11] Clearly, religious exceptionalism factors into these scenes. While the narrative belittles Christian superstition regarding angels, the groups targeted for Frank's manipulation would be, for many Americans, outsiders: the Mormon "other," the Catholic "other." As such, these portrayals are consistent with the broader post–Civil War US construction of an American identity that excludes not only non-Christians but also Christian faiths outside a narrow Protestant spectrum.

But another, more significant element is present here. Frank Reade Jr., while he appears to limit such pranks to outsiders, has few qualms about engaging in behavior that might strike some as blasphemous—a consistent trait in the first decade or more of the series. He does not engage in any behavior that would overtly mark him as Christian. He does not attempt to proselytize any of the various native peoples he meets in the series. He isn't depicted as praying, attending church regularly, studying the Bible, or any of the other traits used by nineteenth-century authors to indicate normative Christian piety. He seems a nonpracticing, generic Protestant, aligned with the Anglo-American norm in only cursory ways, neither a missionary nor a complete materialist.

Despite Frank's lack of overt practice, Christianity becomes tied much more closely to the explorers' travels as the series proliferates. These elements appear in one of the earliest stories to feature a religious subtext. In *Frank Reade, Jr., in the Sea of Sand* from August 1893, Reade meets an explorer named Washington Whitwell in Chicago. Whitwell has an ancient piece of vellum found in Syria that has Hebrew characters written on it; he claims it is evidence of a lost race in the "southern part of the Great Sahara" who are "as civilized as were the Jews in the time of Christ."[12] While they agree that the location is virtually inaccessible by land, Reade suggests that his new airship will permit them to explore the region. The plot laid out here is a lost-race narrative, part of the literary fad popularized by the enormous transatlantic success of H. Rider Haggard's *King Solomon's Mines* in 1885.[13] Lost-race tales utilized an exploration narrative similar to Edisonades, frequently portraying travelers who encountered new civilizations in uncharted territories, but they did not possess the Edisonades' fundamental technophilia and unreflective celebration of the independent inventor. Lost-race novels have been directly connected to nineteenth-century scientific debates; Carter Hanson, for example, has noted the popularity of lost-race novels in Britain, arguing that these works "address profound anxieties about Darwinian relativism and the racial amalgamation of British society."[14] As products of the same cultural moment that Hanson observes, Edisonades, like lost-race novels, had potential to work out such anxieties narratively. Rather than rejecting biblical histories in favor of evolutionary science's alternative narrative, these novels portray technocratic exploration as a means to reestablish biblical authority in matters of history and race. They represent the conflicted approach to science found in Edisonades at large and play out the tension between science and religion found in the larger American culture of the time.

Frank Reade, Jr., in the Sea of Sand does this from the onset. As they fly from the United States to Africa, we learn rumors about the civilization they hope to find. It occupies land where the "Malakites" once flourished and traded with the Syrians "eighteen hundred years" ago, but the area was wiped out by an earthquake and became known as "the Sea of Sand." No one has ventured there since (4). Flying above their destination, they see two armored warriors, "powerful in frame, and of an olive hue in skin, dressed in part armor . . . much after the fashion of the Roman centurions in scriptural times" (14). They hope to find more of such people when they land. Upon making camp, however, they are attacked by twenty "savage-looking" giants, with "scraggly beards" and "goat skin" clothing (15). The aeronauts realize that there are "two different races" at odds in this lost area: the giants are called Barokites, and their centurion-like opponents are the Malakites (16).

Whitwell attempts to communicate with one of the Malakites, eventually addressing him in Hebrew. The Malakite immediately responds and tells a lengthy tale. Whitwell informs the group: "We are in a wonderful country, governed by King Lodom, a lineal descendent of David. This man is an out and out Hebrew and he, with his people, still cling to the manners and cus-toms as well as the old faith of Abraham and Isaac"(18). The text elaborates: "Here was a most wonderful discovery. One of the lost tribes of Israel so often mentioned in Holy Writ was found" (18). This element exceeds the religious undercurrent of hallmark texts like *King Solomon's Mines*, where the heroes discover tangible evidence of biblical history but the area itself is populated by natives without a direct connection to that history or even an awareness of its importance.[15] The Malakites are living history, a direct con-nection to biblical times, preserved and ready for study.

The story proceeds in the standard manner of lost-race adventures. Our heroes are welcomed by the natives who need their technological assistance in their war, an alliance that John Rieder has shown is a central element of most lost-race narratives.[16] Reade shows off his airship by giving King Lodom a ride, and the king gratefully provides him with a "diamond of the size of a wallet" as a gift (23). After spending an idyllic week with the Mala-kites, the Americans are called into duty because the king is kidnapped by the Barokites. These savage giants attack the city, and Reade's counterattack is fairly emblematic of the action sequences of the entire series. He mans his airship and takes charge of a swivel gun that fires electric charges.

> The Barokites were thousands in number, yet the electric gun mowed them down as a scythe cuts grass. Yet in their headlong valor they charged. . . .
>
> [Frank] gave Barney the signal, and the rotascopes began to revolve and the ship arose into the air. . . .
>
> Up, up the air-ship went.
>
> When fifty feet in the air, knowing that the bows and arrows of the Barokites could do no harm, Frank Reade, Jr. held the ship suspended.
>
> Then he worked the electric gun, and before such a fearful instru-ment of death the Barokites could not stand. (23)

In the Barokite adversaries, we find the novel's predominant appeal to biblical history, one that will become a standard in the series. The Barok-ites seem to have their origins in the tales of giants from the Old Testa-ment: the Nephilim and the Rephaim. At least one early science-fiction text that Senarens would have known featured a portrayal of an antediluvian savage as a giant: Jules Verne's *Journey to the Center of the Earth*, translated into English in 1871. That text, however, makes no specific connection be-tween its fleetingly glimpsed subterranean giant and the biblical tradition beyond describing him as "antediluvian."[17] Senarens's connection is more explicit. By tying his lost tribe to King David, he implicitly connects the Barokites to the biblical Rephaim. His more Bible-savvy readers would know Genesis 6:4's reference that "there were giants in the earth in those days," and that their presumed descendants were defeated in Bashan by the Israelites in the Book of Deuteronomy.[18] In Senarens's era, these ideas received news coverage when a new translation of the Bible was released.[19] Lawyer and Bible scholar A. H. Dana wrote a multi-part analysis of this new version for the *Brooklyn Daily Eagle* in January 1887, which prominently mentioned the word "Rephaim" as an example of a term translatable in a variety of ways. "Rephaim" meant either "dead things" or "giants."[20] Scholar Ronald S. Hendel analyzed this dual meaning, and his findings give perspective to anyone who might think it a stretch to portray Old Testament giants as token intimidating "bad guys" in a dime novel. Hendel recognized that the role of the Rephaim encompasses both meanings of the term: they are giants meant to be enemies made obsolete by the power of God's people. Hendel concluded, "The function of the Nephilm-Rephaim in all [biblical] traditions is constant—[While powerful and terrifying] they exist in order to be wiped out: by the flood, by Moses, by David, and others. The function of the Nephilim in Israelite tradition . . . is to die."[21] By having Reade Jr. execute them en masse with his electric gun, the series unwittingly joins a longstanding tradition. He confronts and kills the Bible's most generic adversaries.

In *Sea of Sand*, our heroes feel connection to the Hebrew Malakites, immediately becoming their friends and protectors. The Malakites are more recognizably civilized than the Barokites; they have cities, tools, all the trappings that Westerners would equate with society. Not surprisingly, given their reputation as proto-imperialist propaganda, technocratic dime novels often equate friendship and protection with the ability to use advanced technology to uphold the social status quo with violence. Reade and company, however, feel a connectedness directly because of a shared Judeo-Christian heritage. Even more importantly, however, the Americans recognize King Lodom's authority because of his blood ties to the Old Testament's King David. While the King obviously values Reade Jr. for his airship's military might and the promise of wiping out his adversaries, the Americans in the group are awed by the kingdom's historical resonance. They defer to these people and offer their services in part because living among them "seemed like being carried back into the old Jerusalem of which we are told by Holy Writ" (20). Almost immediately, all members of the party recognize the larger value of their discovery. When Frank calls the discovery "wonderful," Whitwell notes, "Of course it is, and quite invaluable to science. How the religious and scientific world will be electrified when they hear of this won-

derful bit of exploration" (18). Whitwell's telling comment conjoins the bifur-
cated worlds of religion and science; the discovery will be of value to both
realms, and he understands they will be "electrified" by confirmation of biblical historical reports. Later, Frank Reade Jr. says, "What an incalculable
benefit this will be to bibliographers and historians. . . . They can come here
and study the Hebrew life just as it was in the time of Christ" (20). The protagonists immediately understand that their discovery will impact multiple
scientific and scholastic disciplines.

Despite this, they do not share their findings with the world at large.
At first glance, this would seem akin to the novels' formulaic treatment
of machine power. Like the technological transformation promised—but
never delivered—by Reade's inventions, the narrative suggests a potentiality wherein explicit confirmation of biblical history can be made on an
international scale via the normal, authoritative channels of "bibliographers
and historians." In fact, however, the text explicitly gives a reason why this
living archeological discovery should remain secret, and it does so by reiterating the series' previous skepticism regarding imperial power. Near the
story's end, Reade and company conclude that they must not reveal the
whereabouts of the Malakites for fear that they will be at the mercy of non-
Christian invaders. "We can never hope to link this lost nation with our
people in this generation, or at least so long as the Turks hold Palestine
and the main country of the East. . . . The Khedive would send a conquer-
ing army down here and make all this country subject to his dominion. The
Malakites could not help being slaughtered, for their weapons are as nothing
compared with the modern engines of warfare" (28). Of course, Reade's own
slaughter of the Barokites underscores this. Reade is fearful of expansionist
impulses of the Turkish Muslim government. While Frank's opinion could
be construed as American Judeo-Christian exceptionalism, it resonates with
a general mistrust of empire in other stories that will become more prominent in later stories, including *Frank Reade, Jr. in Cuba* and two subsequent
biblically based lost-race storylines.

In November 1893, just a few months after *Frank Reade, Jr. in the Sea of
Sand*, the Reade series published a two-part cliffhanger featuring another
Old Testament lost race and makes its use of the Rephaim even more explicit. *Frank Reade, Jr., and His Electric Coach; or, the Search for the Isle of
Diamonds* sends the protagonist to Mexico, this time piloting a four-wheeled
overland vehicle that is part boxcar, part tank. Reade is told that the location
is inhabited by a race of giants that are believed to be "one of the lost tribes
of Israel mentioned in the Bible."[22] When they cross a bridge to the island,
they encounter "an enormous sized man. . . . His skin was creamy white,
his hair was long and tawny, and the mode of his features, which were hair-

less, was rather Jewish, and his eyes were blue. In a word the giant looked like an albino savage" (I:10).

The savage is named Isaac, the king of a tribe of lost Israelites. Unlike the Barokites from the previous Reade novel, these giants *are* the lost tribe. They speak Hebrew, and their civilization is filled with lost-race novel clichés, including houses adorned with jewels. Reade's group determines that it would be "purely rank robbery" to attack these people and take their diamonds. Instead, he uses the electric coach to defend them from Mexican bandits (I:20). Reade puzzles over their enormous statures and their Jewish customs, but quickly comes to a conclusion: "By jingo, I've got the key to explain their size, if they are descendants of the ancient Israelites. In 1452 B.C. there was an Amorite chief, ruling from the Jabbok to the foot of Hermon, and his name was Og. He was one of a giant race of Rephaim, whose stronghold was a remarkable district called Argob by the Hebrews, which means stony. His iron bedstead was nine cubits long by four wide. I'm under the impression that the tribe on this isle are descendants of his race" (I:21).

Of course, Senarens equating the Rephaim with a lost Israelite tribe is problematic, leading E. F. Bleiler to wryly note that the writer "should have read his Old Testament more closely."[23] The reference to Og and the Rephaim comes from Deuteronomy, suggesting that Senarens did, in fact, consult the Old Testament in the process of writing. The author lifts details directly from the King James Bible, as where Deuteronomy 3:3 states: "So the Lord our God delivered into our hands Og also, the king of Bashan, and all his people: and we smote him until none was left to him remaining."[24] This military achievement is impressive because of Og's heritage and the fear he initially instills in the Israelites, hence the reference to his size: "For only Og king of Bashan remained of the remnant of giants; behold, his bedstead was a bedstead of iron . . . nine cubits was the length thereof, and four cubits the breath of it."[25] Defeating Og represents a final defeat of the giants. Similarly, the geographical locales Senarens references are from the same section of Deuteronomy; the lands the Israelites conquer includes Og's land by "the river Jabbok" (Deut. 3:16) and "from Aroer . . . even unto Mount Sion, which is Hermon."[26]

What should we make of Frank Reade Jr.'s abrupt and strangely detailed deployment of scriptural knowledge? Nowhere in previous novels in the series is he portrayed as a practicing Christian, let alone one who would know precise details including obscure dates. Why does it appear in *Sea of Sand*? The obvious answer is narrative efficacy. It's convenient for him to know this, and it moves the story along. Of course, this is not necessarily a slight of Senarens's artifice, and the heavy-handed use of coincidental knowledge is not limited to dime novels. Mark Twain uses the same sudden recall of pertinent knowledge in his technocratic masterpiece, *A Connecticut Yankee in King Arthur's Court*, when Hank Morgan suddenly recalls the date of an sixth-century eclipse to pass it off as his own magical act. This bit of authorial contrivance seems unlikely, but the plot hinges on it. A charitable reading might argue that both Morgan's and Reade Jr.'s knowledge is consistent with their characterization: both protagonists are intelligent and well read, although their practical technological prowess overshadows their more academic learnedness. Reade's specific mention of locales such as Jabbok and Hermon portray him as a well-read young man with an excellent memory of biblical history. Another reason, however, must be considered. What little plausibility this science has, once again, comes from the series' appeal to popular Christianity. More importantly, the scene indicates that, at minimum, Senarens thought it would seem reasonably plausible to readers if Reade had memorized dates and locations from the Bible. This, of course, presumes a readership schooled in the Bible's history, likely a safe bet in the United States of 1893. In Frank Reade Jr., Senarens imagines a character with biblical knowledge but without other overt expressions of Christian religiosity—and imagines a readership receptive to this character. As Sara Lindey has shown, dime novel readers frequently idolized the genre's youthful heroes, using characters' names as their own in correspondence and asking questions to help them pursue a similar course in life, using the editors as "not only as monitors of their physical and mental development, but also as career counselors."[27] Under these circumstances, it is not a stretch to suspect that audiences saw Reade's blend of technocrat, philanthropist, and well-informed Christian as an ideal, a specific American "type" to be achieved.

An even more provocative connection comes in the oddly precise date that Reade provides in his exposition: 1452 B.C. Here, we find the Reade novels engaging in a blend of historical research and fiction that persists in American conversations about religion and science. Presumably, Senarens pulled this date from the same Bible he used for the other pieces of research shown in *Sea of Sand*. In fact, many editions of the King James Bible came with annotations that utilized the dating method developed by James Ussher, the seventeenth-century Irish archbishop who famously used biblical scholarship and historical evidence to date Old Testament events, including the creation of the world in October 4004 B.C. Ussher's dates were incorporated into many annotated Bibles into the nineteenth-century. For example, an 1860 study Bible, published by Eyre and Spottiswoode in London, begins with a recurring marginal header at the top of each page, noting the first chapter of Genesis as "Before Christ, 4004." Each page comes with a reiteration of Ussher's calculations, presented in the upper corners of

the marginal notes. As would be expected, Deuteronomy 3 is noted as occurring "Before Christ, 1451." It is fairly certain, then, that Senarens drew his
particular date from such a study Bible.

For Senarens, the Bible was both a source of historical fact and an appeal
for verisimilitude. He utilizes the Ussher dates to make his hero's encounter
with giants seem at least passingly plausible to nineteenth-century American readers. In 1894, Ussher's ideas were ubiquitous enough to be inserted
into a dime novel plot with little fanfare or apparent controversy. They were,
in fact, presented as biblical canon, with no attribution in common Bibles
distinguishing it from the sacred text around it. Ussher's scholarship gained
attention in our era when they were translated and published in full as *The
Annals of the World* in 2003 by a creationist religious press promoting its
use as a textbook.[28] In this scenario, we have a nineteenth-century science-
fiction writer explaining his hero's encounter with a race of giants by using
source material that is still deployed in today's creationism versus evolution
debates. In *Sea of Sand*, Reade recalls very specific scriptural history that
isn't literally "scriptural" at all, though given the presentation he and his author might be excused for not realizing it. The example demonstrates the
power of textual inclusion where the Bible is concerned, explaining at least
partially Ussher chronology's persistence in the last hundred and fifty years
of discussion about biblical accuracy.

The episodic, two-part *Electric Coach* story provides less specific description of the biblical society than *Sea of Sand*. Isaac the giant alternates
between piety and savagery, perhaps indicative of Senarens's conflation of
Rephaim and ancient Israelites. A volcano destroys the hidden city and kills
most of Isaac's tribe, but not before Frascuelo—the bandit who has pursued
Reade throughout the story—steals many of the hidden city's diamonds.
Isaac survives the volcano and acts in violent outbursts at least in part because he is tormented by the loss of his people. Enraged at Frascuelo, Isaac
devotes his life to killing the bandit (I:28). After witnessing a series of confrontations between Isaac and Frascuelo, Frank comes to think that Isaac is
capable of violence and torture because his tribe was "without Christian enlightenment" (II:14). The storyline culminates with Isaac throwing Frascuelo
into a pit of snakes to die (II:20). After this, Isaac cries out, "Oh, God! Great
is thy power; merciful thy precepts; wonderful they grace. My people can repose in peace" (II:20). He chooses not to leave for civilization with Reade,
and remains "a massive commanding figure . . . with tearful eyes and clasped
hands raised heavenward" (II:21). While capable of violence and torture that
Reade deems un-Christian, Isaac is pious and God-fearing in his faith in a
manner the text consistently portrays as admirable.

One additional example shows the remarkable consistency with which

Old Testament history was used in the Reade technocratic exploration novels. *The Mysterious Mirage*, from August 9, 1895, features Reade exploring Egypt in his heavily armed Overland Chaise. He is working with explorer Colonel Dustin and newspaper reporter Theo Wilton, helping them find a mysterious city in the Sahara. As in previous Reade stories, a biblical reference is provided and directly aligned with scientific study; Dustin convinces them to brave the Sahara to find this city: "Think of what a mighty discovery it will be for science and for the world. . . . Who knows but that this may be the city and region of Ophir described by Solomon, and which no man has ever located?"[29] Ophir is a gold-rich land mentioned in Scripture, most notably as a location of gold presented to Solomon by the Queen of Sheba in Second Chronicles.[30] It is also the location mentioned as the site of Solomon's Mines in Haggard's novel, and it is impossible to know if Senarens used it in his plot because of Haggard's influence or his own scriptural research.[31]

Even if the biblical reference is second-hand from Haggard, Senarens veers from the approach of *King Solomon's Mines*. The journey is simultaneously a search for material gain, an attempt to fill a gap in scientific geographic knowledge, and a vindication of Judeo-Christian tradition. Senarens's explorers do not find gold or adventurous conflict in the area, nor is the city they find actually Ophir. First, they discover skeletons—fourteen feet in length—locked in a wrestler's death grip. "What a race of giants they must have been," says Frank's comrade (10). As with *Sea of Sand*, the presentation of giants provides a tacit link to Old Testament narrative, one that becomes explicit as Frank and his companions find the city for which they searched. The citizens are not giants, but a light-complexioned, Hebrew-speaking race called the Habanites (11). They are portrayed, not as another lost tribe, but as *the* tribe, an "undoubtedly pure Hebrew nation" with no interaction with the outside world. "God's chosen people!" exclaims Frank, "so we may imagine how the people of Israel looked in the days of Moses" (11). Unlike the besieged Malakites, the Habanites live in peaceful isolation, with none of the internal strife that necessitates the protagonists' action as found in other lost-race novels. In *The Mysterious Mirage*, Reade and his Western companions are awed by the peaceful, gentle utopia of the Habanites wherein, we are told, "No word of quarrel or blasphemy was to be heard, and every man was polite to his neighbor" (12). Wilton contrasts them with nineteenth-century Jews, noting that "we are apt to consider the Hebrew, the Israelite and the Jew as all one race, dark-skinned, coarse-featured and enemies of Christ"; the texts stops short of outright condemning such blatantly antisemitic generalizations, instead focusing on the Habanites' "pure" bloodlines and moral flawlessness (11).

While in previous adventures, Reade had considered the benefits of revealing the lost race to Western scholars, he never considers it here. Instead, he immediately makes the same decision to keep the location secret that he made in *Sea of Sand*—even extending that work's understated anti-imperialist message. Their group has a run-in with a Bedouin tribe in the area on the way to the city, and they tangle with them again on the way back. The colonel fears the Arabs of the area are too vicious and would destroy the Habanite utopia.[32] "It would be an awful pity for some of these same tribes to find that valley," he notes (12). The discussion takes a turn when the reporter Wilton adds that "it is not altogether these tribes of the desert you need fear. . . . There is England, France or Germany, whose methods in every part of the world are unscrupulous. You would see their soldiers in those sacred temples of this perfect Hebrew race before you could say Jack Robinson. It would then become an English, French or German colony or protectorate" (12).

Imagining a biblical utopia brings forth another of the series' explicit anti-imperialist statements against Europe's "unscrupulous" exploitation of lands around the world. The heroes simply do not want the Habanites to be corrupted. "They worshiped one God, and lived in his glory," the story notes approvingly (12). Even more provocatively, we are told the Habanites are "a race of people almost perfect in Christian faith in practice and in profession" (12). Ironically, our protagonists and the narrator identify this civilization as "Christian" when it allegedly hasn't changed since the "days of Moses." And this dichotomy is part of the recurring narrative's thrust. In the Frank Reade Jr. novels, we find a world where lost Jewish tribes are immediately looked upon by their Western discoverers in relation to Christian history. They are a living connection to the past. John Rieder has noted that lost-race stories often portray the discovered race as prehistoric "other"—basically viewed by the Westerners the same way a colonizer views the colonized.[33] In these Frank Reade Jr. stories, however, the discovered other is valued as a link to a shared spiritual heritage, one that is respected and defended. Unlike the Catholics and Mormons who are portrayed as ripe for mockery in the series, Senarens depicts two of the three Jewish communities with ties to prehistory as sacrosanct, and they are incongruously viewed by the protagonists as closer to mainstream Protestant Christianity than those other Christian sects.

When the technocratic exploration narrative of the Reade novels uses the Bible as a historical source, it reaffirms the Bible's status as historical text. Ussher's chronology, for example, continues to be treated as fact by twenty-first-century Christians at least partly because of its repeated articulation in popular culture outlets for over a century. Senarens's use of Ussher suggests that it was treated as historical fact in his era, even by technological writers, because of its inclusion in study Bibles. It results in a mutually reinforcing relationship between the Ussher chronology and the popular literary work incorporating it, spreading and sustaining its influence. True, we can read this use of the Bible in proto-science fiction as mere plot devices, used for verisimilitude by a writer looking for a common historical element for his audience. It can even be read as simple borrowing and as embellishing the mode of Haggard's lost-race novels. However, the later Frank Reade Jr. novels articulate a consistent subtext, one in which technologists encounter "proof" of biblical history. The stories promote these encounters as significant, each one a "mighty discovery . . . for science and for the world." They do not present a foundation-shaking portrayal of science or the potentiality of technological travel. Instead, the discovery is always a reaffirmation, a discovery of evidence that validates the earlier, biblically based view of history to which Americans had grown accustomed, not the radically rewritten version of history presented by nineteenth-century science.

A final irony is worth noting. Overt connections between dime novels and Christianity were being made in the 1880s, but in a wholly oppositional way. In 1883, Anthony Comstock published *Traps for the Young* (1883), a condemnation of what he called "Evil Reading." The book holds a position for nineteenth-century dime novels that is roughly analogous to the place psychologist Fredrick Wertham's book *Seduction of the Innocent* (1954) holds in the history of the twentieth-century comic book; it is a highly sensationalized screed against a literary art form on the basis that it promotes degeneracy among young people, one that tainted the form for decades and resulted in some changes in the kind of material companies printed.[34] Comstock, a New York postal inspector, filled his book with Christian piety and a tone of moral authority. His chapter on "Half-Dime Novels and Story Papers" begins by outright asserting that Satan was behind the popularity of dime novels, "resolved to make the most of these vile illustrated weekly papers, by lining the news-stands and shop-windows along the pathway of children from home to school and church."[35] Comstock recounts plots that rely on violence and reward criminality: "these stories breed vulgarity, profanity, loose ideas of life, impurity of thought and deed."[36] He follows with reports of rises in juvenile crime. Comstock would presumably be shocked by the notion that some of these same, violent dime novels could be a conduit for advocating scriptural credibility. And yet, by the 1890s, that was exactly what was happening in the pages of the *Frank Reade Library*. It is also impossible to know if the incorporation of biblical history was in part a reaction to protests such as Comstock's, but it seems unlikely given that the novels mentioned in this chapter were all composed ten years or more after *Traps for the Young* appeared. Bleiler has noted that the violence and racial humor in the series was tempered as Senarens matured at least in part due to possible complaints from readers.[37] Still, there is nothing to suggest that Senarens had a larger goal than to simply use the Bible and its stories as a link to history, under the assumption that his readership would go along with it.

Ultimately, as technocratic exploration novels grew in popularity and their narrative components began to filter into American literature at large, this element crops up more and more. The technocratic exploration tale becomes a venue for religious commentary, most often deeply conservative, literal readings of Scripture. This combination of technophilic possibility and Judeo-Christian certainty proves alluring for writers again and again during the period. Writers wishing to weave a tale featuring a traveler in a strange, utopian land or an inventor exploring remote locales find it difficult not to appeal to religious tradition in their work, as Senarens does. And, as we will see, writers interested in voicing their concerns on religious matters seem to recognize the technocratic exploration narrative as an appropriate, popular outlet for their ideas.

5
Confronting "Fol-de-Rol"
Mark Twain, Technocracy, and Religion

Mark Twain's place in the Edisonades' history has been most frequently limited to a single book: *A Connecticut Yankee in King Arthur's Court* (1889).[1] SF scholar John Clute mentions the book's primacy in defining Edisonades, particularly the rhapsodic language Twain's character uses when he describes technology, stating that "the resemblance between the Boss protagonist of that novel and the self-image of Edison expressed in his writings is most striking" (369). Protagonist and narrator Hank Morgan embodies the confident, technologically savvy, and imperialistically minded hero of Edisonades as he attempts to democratize Arthurian England by forcefully, yet secretively, introducing nineteenth-century technology and political concepts into the sixth century. While there is no hard proof that Twain read inventor series such as those featuring Frank Reade Jr. and Jack Wright, he knew dime novels and used their themes and contents as fodder.[2] For example, he name-dropped the title of dime novelist Ned Buntline's non-Edisonade *The Black Avenger of the Spanish Main* in *The Adventures of Tom Sawyer* (1876), offering Buntline's novel as shorthand for the kind of bloody adventures Tom enjoys.[3] In 1881, he had publisher James R. Osgood provide him sea adventures, particularly William Clark Russell's *A Sailor's Sweetheart* and George Cupples's *Green Hand*, likely with a plan to satirize the genre.[4] (These latter works were part of *Harper's Franklin Square Library*, part of the cheap reprint publishing market that was conflated, in many Americans' minds then and now, with original dime novel productions like the *Frank Reade Library*.)[5] Comparing Twain's work with dime novels is, at first glance, somewhat inexact. Dime novel authors worked hurriedly, generating thousands of words in days for regular monthly or weekly publications, while Twain spent over five years—the better portion of the late 1880s—working on and off writing *A Connecticut Yankee*. Similarly, the dime novels' narrative canvas was necessarily episodic, presenting adventures in installments with little consistent, long-term character development. Twain's longer, first-person narrative allows frequent moments of interior reflection by the protagonist, including instances where he elaborates on the broader, cultural ideas that inform his grand schemes. Despite these obvious differences, the core is the same. Morgan's technological shenanigans include using blasting powder and lightning rods to destroy the tower of court magician Merlin and gaining prestige by ascribing the pyrotechnics to his own, superior "enchantments" (56–59). Morgan also plays the same game that Frank Reade Jr. occasionally plays, passing off his use of technology as spiritual power in order to influence or intimidate a superstitious audience that he views as his inferiors.

Twain digs deeper than the Edisonade dime novels when it comes to considering larger implications of manipulating religious faith and superstitions. In fact, Twain's entire body of work offers a sustained contemplation of the contradictions of Christian faith and religious belief in general; it can be found in his early satire of Christian religious pilgrims in the Holy Land in *The Innocents Abroad* (1869) as well as in his later writings such as *Letters from the Earth* (drafted in 1909, but unpublished until 1962 due to its controversial nature). Pinpointing Clemens's religious beliefs has been difficult, as the range of interpretations that have appeared in the past decade suggests. Lawrence Berkove and Joseph Csicilla find him a "heretical" Calvinist with a remarkably consistent "countertheology" based on God's indifference.[6] Tracy Fessenden sees a more malleable figure whose disbelief results in "a personal and artistic unraveling."[7] Joe B. Fulton sees him primarily as a parodist and burlesquer of religion who, nevertheless, maintained his Presbyterian beliefs at least partly because he saw "deviation from the 'mother vein' of the church as foolish [and] dangerous."[8] Harold Bush contrasts reports of Twain's disbelief with evidence from individuals such as his minister Joe Twichell, concluding that Twain had "strong religious proclivities throughout his life" and likely never rejected faith in practice regardless of his statements otherwise.[9] While his private life saw prolonged periods of doubt and spiritual longing, Twain the writer was a keen observer of American faith and morality. At the same time, Samuel Clemens had a lifelong fascination with technology and a late-life passion for international politics that flourished when he became involved with the Anti-Imperialist League.[10] His outspokenness regarding US involvement in foreign countries and his essentially realist literary core lend gravitas to his technological novels, providing a level of characterization that explicitly wrestles with the imperial ramifications of technology and expansion. He understood that technocracy writ large would have implications for religious authority, and his portrayal of this head-to-head confrontation makes up much of *A Connecticut Yankee*'s text and provides the entire impetus for its denouement. By adding religion to the lists of concepts that the technocrat can either reinforce or oppose, Twain's stories focus on technology's ability to create stasis rather than revolution. As with the Reade dime novels, technology does not open up new possibilities or challenge the status quo. Rather, Twain picks apart the imperialist tendency to use technology to recreate existing social circumstances and reinforce prevailing Protestant American beliefs.

To show this, I wish to examine not only *A Connecticut Yankee*, but also the two Tom Sawyer stories that bookend it: the unfinished *Huck Finn and Tom Sawyer among the Indians* (drafted in 1884) and *Tom Sawyer Abroad* (1894). In addition, one other technocratic exploration novel shaped Twain's understanding of the narrative's implications on religious faith: the unpublished polar-exploration manuscript written by his brother, Orion Clemens, in 1877. Only by understanding the exchanges between Samuel Clemens and his brother can we fully comprehend the extent of Twain's religious skepticism and his deep mistrust of technocratic fiction—the twin engines that powered *A Connecticut Yankee in King Arthur's Court*.

Orion Clemens's Manuscript and "That French Idiot"

An illuminating example of Twain's understanding of early science fiction can be found in his correspondence with Orion Clemens. Contrary to the then-prevailing American familial standard, Samuel Clemens, rather than his eldest brother, became the de facto head of his extended family. Over the years, he grew increasingly frustrated by Orion's financial and emotional dependence. In 1877, Orion wrote to his famous literary sibling asking him for help constructing and publishing an adventure novel entitled *The Kingdom of Sir John Franklin*. Orion based his idea on the real-life British explorer who died in 1845 while trying to discover the Northwest Passage.[11] In Orion's fictional tale, Franklin's expedition culminates in a trip into the earth's core. Orion suggests, somewhat sheepishly, that he and Sam collaborate in the writing and share the profits of this hollow-earth adventure, adding, "Couldn't you imagine lots of queer adventures and romances under such circumstances?"[12]

What Orion suggests, then, is plainly a technocratic exploration novel. As Sam immediately noted, Orion's idea was not blindly original. Hollow-earth stories had a tradition going back to *Symzonia*, an 1820 novel featuring a utopian society at the earth's center. *Symzonia* was presented as the notes of a "Captain Adam Seaborn" but is commonly ascribed to John Cleves Symmes Jr. and thought to be a promotional device for his hollow-earth theory and the polar exploration he and Jeremiah Reynolds planned to prove it.[13] The work popularized the concept of "Symmes's Hole," an entry point at each pole that granted access to the world below. Symmes's work inspired, among other works, the polar exploration portions of Poe's *Narrative of Arthur Gordon Pym*.[14] And yet, an examination of Orion and Sam's interchange gives us insight not only into Twain's subsequent portrayal of technological adventurers who travel to distant locations, but also the place of both Clemens brothers in the broader development of the technocratic exploration novel. In some ways, Orion Clemens is ahead of the game in his conceptualization of how technocratic exploration novels can operate culturally. The excerpts of Orion's drafts that still exist—and his own commentary about the full manuscript that was lost—portray a writer attempting to explicitly insert religious commentary into the genre. Moreover, Sam's comments on his brother's ideas articulate something about *his* unique approach to the same type of story, clarifying just how Mark Twain approached narratives that conjoined religion, technology, and exploration.

Sam's responses to Orion's proposal are indicative of his frustration regarding the older brother he generally perceived as a ne'er-do-well and whose increasing neediness made their relationship strained at best. His December 1877 reply to Orion dismisses the idea of collaboration and tells him to write the book himself "if you can drop other things."[15] It appears Sam saw this as another of the countless projects his brother would undertake and not finish. Orion seems aware of this, and his letters are filled with indications that he is working hard and that note his meticulous revision process. His letter from December 1877 features six and a half pages of fairly standard polar adventure, beginning with an explorer en route to China discovering a mysterious stranger in a canoe alongside his ship. The occupant is an "Esquimaux" Indian who was part of Sir John Franklin's 1845 party. He relates his story, noting Franklin's party seeing ghost-like apparitions and five members becoming insane.[16] Orion sent more excerpts with page numbers from the original copy in brackets; the letter from January 24, 1878, for example, begins on page 34 of the text and continues for several pages, adding, "I have reached the sixty-sixth page."[17] These excerpts are the only portions that remain.

In a letter from February 5, Orion gives his most clear summary of the entire work in the context of mentioning another problem that has led to his revisions: "In the part re-written there are some curious coincidences with Jules Verne's 'To the Centre of the Earth,' though when I wrote my rough draft I did not even know there was such a story."[18] He then goes on for a page and a half, noting similar plot elements between the two works—such as a broken compass that leads the heroes astray—and similar findings in their respective hollow earths, such as prehistoric monsters. Orion gives details by comparing Verne's story unfavorably to his own: "His travelers preposterously go down an extinct volcano. . . . Mine go in at Symmes's Hole. He finds a gorilla 14 feet high, of which he gives only a partial description, and the thing turns out to be a dream. My gorilla is fully described . . . but . . . is not an ape, as his is, mine is a gentleman; he is primitive man with pictures, statues, a daughter who plays music, a house."[19] From this we see how Orion conceptualizes his project, incorporating Darwinian ideas of human descent into a fantasy tale, using Verne as contrast to describe his method.

Verne was a household name by 1878, at least in part because his material was dumped on the American audience—twelve novels in two years—from 1872 to 1874.[20] Moreover, his work was poorly translated, with entire chapters removed, new material added, and significant political/scientific commentary whittled down to nothing.[21] For example, translator Lewis Page Mercier, a minister writing under the pseudonym Mercier Lewis, removed sections of Verne's work that could be deemed controversial.[22] In *20,000 Leagues under the Sea*, he omitted sections in which the protagonist explains how geology disproves the biblical creation story and a scene in which Captain Nemo's cabin is found to contain portraits of patriotic heroes including Poland's Kosciusko, Greece's Botzaris, America's Washington, Lincoln, and—more provocatively—abolitionist John Brown (289). Anything so potentially inflammatory was excised, at least in part because of the publisher's determination to market Verne to juveniles. Most Americans reading Verne in translation during the 1800s likely had no idea that the author was engaging with questions of faith and empire so pointedly in the original French. Verne's *Journey to the Center of the Earth* (published in French in 1864 and translated into English in 1872) suffered a similar fate. The youthful protagonist's dream sequence of a giant "gorilla"—so prominently mentioned by Orion Clemens in his letter to Sam—was, in fact, the addition of an anonymous translator.[23]

Such developments partly explain why an American writer such as Twain could dismiss Verne so completely. By this point in his life, Samuel Clemens had written dismissively of Verne in his notebooks, indicating that he had to scuttle a story about a balloon voyage mid-draft because Verne's *Five Weeks in a Balloon* was published.[24] And he subsequently ended his *A Murder, A Mystery and A Marriage*, first proposed to W. D. Howells in 1876 and posthumously published in 2001, with a chapter-length dig at Verne in which the villain tosses the author out of a balloon.[25] Orion's letter presents a confluence Sam Clemens couldn't resist: a chance to savage Verne and to dismiss the goals of his clingy older brother. Sam's letters to his mother suggest that he took Orion's claim to have been unaware of Verne with a grain of salt. On February 23, 1878, their mother inquired as to Sam's thoughts about his brother's manuscript. He replied: "I begin to fear it is going to be only a wandering, objectless, motiveless imitation of the rampaging French lunatic, Jules Verne. I *saw*, in the first place, that he was walking gaily along, *exactly* in the Frenchman's footsteps, & with the air of a man who wasn't aware that there was anything to be ashamed of about it. . . . Orion sends his hero down Symmes's Hole in to the interior of the earth . . . he meets & talks with a very gentlemanly gorilla; he sees & elaborately describes a pterodactyl, &c &c . . . Can you imagine a sane man deliberately proposing to retain these things & print them, while they already exist in another man's book?"[26]

In his February 21 reply to Orion, Sam tells him, "Everybody would say the ideas were Verne's & nothing but the expansion & elaboration of them yours." After accusing him of "poaching on Verne's peculiar preserve," Sam Clemens seized on the same "talking gorilla" element he'd mentioned to their mother and gave his brother the following advice: "Why don't you find Verne himself down there? Why don't you handle your gorilla for all he is worth & when you have got the good of him, let the reader discover it is Verne in disguise. I think the world has suffered so much from that French idiot that they could enjoy seeing him burlesqued—but I doubt they want to see him imitated."[27] Sam makes an additional suggestion: "You give me a most unsatisfactory idea of the story, sending it in random snatches. Don't do that. Send it all at once."[28]

It may be fair to say that Orion surprised his brother. Within a week, he wrote back stating that he had written one hundred and sixty pages. This is the point where they begin to discuss portions of the manuscript that no longer exist. Here Orion notes a major shift in his content: "I shall strike out where I am anticipated by Jules Verne." He notes a new approach: "I find two hells in the middle of the earth, one ancient one, the other a modern improvement. I shall put Verne in the last for telling lies and misrepresenting nature. I have been led into that much religion, though I have not been unmindful of your charge to let it alone. The interest of the times, however, in that particular subject, I hope will justify it."[29]

"The interest of the times" is a provocative phrase, particularly considered in light of later events in Orion's life. It's clear that, not for the last time, Sam had warned him to avoid writing about religion. In March 1879, one year after he wrote *The Kingdom of Sir John Franklin*, Orion was excommunicated from the Presbyterian Church by the elders of his Keokuk, Iowa, church. This is primarily due to a speech he gave titled "Man the Architect of Our Religion," in which, according to Sam, Orion addressed the Darwinist agnosticism of Robert Ingersoll.[30] The lecture seems to have made public thoughts that he had shared only with Sam and his pastor. Two years earlier, he had attempted to resign from the Presbyterian Church but was convinced to stay. In 1879, the session tried him on charges that his speech questioned basic Christian principles such as divine inspiration of the Bible and the equality of Christ with God.[31] Church session minutes of April 29, 1879, say the speech was "from its whole scope a denial of the fundamental doctrines of the Church."[32] Orion's public humiliation led Sam to write one of his more encouraging letters: "If you made a square deal & told honest thought in the lecture, I wouldn't care what people say. . . . Your heresy won't damn anybody that doesn't deserve it perhaps . . . you showed a deal of moral courage to deliver it."[33] Orion's Sir John Franklin manuscript predates this bit of brotherly approval, but the "blasphemies" that Orion made public in 1879 seem to be given a first draft in that literary work.

By March 1878, there is clearly more than a talking gorilla at stake for Orion Clemens. He states, "I mean to put out the fires of hell, and this is the gist of the Kingdom of Sir John Franklin."[34] In an addendum dated March 19, Orion notes his wife's response to the work. "Mollie read to the hanging scene, and laid down the manuscript, shocked and despondent at its . . . heresies. . . . But why should not people be brought to face and realize what they profess to believe? It is radical, but it is the honest expression of my thoughts, and I have an idea that there is just now being opened a market for that description of honesty."[35]

Between Orion's description of purpose, Mollie's reaction, and Sam's subsequent comments, the manuscript's content becomes clear. Orion sent the entire manuscript to his brother and Sam offered feedback about passages. According to the Mark Twain Papers at the University of California, Berkeley, about 60 percent of the enclosure Sam sent with page-specific comments is missing, but the individual notes that survive are telling. Sam declares it "too crude" to offer to a major outlet but also "*less* crude than I expected it to be, & considerably better work than I believed you could do."[36] He puzzles about the respective troubles of fictionally depicting Heaven and Hell, noting his own attempt to write a "Journey to Heaven" that had given him fits every try. "I have suggested that you vastly modify the first visit to hell, & leave out the second visit altogether. Nobody would or ought to print those things. . . . In my opinion, you will find that *you* can't write up hell so it will stand printing."[37]

Apparently both Jules Verne *and* Jesus Christ make appearances in Orion's novel, although both appear in a less-than-savory light. As Orion promised, Verne is in Hell, although Sam says that "one should not call Verne harsh names. His crime should be sarcastically *suggested* rather than *told*." The use of Christ, however, provoked Sam enough to produce one of the most revealing notes about his own professed beliefs at that time. He states, "Neither Howells nor I believe in hell or the divinity of the Savior—but no matter, the Savior is none the less a sacred Personage & a man should have no desire or disposition to refer to him lightly, profanely, or otherwise than with the profoundest reverence. The only safe thing is not to introduce him or refer to him at all, I suspect."[38] Sam notes that much of Orion's portrayal of a church is "not good enough or interesting enough to retain." Among his commentary are phrases such as "too vivid" or "generally too strong." Orion's final version, it seems, erred on the side of excess in its religious commentary. Regarding something unspecified on page 300, Sam states "This is simply offensive."[39]

The evidence shows that what Orion sent Sam was not merely a journey to the center of the earth, but a strident articulation of religious doubt. His exploration narrative is ultimately used to enable theological commentary. These are not the "queer adventures and romances" he mentioned in 1877, but something else. His conflation of "primitive man" and a "gorilla" show Orion injecting evolutionary ideas into the tale, an approach that—to Orion at least—was superior to Verne's naturalistic cataloguing. Orion's understanding that there could be "a market for that" and his appeal to "the interest of the times" shows his anticipation of the scores of stories that would be published in the next two decades that cover similar ground, including the Frank Reade serials of the 1890s. He understood that sending explorers on a scientific journey could facilitate a reconsideration of existing dogma. This is the same approach used by later technocratic exploration novels, but to different ends. Orion idiosyncratically expresses heretical doubt rather than the conservative rearticulation of biblical authority found in the Edisonade dime novels and similar, later works.

What is interesting about Samuel Clemens's comments, then, is his discouragement of this approach. The writer we find in these letters values concision and suggestion, someone who promotes approaching sensitive topics in elliptical ways. Moreover, the letters showcase Sam's discomfort with the use of such a story for religious ends. It is significant because, as we know, Mark Twain absolutely *did* use technological tales for religious commentary in subsequent novels. Despite his own fascination with science and technology, he apparently saw a distinction between his work and Verne's. His uncomplimentary assessment of Verne as "that French idiot" indicates a lack of respect for the brand of technophilic storytelling that Verne used. In fact, despite his interest in technology and his ability to write enthusiastically pro-science characters, Clemens had mixed feelings about science in general.[40] "Science" for Samuel Clemens represented many things, as it probably did for most nineteenth-century Americans. And yet, by suggesting that his brother "burlesque" Verne, Clemens reveals a great deal about his own artistic approach. In fact, Twain would eventually heed his own advice. In 1878, Twain began writing *A Connecticut Yankee*, originally conceived as a burlesque of Mallory's *Le Morte d'Arthur* during his lecture tour in 1884–1885 with G. W. Cable, who recommended the book to him. Clemens read the book, and his first response was pure enjoyment.[41] Shortly thereafter, Clemens wrote a note that an upcoming story should "have a battle between a modern army, with gattling guns . . . [and] Middle Age Crusaders."[42] He also made his famous notebook entry about a "dream of being a knight errant in armor in the Middle Ages. Have the notions and habits of thought of the present day mixed with the necessities of that. No pockets in the armor. No way to manage certain requirements of nature. Can't scratch. . . . Always getting struck by lightning."[43] The notebook entry shows Clemens thinking through the comic possibilities of approaching Mallory's work from a contemporary perspective. His logistics veer from practical ("no pockets") to the somewhat absurd ("always getting struck by lightning"). As this example shows, Clemens used a process that was not driven by a set formula as much as a desire to play with, and frequently mock, the formulas he found elsewhere. To fully flesh out *A Connecticut Yankee*'s satire, however, he would need to add religion to the mix, something that, as his correspondence with Orion demonstrates, he knew could be trouble.

Twain, Dime Novels, and Religion in Context: Among the Indians

Twain's first major articulation of exploration and religious commentary coincides with his use of dime novels and frontier literature as he prepared to write *Huck Finn and Tom Sawyer among the Indians*. Twain sent a request to his nephew/publisher Charles Webster: "Send to me, right away, a book by *Lieut. Col. Dodge USA.*, called '25 Years on the Frontier'—or some such title. . . . I want several other *personal narratives* of life & adventure out yonder on the Plains & in the Mountains, if you can run across them—especially life *among the Indians*. . . . I mean to take Huck Finn out there."[44] Clemens requested "personal narratives" from Webster, and these appear to be his primary source material for *Huck Finn and Tom Sawyer among the Indians*. Like the sea novel reprints Twain ordered from Osgood in 1881, first-person histories such as Dodge's work were frequently lumped in with frontier-based dime novels by writers such as Ellis by the American public and press.[45] While sensationalized, Dodge's book, *Our Wild Indians: Thirty-Three Years'*

Personal Experience among the Red Men of the Great West (1883), represents the kind of overt debunking of Cooperesque notions of the frontier
that Clemens surely appreciated. Dodge's chapter on the fates of white captives specifically names Cooper, stating that "Cooper, and some other novelists, knew nothing of Indian character and customs when they placed their
heroines prisoners in their hands."[46] Dodge's accusation no doubt applies to
not only Cooper but the dime novelists who emulated him.[47] While Twain
may not have consulted actual dime novels for source material, he certainly
crafted his tale with an understanding of Cooper paired with a counter-ide-
ology borrowed from the pages of Western explorers' dime novel–like personal narratives.

Huck Finn and Tom Sawyer among the Indians is the first work where
Twain confronted frontier exploratory tropes and assessed the role of both
religion and technology in facilitating such expansion—the same technique
he would refine in *A Connecticut Yankee* and *Tom Sawyer Abroad*. In Twain's
science fiction, technology's ability to create new knowledge is hampered by
peoples' established conception of the world. His technocratic protagonists
cling to their own prejudices and their existing conceptions of identity, finding ways to use technology so that it reinforces these ideas. Before he fully
utilized this approach in *A Connecticut Yankee*, however, Twain drafted a
story that addressed how exploration could actually shape a traveler's worldview and change him. Begun in early 1884 and left unfinished in August of
that same year, *Huck Finn and Tom Sawyer among the Indians* begins with
Tom Sawyer, Huckleberry Finn, and Jim preparing to leave their town to see
the West. Huck narrates the tale. Tom desires to light out for the territory,
but he must convince Huck and Jim to join him. Jim protests the most, noting that he has no desire to make acquaintance with Indians. He says, "Ef
dey ketches a body out, dey'll take en skin him same as dey would a dog.
Dat's what I knows 'bout 'em." Tom's reply: "All fol-de-rol" (34). Twain sets
the stage in the same manner he ultimately uses in *Tom Sawyer Abroad*, with
Tom presenting his romanticized outlook and Jim voicing practical concerns
that are immediately dismissed by the book-smart white youth. In fact, the
impression of Indians that Jim voices coincides directly with the portrayal
of Indians in Dodge's book.[48] Tom responds with a page-long description
of how Indians are "the noblest human beings that's ever been in the world"
(35). Jim is won over, concluding emphatically, "I doan' want no likelier folks
aroun' me d'n what dem *Injuns* is" (37). Off to the Plains they go.

Huck, Tom, and Jim meet up with a family, the Mills, and request to
join them during their journey to Oregon (40). One of the Mills daughters,
Peggy, is the sweetheart of a skilled frontiersman named Brace Johnson,
who is scheduled to join their party later. Johnson is an experienced Indian

fighter, and very much a "big, and fine, and brave, and good" young Anglo-American in the tradition of Leatherstocking and Baldy Bicknell from *Steam Man of the Prairies* (42). When the group encounters an Indian party—much to Tom's delight—Peggy explains Johnson's dislike of Indians, noting that she wishes "he could see that Injuns was just like other people" (46). The Indians they have met, however, eventually kill the Mills parents and kidnap Peggy and Jim. When Johnson arrives, Huck and Tom follow him in a revenge/rescue mission not unlike the one at the end of the first Frank Reade Jr. story. As they begin tracking the Indians, Huck wonders about the small dagger Peggy had shown him—a gift from Brace Johnson to be used for suicide in case of Indian attack—and asks Johnson why "he actually hoped Peggy *was* dead" (54). Huck spares the reader the details, saying nothing more than "he explained it to me, and then it was all clear" (54).[49]

Johnson's hard-earned frontier knowledge sets the contrast to Tom Sawyer's naiveté. Johnson, Huck tells us, "talked about Injuns . . . the same as if he was talking about animals" (61). Tom must confront his misconceptions. After the raid, Huck asks a seemingly innocent question and receives a telling reply:

"Tom, where did you learn about Injuns—how noble they was, and all that?"

He gave me a look that showed me I had hit him hard, very hard, and so I wished I hadn't said the words. He turned away his head, and after a minute he said "Cooper's novels," and didn't say anything more." (50)

Just as *A Connecticut Yankee* pokes fun at Mallory's *Le Morte d'Arthur*, *Huck Finn and Tom Sawyer among the Indians* sends up Cooper and the numerous dime novels that used Cooper's formula, first by burlesquing their frontier tropes and then by explicitly stating how incorrect their portrayals of the frontier are when compared to perceived reality. In many ways, the unfinished novel works through ideas that would become his later essay "Fenimore Cooper's Literary Offenses," written for the *North American Review* in 1894.[50]

One might suspect that, given his focus on debunking Cooper, Twain would highlight the negative portrayals of Native Americans presented by Dodge. Instead, Twain found something in his research that piqued his interest: Dodge's portrayal of Native American spiritual beliefs. Twain wrote the following note in his copy of Dodge's *Our Wild Indians* in preparation for *Huck Finn and Tom Sawyer among the Indians*: "Our illogical God is all-powerful in name, but impotent in fact; the Great Spirit is not all-powerful but does the very best he can for his injun and does it free of charge."[51] Twain's portrayal of Native American faith obviously oversimplifies the wide range of actual beliefs across Native American tribes; as Axel Knoenagel has stated, it is "only replacing one stereotype for another."[52] Nevertheless, in Dodge's work, Clemens found at least one area where the Indian outlook represented what he viewed as an improvement on the white Protestant worldview he had inherited.

The influence of this idea seeps into Twain's portrayal of Brace Johnson who, despite his distrust and hatred of Indians, has nevertheless adopted their religious views. Huck explains that Johnson has lived with Plains Indians long enough to have "some of their ways" including their spiritual beliefs: "And one of the things that puzzled him was how such animals ever struck such a sensible religion. He said the Injuns hadn't only but two Gods, a good one and a bad one, and they never paid no attention to the good one, nor ever prayed to him or worried about him at all, but only tried their level best to flatter up the bad god and keep on the good side of him; because the good one loved them. . . . Brace thought more of the Great Spirit than he did his own mother, but he never fretted about him" (61–62). Johnson's attempt to "flatter up the bad god" impacts their adventure. Johnson loses track of the days and eats meat on a Friday. Swearing off meat on certain days is one way Johnson hopes to appease the unnamable "Bad God," and he tells Huck and Tom that the "best way" to appease the Bad God is through self-denial, "same as you do in any religion" (62). When Tom goes missing later, Johnson attributes it to the Bad God getting his revenge.

Despite the jab at religion's tendency to equate self-denial with appeasing God, Brace Johnson's faith is clearly *not* the "same as" the religion of Huck, Tom, Jim, or the Mills family, or any of the numerous Oregon Trail pioneers they represent. Indeed, Johnson is the only character who, in Twain's terms, actually knows the score. He is the one that Peggy Mills and her family plan to rely on during their journey West until the Indians attack before he arrives; he is the character the boys rely on after tragedy strikes. Huck recounts Peggy's description of him as a man who learned all about "trapping, hunting, scouting, fighting . . . [and] knowed the plains and mountains and the whole country, from Texas to Oregon" (42). Johnson's common sense and know-how lend credibility to his decision to practice "injun" religion. He has traveled and experienced the full spectrum of frontier life in a way that Tom and Huck have not. Albert Stone notes that Brace Johnson's spiritual beliefs "provide excuse for voicing the marked relativism [Twain] himself felt" (178). In fact, Johnson's decision is echoed in the sentiments of the Connecticut Yankee himself, Twain's protagonist Hank Morgan, who declares that "man is only at his best, morally, when he is equipped with the religious garment whose color and shape and size most nicely accommodate themselves to the spiritual complexion, angularities and stature of the individual who wears it" (81). In Brace Johnson, we find these ideas played out on an individual level. While Johnson never explicitly states why he has converted to "injun" religion, Huck's summary of his ideas makes a few things clear. In its ability to provide a clear explanation of good and evil, the religion suits Johnson's needs. The Indian religion simply extends into the spiritual realm the kind of physical activities that define Johnson's character. Its systematic approach, where the good occurs naturally and the bad can be circumvented through skilled action that appeases a "Bad God," surely appeals to the self-reliant outdoorsman whose entire survival relies on reading the natural environment and knowing what to do in dire circumstances.

In *Huck Finn and Tom Sawyer among the Indians*, the frontier provides a locus where beliefs are challenged and, in some cases, refined. Tom loses his romanticized vision of Native Americans; Brace Johnson, in contrast, discovers a religious view that he finds superior to white Christianity. He allows the frontier to change his worldview. But Brace Johnson is not a Twainian technocrat. In many ways, Johnson presents a stark contrast to the heroes of *A Connecticut Yankee* and *Tom Sawyer Abroad*, whose reliance on their prior understanding of history and their own American identity actually thwart their technocratic plans.

A Connecticut Yankee: Adding Technology to the Mix

The transition between *Huck and Tom among the Indians* and *A Connecticut Yankee* involves two elements. First, it presents what Tom Quirk has called "Twain's shift of interest from individual moral nature to a social psychology."[53] It is one thing for Brace Johnson to change his "religious garment"; it is quite another thing for Hank Morgan to enact nationwide religious reform, to surreptitiously attack the Church and expound at length on the best methods to undermine it. Second, Twain makes technophilia one of the defining elements of his protagonist, and Hank Morgan's reforms stem from his desire—and his ability—to reproduce nineteenth-century technology in sixth-century Britain.[54] Underlying *A Connecticut Yankee* is the notion that these two elements are tied together, that reform means simultaneously undercutting spiritual authority and introducing new technology, and more importantly that the Church will be threatened—perhaps quite justifiably—by science and technology and will attempt to quash it.

Hank Morgan reaches Camelot through the very unscientific means of "transmission of epochs—and bodies" that occurs after he is knocked in the head by an angry subordinate at his job at the Colt Arms Factory in Hartford (2–5). Once there, he brazenly concludes that he is uniquely suited to lead: "If . . . it was really the sixth century, all right, I didn't want any softer thing: I would boss the whole country inside of three months; for I judged I would have the start of the best educated man in the kingdom by a matter of thirteen hundred years" (17).

Morgan first uses his knowledge to predict an eclipse, declaring it to be a demonstration of his magical powers (46–48).[55] He appeals to the Arthurians' superstitions to gain clout and persuades them to recognize him as "The Boss," a position "equal to the king" in power (63). Morgan then puts into use his skills from the Colt Arms Factory where, he tells us, "I could make anything a body wanted . . . and if there wasn't any quick and new-fangled way to make a thing, I could invent one" (4). He creates a patent office and a regular newspaper. Near the end of the book, after he has spent multiple years transforming Camelot, he notes that he has brought to the kingdom "the telegraph, the telephone, the phonograph, the type-writer, the sewing machine" and a fleet of steamships, with which he hopes to launch an expedition "to discover America" (397–98). Along with these come institutions of social reform, including "a teacher-factory and a lot of Sunday schools" (81). His ultimate plan involves two elements: first, "to overthrow the Catholic Church and set up the Protestant faith on its ruins," and second, "unlimited suffrage . . . given to men and women alike," culminating in a "Republic" after King Arthur's death (398–99).

As a number of scholars have observed, the story above plays out a remarkably straightforward imperialist narrative: an outsider—armed with science and technology superior to the culture he has entered—proceeds to set up a system wherein he has all authority and then reaps the benefits of that authority, all the while shaping the culture so that it more closely resembles his own. Even the earliest nineteenth-century reviews overtly recognized the text's criticism of the US circa 1889, understanding that, while part of the story's thrust came from an outright celebration of nineteenth-century culture over the medieval worldview, its critique was more expansive. Howells's January 1890 review in *Harper's* called the book "an object-lesson in democracy. It makes us glad of our republic and our epoch; but it does not flatter us into a fond content with them; there are passages in which we see that the noble of Arthur's day, who battened on the blood and sweat of his bondmen, is one in essence with the capitalist . . . who grows rich on the labor of his underpaid wagemen."[56] José Martí, whose writing always kept a keen eye on US imperialist tendencies, highlighted the book's critical element and explicitly marked it as a potentially anti-imperialist text: "So skillfully does he develop his theme that the salient character of that age of kings and bishops, peasants and slaves, proving to be a picture of what is beginning to be seen in the United States, is more than a mere copy."[57] While the novel predates the Spanish-American War and Twain's public assertion of himself as an anti-imperialist, many contemporary writers see it as implicitly critical of US imperial expansion as well.[58] Hsuan Hsu states, for instance, "Although *A Connecticut Yankee*'s references to imperialism are often circuitous, they are also more ubiquitous and compelling than its references to antebellum slavery and Gilded Age capitalism."[59] Such readings indicate that we must read Morgan's imperialistic assertions critically and skeptically, much the way we see Tom Sawyer's faith in "Cooper's Indians" as a belief to be dismantled rather than vindicated. The tale's conclusion highlights these complexities by showing the results of Morgan's attempts at progress. Ultimately, his reforms fail. The Church issues an Interdict, quickly bringing England back to status quo despite Morgan's small and technologically enabled armed resistance. John Carlos Rowe has suggested that the ending calls into question the entire technocratic imperial enterprise: "There is little evidence that the boys and teachers 'trained' under the new educational regime have learned anything beyond the mere manufacture and operation of the new technologies; they are still profoundly dependent on the ruler [Morgan], who has simply exchanged his crown or miter for the scientist's laboratory coat."[60] Other writers have suggested that the pessimism of the final chapters is more a result of Twain's lengthy composition process, and the travails of his personal, financial life during that time, than his genuine skepticism about the value of Morgan's endeavor.[61] Even critics inclined to read Hank Morgan's pontifications as proxy for Twain's own views seem to agree the book is about the futility of imperial endeavor rather than a justification of it. Despite Morgan's supreme confidence, his technocratic plans are doomed.

One example showcases Morgan's overconfidence in technology and his perception of how it can and should act as a cultural force. Near the end of the book, Morgan wins a jousting tournament by shooting knights with a makeshift revolver. Hank sees this as a victory over not only "knight errantry" but over Merlin, who has publicly offered his magical services to Morgan's challengers. Morgan gloats, "Somehow, every time the magic of fol-de-rol tried conclusions with the magic of science, the magic of fol-de-rol got left" (393). Interestingly, Twain has his Yankee protagonist use the same dismissive term—"fol-de-rol"—that Tom Sawyer deploys in *Huck Finn and Tom Sawyer among the Indians* to counter Jim's views of Indians. Both Tom and Hank are charismatic figures, performers, and dreamers who don't fully grasp the limits of their own knowledge. For Hank Morgan, the narrative that he has consumed is not a Cooperesque version of the noble savage myth but a post-Enlightenment narrative of science and progress in which technologically advanced individuals (or countries) have the right to be "the Boss."

From this cultural assumption about the power of science and technology comes a perception of science's enemies. Morgan's biggest threat is not Merlin, or the knights, but the Church. "I was afraid of a united church," he plainly states, "it makes a mighty power, the mightiest conceivable, and then when it by and by gets into selfish hands, as it is always bound to do, it means death to human liberty, and paralysis to human thought" (81). Morgan's sense of inevitability, of his playing out some master narrative, becomes clear here. Just as "the magic of science" will win out "every time," so too is religion "always bound" to be used by "selfish hands" to crush free-thinking individuals. Because of his commitment to this conception of the world, Hank presumes that he must inevitably fight the Church. Hank consistently aligns the Church with the "magic of fol-de-rol" that exists to be undermined, and this must be done in small, careful steps through the deployment of science and dissemination of information facilitated by technology. As a result, Hank Morgan undertakes many of these reforms in *secret*, attempting to slowly roll out his nineteenth-century technology and to undertake his program of religious and political reeducation in "various quiet nooks and corners" (80). By portraying this explicitly, by making it integral to the novel's plot and the ultimate downfall of its protagonist's plans, Twain lays out an element that the broader Edisonade only provides in small glimpses. Twain's Yankee assumes, with no real evidence from Arthur's times, that the Church will be hostile to his plans and perceive him as a threat to its power.

Morgan, then, is a secularist. His model to counter the Church comes directly from his experience as a nineteenth-century American, particularly as a Protestant in a nation where the press and public opinion were frequently anti-Catholic.[62] Moreover, he articulates almost note for note the formations of secularism that Tracy Fessenden has itemized, a narrative that "begins with the flowerings of intellection and creativity, within and against the structures of the Catholic Church. . . . The story continues in the Reformation, which upended the spiritual and political hegemony of Rome, and in the treaties that ended the so-called Wars of Religion by carving out separate domains of religious and political authority . . . [that] lays the ground for democracy and Enlightenment."[63] As Fessenden points out, this cultural narrative has been reiterated so many times that modern Americans take it as a given. Once Hank Morgan assumes the Church is his enemy (that is, *immediately*), he states his solution: "I had started a teacher-factory and a lot of Sunday schools the first thing; as a result I now had . . . a complete variety of Protestant congregations all in prosperous and growing condition . . . I could have given my own sect the preference and made everybody a Presbyterian without any trouble, but that would have been to affront a law of human nature: spiritual wants and instincts are as various in the human family as are physical appetites, complexions, and features, and a man is only at his best, morally, when he is equipped with the religious garment whose color and shape and size most nicely accommodate themselves to the spiritual complexion, angularities and stature of the individual who wears it" (81). Such is Hank Morgan's view of religious tolerance. Its tenets—taught to Arthurians in secret locales so closely aligned with technocracy that he calls them "factories"—are the wholesale assumptions of secularization.

Morgan struggles internally when he sees honorable or helpful priests.[64] He grudgingly admits that his interactions with individual priests "showed that not all priests were frauds and self-seekers, but that many, even the great majority, of those that were down on the ground among the common people were sincere, and right-hearted, and devoted to the alleviation of human troubles and sufferings" (160–61). He continues that same paragraph, however, by concluding that these good priests may, in fact, be a hindrance to his plans: "for it was just the sort of thing to keep a people reconciled to an Established Church. . . . Concentration of power in a political machine is bad; and an Established Church is only a political machine . . . an enemy to human liberty" (161). For Morgan, the corrupt nature of the Church trumps the goodness of its individual members, providing further justification for his actions.

All this could easily be read as Twain editorializing, voicing a modern, progressivist secular narrative he and other Americans took for granted. And, indeed, it has been.[65] Such readings, however, typically do not take into account Twain's writings to his brother and his *Huck and Tom among the Indians* manuscript. Read in contrast to Brace Johnson's unorthodox (for a Westerner) religious views, Morgan is more precisely understandable for the cipher that he is. While Johnson has every bit of the expansionist mindset that Morgan has, his religious practices and piety are a reversal of the Western norm. Morgan, in contrast, sticks to his beliefs about religion doggedly. The possibility that he will somehow have a Brace Johnson-like conversion to his new world's religious views is highly unlikely and never even suggested. By the time he wrote *A Connecticut Yankee*, Twain had slightly altered his own Calvinist religious garments, leaving the Presbyterianism of his youth, adopting his wife Olivia's Congregationalist denomination, and becoming a regular attendee of Joseph Twichell's Asylum Hill Congregationalist Church in Hartford.[66] Morgan, however, lauds himself for being a tolerant "Presbyterian," a member of the same sect that had, ten years earlier, excommunicated Orion Clemens. Other explicitly Presbyterian characters in Twain's later work include the vivisectionist father who blinds and kills the family dog's puppy in "A Dog's Tale" (1903). Clearly, the label did not signify tolerance to Twain, though he understood early on that growing up in that particular denomination would always make it part of his religious DNA.[67] The author understood that frontier exploration could change a person's views about mainstream Protestant Christianity; he had worked that out partly in *Huck Finn and Tom Sawyer among the Indians*. Such is not the case for Hank Morgan on the Arthurian frontier. Instead, Twain deliberately forges a character who acts out in a manner that embodies American nineteenth-century training and presumptions.[68]

If we view the book as both inherently critical of the imperial venture and presciently aware of the way technology enables that endeavor, then it becomes particularly essential to consider exactly how Hank Morgan enacts his plans. Morgan plainly understands that the correct deployment of technology can expand power on an individual scale, mirroring a view shared by the Frank Reade novels. Two of Morgan's reforms reveal his conceptualization regarding precisely *how* technology can, or should, be utilized. When Morgan restores the fountain in the Valley of Holiness and when he establishes a newspaper, he operates in a methodical manner with elaborate digressions into the philosophy behind his actions. Both cases illustrate Hank Morgan's perception that science and religion must conflict and how that impacts an imperial enterprise facilitated by technology.

During his knight-errant mission, Morgan prepares to visit a holy site with an allegedly miraculous fountain. Upon arrival, he finds out that the fountain is dry, and must confront an unusual Church policy as a result. Morgan learns that the Church treats bathing as a sin, and has promoted the idea that the drying up of the fountain was caused by bathing (201). By the 1880s, bathing had cultural connotations of hygiene, class, and even religiosity.[69] For Morgan, the notion that the organized Church would prevent bathing is not just an example of its unyielding and tyrannical influence on the minutiae of sixth-century lives, but potentially an affront to his understanding of Christianity's connection to hygiene. Morgan uses the situation with the fountain as an opportunity to build up his technocratic reputation. He secretly sends off to his "Chemical Department, Laboratory Extension" at Camelot for plumbing supplies and two assistants (202). Although he works with the priests, Morgan appeals to their superstition rather than their scientific curiosity by outright encouraging their notion that he is working "enchantments" (205). He does this with performative flourishes. Morgan tells the reader, "As a matter of business it was a good idea to get the notion around that the thing was difficult. Many a small thing has been made large by the right kind of advertising" (210–11).[70] His small crew covertly installs a pump and some lead pipe, then places colored rockets wired to a battery; the latter is necessary only for show (219). Rather than simply repair the fountain, Morgan sets up a noisy charade: "When you are going to do a miracle for an ignorant race . . . play your effects for all they are worth" (219). And so, he performs his work in public, launching the rockets in sequence each time he speaks one of a series of German tongue-twisters he claims are spells (221–24). In this endeavor, then, Hank Morgan uses two types of technology—plumbing and fireworks, technology-as-repair and technology-as-pageant, respectively—and maintains the public illusion that they are magic that only he can control. Just as he has discreetly sent for assistants with supplies from his secret factories, so too does he secretly let some of the monks in on the mechanism behind his performance. He states, "I took along a nightshift of monks, and taught them the mystery of the pump, and set them to work. . . . To those monks, that pump was a good deal of a miracle itself" (224). At best, this action shows Morgan's willingness to spread information about science and technology to groups who need it while he reserves any large scale revelations about where his "enchantments" come from in order to lessen possible resistance to the status quo.

After fixing the fountain, however, Morgan takes an extra step by using the prestige he has gained to further undermine the Church's authority. By this point in the book, he has already attempted to undermine knighthood by turning knights into walking billboards for products like soap and toothpaste. He ties his latest plan to that strategy:

> My influence in the Valley of Holiness was something prodigious, now. It seemed worthwhile to try to turn it to some valuable account. The thought came to me the next morning, and was suggested by one of my knights who was in the soap line come riding in. . . . So I sounded a brother:
> "Wouldn't you like a bath?" (226).

He invites the Abbot and monks to take baths in the water, despite their fear that this behavior will "drive away the blessed water again" (227). Morgan promises that he has "knowledge" that informs him that bathing is not the sin that caused the water to stop. The technological improvements he has made have established his reputation as an enchanter so much that he can claim special information about sin, essentially giving him the role reserved for priests. Morgan's focus appears to be about helping the locals. The priests *want* to bathe, but their religious faith forbids it. Morgan uses his technological feat of fixing the fountain—passed off as supernatural power—to erode the priests' faith in the Church's authority on supernatural matters. He helps them do what they want only by shifting their reliance on the Church to reliance on him. In *A Connecticut Yankee*, Twain makes cleanliness an outward example of colonial power that vindicates the individual's rights over the Church's rights, but also shows how such reforms fail when enacted by an Edisonian technocrat who is more interested in enforcing his own view of history than on genuinely assisting the individuals in question.

Morgan's subsequent acts build on this character flaw. He reports the restoration of the fountain in one of his other great technological undertakings: the newspaper. The establishment of a newspaper further demonstrates how Morgan uses technology to divergent means, hoping to simultaneously enact reform and maintain exclusive control over the kingdom. Morgan engages in many of his most florid descriptions of democracy's value when he speaks about newspapers.[71] Bruce Michelson has pointed out that Morgan understands news primarily as a consumer; while he has training in munitions and mechanics, he is not a trained printer or journalist.[72] Merely by being a reader of American newspapers, Morgan thinks that he can bring journalism to Arthur's England. Newspapers figure into one of the book's passages where Morgan most directly outlines his plans: "The first thing you want in a new country, is a patent office; then work up your school system; and after that, out with your paper. A newspaper has its faults, and plenty of them; but . . . You can't resurrect a dead nation without it" (74). Because of this worldview, the paper becomes a central part of Morgan's reform plan. Indeed, Morgan holds a faith in the newspaper's place in society typical of nineteenth-century Americans. The number of daily newspapers quadrupled from 1870 to 1900, partly due to the foundations laid in the early republic that included colonial arguments limiting libel, the First Amendment, and low postal rates to support a free press during the 1790s.[73] While muckraking and jingoism tend to define the 1890s period defined by William Randolph Hearst's and Joseph Pulitzer's sensationalized papers, journalists of the era had a growing desire to stick to the facts and increasingly promoted themselves as problem-solvers because of their ability to get information to the public.[74] As an 1880s news consumer, Hank Morgan conceives of newspapers as a tool to right social wrongs and a vital emblem of democratic society.

Samuel Clemens's fascination with the press, particularly technology's ability to aid or limit free speech, extends back to his days as a printer's assistant in Hannibal. The result made him simultaneously enamored with new technologies and skeptical over their correct usage.[75] By the time he wrote *A Connecticut Yankee*, Twain had heavily invested in a new technology designed to facilitate printing: James Paige's compositor. Twain's initial, unbridled enthusiasm for the compositor represents a triumph of Twain's technophilic enthusiasm over his skepticism for many Twain scholars, and the near-mythic failure of this investment haunts many scholars' readings of

A Connecticut Yankee.[76] Twain began writing the book enthused about the compositor's financial prospects and even considered retiring from writing to live off the profits of his investment. But the machine never worked correctly and required constant infusions of money to retool it. Near the end of 1888, Twain's frustration grew and he noted "the thing has gone straight downhill toward sure destruction."[77] Indeed, the culmination of these bad investments bankrupted him.

In practice, however, Morgan's re-creation of modern journalism rests on technology's ability to undermine the Church, essentially replacing one type of supernatural belief with another. Surprisingly, Morgan begins his endeavor by finding an "intelligent priest" to begin writing information about tournaments (74). Morgan notes that the priest is detailed and precise because his work in the Church is directly related to swindling mourners out of money: "He had kept books for the undertaker-department of his church when he was younger, and there, you know, the money's in the details; the more details, the more swag: bearers, mutes, candles, prayers—everything counts; and if the bereaved don't buy prayers enough, you mark-up your candles with a forked pencil, and your bill shows up all right" (74). From its very inception, then, the newspaper operates as a method to transfer power away from a Church that is assumed to be corrupted by money and power and reallocate its resources to a more democratic institution: the free press.

How free is Hank Morgan's press? Tellingly, one of his first actions in the book's latter portion is a darkly comic act of prior restraint. It comes after Morgan has ended knight-errantry and publicly revealed the secret elements of his master plan, including schools, mines, and factories. Sir Dinadan the Humorist prepares a book of jokes, including one "gray-headed" joke that has plagued Morgan for his entire stay in Camelot. "I suppressed the book and hanged the author," he announces (397). While this occurrence represents a comic culmination of Morgan's frustration with stale humor and is perhaps more than anything indicative of Mark Twain's inability to pass up a joke at its expense, it also presents a dictatorial action against free press and a truly self-contradictory act on the protagonist's part. The joke may be too good to pass up, but it also underscores Morgan's unreliability as a democratic role model. Such an action further supports the notion of Rowe and others that Morgan represents Twain's mockery of the would-be democratic imperialist. Morgan, then, does not have a consistent view on the press's power or the liberating aspects of a free press.

Between these two events—the use of the priest to cover a tournament and the hanging of Sir Dinadan—the actual newspaper is published. In a chapter entitled "The First Newspaper," Morgan is overjoyed to hear the shout of a boy selling newspapers. "One greater than kings had arrived—the newsboy. But I was the only person in all that throng who knew the meaning of this mighty birth," he states, adding, "It was delicious to see a newspaper again" (257). Morgan savors this moment both for the way it reconnects him to his nineteenth-century roots and the special way it reinforces his unique position in sixth century as the "only person" who understands the significance of a daily newspaper. As he sits and reads it, a throng of Britons surrounds him and begin asking about it. "It is a public journal," he states, adding, "I will explain what that is, another time" (261). Morgan conceals the paper's more anti-authoritarian purposes, both in terms of the reallocation of power it presents and its power to influence public opinion. Instead, he notes with glee how the Arthurians call it "a miracle, a wonder! Dark work of enchantment" (262).

Knowing that most of them cannot read, Morgan recounts one of the main stories of the day: an account of "the miracle of the restoration of the well" (262). Always a savvy self-promoter, Morgan reads to them about his endeavors, using the newspaper to further promote the idea that his technological feat was a "miracle." After hearing this story, Morgan states, "So they took [the newspaper], handling it as cautiously and devoutly as if it had been some holy thing come from some supernatural region" (262). Their reaction supports Randall Knoper's claim that "the Arthurians see every one of his commodities as something existing completely autonomously, a fantastic object appearing magically."[78] Morgan seems perfectly content with that reaction.

The portrayal of technology in A Connecticut Yankee involves the simple replacement of one superstition for another, an embodiment of science-fiction author Arthur C. Clarke's famous maxim that sufficiently advanced technology is indistinguishable from magic. Behind Clarke's statement is the idea that an archaic civilization could not comprehend the difference, with the implication that this situation could be manipulated by the advanced civilization. In Hank Morgan's mind, technology is inevitably poised to do battle with the superstitions promulgated by established religious hierarchies, and it does this best by playing up its "supernatural" appearances. Morgan not only passes off a technological feat as magic, he uses another form of technology to reinforce that idea by printing the report in his newspaper. Moreover, that technology serves to undermine the Church, replacing the superstitions of the Church with the unexplained wonders of Morgan's science. In this light, Morgan's power struggle with the "Established Church" represents two well-intentioned oppressors competing for the worldview that will dominate their society.[79] Morgan embodies both the ideas in Twain's labor speech and the larger imperial dilemma, essentially becoming the kind of secretive tyrant he hopes to resist. Ultimately, A Connecticut Yankee presents a critical view of American technocracy by assuming that it will fall prey to the same temptations of power as the institutions it attempts to overthrow.

Perhaps the most provocative assessment of *A Connecticut Yankee*'s approach to imperialism comes from Twain's letter to Howells detailing his frustration that there were "so many things left out" of the final version of the book. "They burn in me," he told Howells, "but now they can't ever be said. And besides they would require a library—and a pen warmed-up in hell."[80] Taking the last phrase as his anthology title, Frederick Anderson sees this line as an indication of Twain's beginning to sense himself as "a reluctant radical [and] an amateur reformer" who would speak out against imperialism and other social ills.[81]

Perhaps surprisingly, Twain ultimately voiced these thoughts in a novel specifically written for a young adult periodical and featuring his most famous protagonists. In fact, as Stone notes, *Tom Sawyer Abroad* first saw print in publisher Mary Mapes Dodge's *The St. Nicholas Magazine*. This periodical was created as part of a larger publishing "counter-reformation," designed to halt the spread of dime-novel reading among adolescents in Twain's era by providing them with more genteel reading material.[82] If indeed Twain's warmed-up pen found its use in his protest writings and essays, it also crept into some of his most apparently bland and market-driven writing. Destitute because of the financial failure brought on by the Paige compositor, Twain had to write for money once again and returned to his plan to continue Huckleberry Finn and Tom Sawyer's adventures. If *A Connecticut Yankee in King Arthur's Court* suggests that technology undermines religion by simply supplanting it with a new kind of superstition, then *Tom Sawyer Abroad* extends these ideas by showing another example of a character whose dogmatic political and cultural views actually limit his ability to conceive of technology's transformative power.

Tom Sawyer Abroad: Expansion, Religion, and Technology

Tom Sawyer Abroad connects all the earlier elements of Twain's understanding of literature, technology, and empire: from his suggestion that his brother burlesque Verne to his disillusionment with US imperialist tendencies voiced in *A Connecticut Yankee*. As in the unfinished *Huck Finn and Tom Sawyer among the Indians*, Huckleberry Finn narrates *Tom Sawyer Abroad*, beginning with Tom's longing to go on a "crusade" (17). Even more than Hank Morgan, Tom Sawyer views violent conflict as a primary means to prestige. Tom is shocked to learn that Huck and Jim don't know what a crusade is. He explains that "a crusade is a war to recover the Holy Land from the paynim [non-Christians]," and is further shocked by Huck's lack of concern about the "Holy Land":

> "What do we want of it?"
> "Why can't you understand it's in the hands of the paynim, and it's our duty to take it away from them."
> "How did we come to let them git hold of it?"
> "We didn't come to let them git hold of it. They always had it."
> "Why, Tom, then it must belong to them, don't it?"
> "Why of course it does. Who said it didn't?"
> I studied over it, but couldn't seem to git at the right of it no way. I says:
> "It's too many for me Tom Sawyer. If I had a farm and it was mine, and another person wanted it, would it be right for him to—"
> "Oh, shucks! you don't know enough to come in when it rains, Huck Finn." (21)

Huck Finn's question about the land's rightful ownership meets Tom Sawyer's scorn. Here, Twain equates the religious concept of a "Holy Land" with imperial endeavor and the broader, Western tradition of tying expansion to religious conflict. As in *Huck and Tom among the Indians*, the base of Tom's knowledge is history books and historical fiction, in this case "Walter Scott's book" (25). The story sets up a recurring motif in which Tom thinks he knows the answers, assuming cultural superiority over those around him, only to be foiled by Jim and Huck who ask, simply and directly, for elaboration beyond his book-smart understanding.[83]

In this instance, Tom attempts to override Huck's common-sense protestations about taking someone else's land or property. He distinguishes the "crusade" he favors from the kind of outright theft Huck sees as analogous to it. When Tom states that, unlike stealing a farm, "this is religious, and totally different," Huck replies with shock: "Religious to go and take the land away from people that owns it?" "Certainly," Tom answers, "it's always been considered so" (22). Taking the land from its rightful owners is acceptable in Tom's terms because it is part of a religious war. Moreover, Tom's appeal to history and his understanding of tradition leads him to ignore Huck's disagreement. Tom focuses on how things have "always been," making him in many ways an arch-conservative resistant to any ideas that challenge his preexisting notions.

Tom's description also prefigures the portrayal of missionaries in Twain's essay "To the Person Sitting in Darkness," published seven years later in 1901. There, Twain the essayist rails against leaders who use religion as an excuse to do violence against another country, even invoking the bigoted, Indian-hating spirit he shared with Colonel Dodge in the process: "What we want of our missionaries out there is . . . that they shall also represent the American spirit. The oldest Americans are the Pawnees."[84] Twain then explains how American missionaries who demand monetary reparations and violent retribution when attacked by locals are analogous to Pawnee warriors who take vengeance by committing violence against "any white person that comes along" and who take "thirteen times" the value of his property.[85] Twain's anger at the dangerous commingling of religious evangelism, violence, and territorial expansion is equally apparent in 1894's *Tom Sawyer Abroad*, with the author using his most famous character as the advocate of the same kind of dangerous ideology he later condemned in "To the Person Sitting in Darkness." Just as Hank Morgan becomes an embodiment of the worst technocratic impulses, Tom Sawyer represents the unreflective, knee-jerk expansionist who seizes opportunity and uses appeals to tradition and religion to justify his acts.

Technocracy, of course, appears in full force in *Tom Sawyer Abroad*. Tom, Huck, and Jim embark on a balloon voyage across the Atlantic that eventually leads them through the Sahara and into the Holy Land itself. Many critics have observed that the structure and concept resemble Jules Verne's *Five Weeks in a Balloon*.[86] It seems Twain finally went back to his planned balloon story after all. The book's scorn for technocrats starts early with its portrayal of the balloon's inventor, a hackneyed caricature of a scientist prone to making interjections about his invention such as "Idiots! They said it wouldn't go; and they wanted to examine it, and spy around me to get the secret of it out of me. But I beat them. Nobody knows the secret but me. Nobody knows what makes it move but me—and it's a new power! A new power, and a thousand times the strongest on earth" (32). While the dialogue is certainly more melodramatic than *A Connecticut Yankee*, the sentiments are taken straight from Hank Morgan's playbook. The scientist jealously guards his secret, tormenting Huck, Jim, and Tom when he finds out that they are on board after takeoff and forcing them to work for him. He eventually succumbs to paranoia, convincing himself that he must alter his course from England and attempting to throw Tom Sawyer overboard during a thunderstorm, and somehow falling out of the balloon himself in the process (60–61).[87]

At this point in the book, Tom Sawyer takes control by figuring out the basics of piloting the airship, and the plot becomes focused on the three friends' episodic adventures on the balloon's flight. Tom dubs himself "Tom Sawyer the Erronort" (75). Twain's creative misspelling of "aeronaut" underscores Tom's youthful unreliability, reminding the reader that Tom is not as well informed as he assumes and that he is prone to "error" because of this trait. Tom's assumption of control over the ship and the group's itinerary indicates his further embodiment of the ready imperialist. Tom frequently stops the action to explain his knowledge of minutiae such as mirages or fleas, declaring his companions "sapheads" or "ignorant superstitious blatherskites" if they don't immediately understand or agree (101, 128). Clearly, Tom has already mastered the exasperated rhetoric of the technocrat, sounding remarkably like the balloon's paranoid inventor in his recurring, casual dismissal of others who don't share his education. While Tom is not an inventor himself, his subsequent mastery of both the flying apparatus and the philosophy behind technocratic exploration bring to the novel a plot and setting congruent to Edisonades.

If there were any lingering suspicions that *Tom Sawyer Abroad* sought to mock American imperialist attitudes, Twain has one last ace up his sleeve when his heroes find the Sphinx. The aeronauts sail around it several times. Then Huck says, "We landed Jim on top of the head, with an American flag to protect him, it being a foreign land, then we sailed off to this and that and t' other distance, to git what Tom called effects and perspectives and proportions, and Jim he done the best he could, striking all the different kinds of attitudes and positions he could study up, but standing on his head and working his legs the way a frog does was best. The further we got away, the littler Jim got, and the grander the Sphinx got" (189–90).[88]

After sailing away, they return to find "two or three wee puffs of white smoke" below the Sphinx and men "hauling a long ladder up onto the Sphinx's back" (193). They realize Jim is under attack by the locals, that the smoke is gunfire. When they pick him up,

> Tom was very indignant, and asked him why he didn't show the flag and command them to *git*, in the name of the United States. Jim said he done it but they never paid no attention. Tom said he would have this thing looked into at Washington, and says—
> "You'll see that they'll have to apologize for insulting the flag, and pay an indemnity, too, on top of it, even if they git off *that* easy." (194)

Tom's urgent, jingoistic response fits perfectly with his views up to that point of the novel.[89] Tom's faith in America's authority is also rooted in military power; the italicized "*that*" in his declaration carries implications of military action, something far worse than reparations. Much as he does during the makeshift escape at the end of *Huckleberry Finn*, Tom Sawyer ignores Jim's understandable fear of bodily harm and instead focuses on the cultural narrative as he understands it.

In this case, Tom's perceptions of their exploration and the Egyptians' attack tie to US policies of Twain's time. Louis J. Budd has noted that the likely inspiration for this scene came from an international incident in 1891 between the United States and Chile "over the mobbing of some American sailors."[90] The "Valparaiso Incident" began when an October 16 wharf-side fight between US navy seamen and Chilean military personnel escalated into a mob attack against the Americans, who were subsequently arrested; the October 17 *Chicago Daily Tribune* headline read, "It Was a Bloody Fray: Americans Stabbed in Back by Cowardly Chileans."[91] Such reports infuriated US citizens and within ten days, both politicians and the public were calling for Chile to make reparations.[92] By October 25, many news articles led with the idea that Chile must apologize and make a reparation payment. The *Chicago Daily Tribune* stated that "the administration does not regard it as a simple street row for which the government cannot be held accountable, but as an insult to the honor and flag of the United States."[93] American papers reported naval buildups and calls for war, but eventually the matter was settled when Chile paid a $75,000 indemnity.[94] Writing in this context, Twain makes Tom a mouthpiece for popular American sentiment. The possibility of military retaliation is so natural for Tom that it remains virtually unstated. Tom's suggestion that Egypt may not "git off *that* easy" represents his understanding that international politics operates best when there is a constant, veiled implication that other countries exist at the pleasure of the United States and may only avoid such conflict if they conform to US demands.

Here, Tom Sawyer demonstrates the quintessential American imperialist's conceptions of how technologically enhanced expansion should occur and what expectations a traveling technocrat should have when he or she reaches the destination. The scene illustrates Tom Sawyer's understanding of international relations, which bears a strong resemblance to his view of the "crusade" in its appeal to both history and authority. Tom assumes that waving the flag alone will protect Jim. If it does not, it becomes a matter of national pride and a subsequent moneymaking venture. "Well, in an aggravated case like this one," Tom tells Huck and Jim, "it [the indemnity] will be at least three dollars apiece" (194). The "erronorts" fly off, literally counting the money before they have it. The ever-practical Jim notes that while he would "take de money," he doesn't care about the apology (194). When Huck asks if all countries make such payments-as-apologies when they have "done wrong," Tom replies curtly, "Yes; the little ones does" and the matter is settled (195). Tom understands their journey in terms of international politics, whereby they have a right to land on a national monument and take measurements and expect not only to be left alone but to be handsomely paid if any of the local populace interferes with their journey. Their new technology does not reorganize the international pecking order; it simply reinforces it.

The formula of Twain's story so closely resembles the Frank Reade template that it is tempting to read *Tom Sawyer Abroad* as one more willful burlesque on Twain's part, to see it as Twain's treatment of dime-novel SF in the manner he had previously reserved for Mallory, Cooper, and other writers. Even if he never read a Frank Reade Jr. dime novel, Twain understood Americans' perception of themselves and how technocracy and imperialism factored into that self-awareness. Like the Edisonades, *Tom Sawyer Abroad* pinpoints the techno-imperial concerns of its era. Unlike most Edisonade inventor heroes, however, Tom does not use the technological transportation as a weapon. As a result, the "erronorts" do not engage in the kind of violent arbitration that is a hallmark of Edisonade dime novels. Edisonade heroes frequently celebrate their autonomy, taking action that governments cannot or will not take. This element of the genre shores up their celebration of individual violence and, in some ways, undermines their actual nationalistic tendencies. Unlike a Frank Reade Jr.-type, however, Tom Sawyer never takes the law into his own hands; instead he makes a traditional appeal to national pride and power.

Only Huckleberry Finn seems to genuinely understand the possibilities of the advanced means of transportation they have discovered. As Earl Briden has noted, Huck is "positioned intellectually between Tom and Jim, sharing a small part of Tom's middle-class education and some of the ex-slave's literalist cast of mind and superstition."[95] However, Huck's willingness to question Tom Sawyer on each issue demonstrates a resistance to his technocracy similar to that found in the Arthurians. While Tom understands the balloon's power only in terms of his own education, Huck counters this. For example, when Tom determines that they cannot use the balloon to carry sand as international commerce because of "duties" and tariffs, Huck quickly points out, "We can sail right over their old frontiers; how are *they* going to stop us?" (174). Huck makes the most reasonable argument, given their technological advantage, but is ignored by Tom who resists any suggestion that doesn't fit his own analysis. Earlier in the book, Huck's perceptions about the logistics of a "crusade" were written off by Tom Sawyer; similarly, Huck's understanding about the empowerment of balloon travel and its potential disruption of the status quo goes unrecognized by Tom.

Ultimately, *Tom Sawyer Abroad* portrays the American technocrat as driven by rationalism informed by religion and popular narratives. Tom Sawyer is both well educated and naïve; he is a talker, a boaster, and casually callous to anyone who doesn't share his ethnicity or beliefs. In one sense, he is a continuation of Hank Morgan, whose unswerving faith in his own abilities to make money and control situations turn him into a proto-imperialist. In another sense, however, he is a more conflicted character who is limited in his ability to understand technology's possibility and the limits of his own country's power because of his existing American identity. Instead of Frank Reade Jr. and Hank Morgan fooling the locals by passing off technology as supernatural power, we find Tom Sawyer deluding himself about the necessity and justification of religious crusades and the right of his nation to demand money.

As *Huck and Tom among the Indians* demonstrates, Twain was capable of creating a protagonist who adapted to religious views that he encountered and found suitable. Tom Sawyer and Hank Morgan are not those characters. Although he does not aspire to the kind of self-aggrandizing reform that Hank desires to create, Tom still respects others only to the extent that they share his worldview. Both protagonists are defined by their desire for power and a zeal for technology that is *limited* by their preexisting worldview, one that is formed by a view of religion as power. Hank Morgan thinks traditional religion must be resisted in his colonial endeavor, while Tom Sawyer views it as an authority that enables that same kind of expansion. In both cases, technology does not transform their views, even as they expect it to transform other people's understanding. Twain's skepticism about human nature, science, and technology results in a portrayal of the limited technocrat, one whose expectation to lead is matched by his inability to consider alternatives outside his existing realm of information.

6
Reconstructing Biblical History
Technocratic Explorations, 1899–1910

The previous chapters have shown the development of the technocratic exploration novel and its engagement with empire and faith in the hands of its most prominent American practitioners: Ellis, Senarens, and Twain. Senarens's output particularly shows that themes of biblical literalism were already encoded into storylines by this period. To fully demonstrate the breadth of the subgenre's spread, and the ultimate religious ends to which it was used, it is valuable to consider works from the turn of the twentieth century, coinciding with the United States' emergence as a global imperial force and the early stirrings of American fundamentalist Christianity, shortly following the appearance of Twain's *Tom Sawyer Abroad* (1894). The 1890s were the real heyday of technocratic exploration fiction, as dime-novel Edisonades appeared weekly from several publishers. Stories featuring boy inventors appeared intermittently throughout the 1880s along with the semi-regular Frank Reade stories; for example, *The Rocket; or, Adventures in the Air*, published in 1882 and reprinted in 1899 with differing pseudonymous authorial attributions, finds a young inventor departing New York in an airship, fighting North Carolina moonshiners, humiliating trigger-happy cowboys in Texas, saving his black sidekick from an anaconda in Mexico, among other adventures in thirty pages of two-column print.[1] The storyline of *The Rocket* differs little from the episodic stories of Frank Reade, but it is presented as a standalone story. After 1890, however, the narrative becomes a cottage industry. Tousey published Senarens's first Jack Wright boy-inventor story in July 1891, publishing over 120 total adventures for that character.[2] Competing publisher Street and Smith created other boy-inventor series at this time. Tom Edison Jr.'s adventures were recounted in the *Nugget Library* weekly in 1891 and 1892, while *New York Five Cent Library* featured Electric Bob in 1893 and continued printing and reprinting his stories in *Brave and Bold* until 1905. The Tom Edison Jr. stories were attributed to "Philip Reade," a name Everett Bleiler notes was likely a pseudonym designed to capitalize on the success of rival Tousey's Frank Reade novels.[3] Despite the character's name, Tom Edison Jr. is never overtly portrayed as the son of the actual famous inventor. Electric Bob's adventures, attributed to dime novelist Robert T. Toombs, featured tank-like inventions frequently in the shape of an animal (a "sea-cat," an ostrich, etc.). Nevins notes that they are likely "satires of the Edisonade genre," and Bleiler suggests they are "tongue in cheek."[4] If parody is a sign of success, Electric Bob proves the Edisonades' mass appeal circa 1893. And, as Twain's career indicates, the hallmarks of these series could be recognized and imitated by reputable authors, even those who may not have ever read one.

This ubiquity enabled writers to blend the material with other ends. We have already seen how the Frank Reade Jr. series blended lost-race narratives of the H. Rider Haggard mold with their technocratic narrative, producing a format for biblical commentary. Feminist utopian texts had a renaissance during this period. Some, such as Mary E. Bradley Lane's *Mizora* (serialized in the *Cincinnati Commercial* newspaper in 1880 and 1881), placed their perfect worlds underground in a hollow-earth akin to works of Symmes and Verne.[5] Lane's novel features a Russian heroine who—while not a technocrat herself—discovers an all-female subterranean technocracy that facilitated, among other things, parthenogenesis that made males obsolete.[6] The hollow-earth motif found favor among religiously conservative writers as well. In 1896, De Witt C. Chipman wrote *Beyond the Verge: Home of the Lost Tribes of Israel*, which featured Israelites in pre-Colombian America seeking refuge inside the hollow earth; William Amos Miller, in 1898, published *The Sovereign Guide: A Tale of Eden*, which posited that the Garden of Eden itself was located beneath the earth's surface.[7] In 1894, business scion John Jacob Astor wrote an interplanetary romance in which earthlings reach Jupiter and Saturn, where they meet spirits of Earth's dead who explain the true nature of Hell, the afterlife, and existence.[8]

Other novels mixed genres with the kind of unoriginality Samuel Clemens feared his brother would fall prey to, but exhibited much more traditional religious ideas than Orion Clemens voiced. A good example comes from Austyn Granville's *The Fallen Race*, published in 1892. Presented as a tale told to the editor of Melbourne's *Argus* newspaper by explorer Dr. Paul Gifford, it features a lost race and hinges on a romance plot between a "white goddess" similar to Haggard's titular *She* and a technocrat akin to Twain's

Hank Morgan. Gifford is lost in the Outback when he discovers the Anonos, a race of furry, globe-shaped creatures ruled by the Great White Queen, a human woman called Azuela.[9] Gifford and his aboriginal servant Jacky-Jacky live among them. During this time, Gifford gains control of the society and defends them from outsiders, partly by passing off Jacky-Jacky as a "Black fire-god" (158–65). He brings technology to the Anonos by starting a mine, building a mansion, and ultimately founding a newspaper (252–66). When he meets Azuela, however, his first action is tellingly *not* technologically oriented but religious: "I endeavored to unfold to this untutored woman the principles of Christianity. As I related, in simple language, how the great Creator, in his infinite love for all his creatures, had sacrificed his best Beloved for their salvation, I could see that the story in its simple beauty worked greatly upon her mind" (138). True to his apostolic namesake, Paul Gifford convinces her with a story of Christ's love that leaves Azuela in tears (138). Granville then drops the Christian conversion subplot until the novel's end, after Azuela and Gifford have wed. Gifford tells us Azuela ordered a church to be built because she "had embraced Christianity, and pledged herself to be a true soldier of the cross" (350). The book's last page reveals that the couple remains among the Anonos, in a society where there is no crime, no divorce, and a free press (350). The ending, then, reconfigures *The Fallen Race* into a kind of utopian pastoral novel despite its early nods to technocracy—with its hero and heroine retreating from modernity into a perfect, secluded world.

Unlike Hank Morgan, Paul Gifford manages to avoid undermining his authority with the locals, eventually bringing the technological trappings to the Anonos without the incipient politics or crime, and forging a political/romantic alliance with Azuela that avoids an outright battle for leadership. Unlike Ayesha from *She*, Azuela is not an awe-striking figure of female power; instead, she is a thoughtful leader loved by the hero for her beauty and easily swayed by him to the Christian faith. This last element of religious conversion showcases the ideological presumptions of the 1890s technocratic exploration tale. As we have seen, religious conversion had been portrayed as a natural component of a technocratic expansion story as early as Washington Irving's work in the 1820s. This element, while absent from Haggard's work and so fraught with presumption in Twain, is presented at face value—as common sense—to *The Fallen Race*'s audience. *Of course*, an explorer would immediately proselytize the lost race's leader before undertaking any scientific, political, or even romantic plans. *Of course*, a Westerner would stay in a society that had all the material, technological benefits of modern society with none of the social problems. To provide a "happy" ending, the work must attempt to resolve all the contradictions of the representative genres of technocratic exploration, lost-race, and utopian pastoral modes. To accomplish this, the intelligent, authoritative leader of the lost race must immediately grasp Christianity's value and convert.

Subsequent novels have similar themes, to the extent that faith becomes a recurring element on some level. In what follows, I want to look at four specific variants of the subgenre from between 1899 and 1903—all aimed at a general, adult readership rather than dime novels' adolescent audience—that incorporate religiosity into technocratic exploration narrative. First, two polar exploration novels—one decidedly spiritual, one satirically secular—show the breadth of religious commentary in these later variants. Anna Adolph's *Arqtiq* (1899) and Albert Bigelow Paine's *The Great White Way* (1901) are both polar exploration novels where American explorers discover perfect, harmonious societies at the pole. They represent, however, a more subversive strain of the narrative by addressing gender equality and Christian evangelism. Two serialized novels from the same era—Garret P. Serviss's *Edison's Conquest of Mars* (1899) and Pauline Elizabeth Hopkins's *Of One Blood, or the Hidden Self* (1903)—take the religious historical discoveries found in 1890s Frank Reade Jr. stories and push them even further, providing conclusive evidence of the Bible's truth through technocratic exploration. Collectively, they demonstrate technocratic invention novels' complex relationship with religious faith.

Gender and Evangelism: Two Polar Technocracies

At first glance, the novel *Arqtiq*, self-published in 1899 by writer Anna Adolph, bears resemblance to Orion Clemens's writing in its polar setting and its visionary religious language, offering what one critic called a "surrealistic dream vision [of a] hi-tech utopia inhabited by ideal people."[10] In fact, *Arqtiq* builds on the Edisonade template by simultaneously presenting a technocratic inventor as the first-person narrator and contemplating religious insights drawn from the remote destination. It differs from previous Edisonades because of its protagonist's gender and its approach to religious conversion. *Arqtiq*'s technocratic hero is a female, a married woman with a great deal of technical know-how and imagination. The story begins with the inventor, who shares the name Anna with the novel's author, planning a polar expedition:

> Always fond of the marvelous, I conceived a strong desire to go to the North Pole.
> To obviate the dangers of the trip I invented a coach, that was also ship and balloon. Its silken canopy is inflatable to strong wings and

wide sails. Its wheels are wide rimmed, to glide over snow, and pan-eled for water paddles. When it is finished and stored I select some friends to accompany me.[11]

Adolph's juggling of sentimental elements and proto-science fiction can be seen here. She has mastered the Edisonades' trope of describing a flying machine with enough plausible detail to mimic it. Unlike Frank Reade Jr., who brings his battle-ready, all-male crew along for each trip, Anna's "friends" are her husband, her elderly scientist father, and a child, her niece Mae Searles, as their "mascot." Thus, the airship is a microcosm of the Victorian-era family, and one trope of boy-inventor novels is replaced by something more genteel than the boisterous shenanigans of Pomp and Barney in a Frank Reade story.

Adolph quickly delivers, then dispenses with, other standards of Edisonades. The group starts their journey in California, they buzz past a railroad train, and later "whirl over the Brooklyn Bridge without minding the many curious gazers" (7). A few mechanical details, like the construction of the airship's interior, are described, but the focus is clearly the destination more than the journey: they arrive at Pole on page 12. Charley, the husband, is surprised there is no open sea while little Mae is disappointed there's not an actual pole sticking out of the ground (13). As they disembark, they hear organ notes, and see a "tall spire, supporting a ring of gold points arising from the valley center . . . [and] a much-alive city" in a valley beyond the snow (13). The city is called "Arc," and it circles "Aurora," the Earth's electric center (14). Buildings are made of ice and enamel (18). Like the Barokites of the Frank Reade series, the people of Arc are giants, and the Americans are "babes to them in size" (14). Conveniently, the first person they meet knows English because his father was an explorer who encountered Westerners while lost from home (15). Anna's group is hosted by a family of savants who help them learn the ways of their world. Adolph quickly establishes that this world is a utopian society.

What follows, however, is an extended subversion of Edisonades' presentation of Christianity. From the moment of their arrival, Anna cannot overcome the thought that she must minister to these people. Like Hank Morgan, she is a technocrat with missionary zeal, and she falls into the same trap as Morgan by simply enacting the cultural values she knows. Her scientist father, however, is apparently an atheist and notes Anna's evangelism with sardonic wit. During a quiet moment, she and her father discuss her views. "Dear father has not God sent us here to convert them?" Anna asks. "Too intelligent," the father replies; "they will convert us" (18). From that moment on, the story becomes a slow conversion narrative where our pious inventor confronts repeated satirical incursions against her religious preconceptions. Indeed, what follows would be merely another perfect utopian pastoral lost-race novel were it not for our narrator. Anna is a woman who has been empowered by technology, who shares a fairly equal footing with her husband and father in the decision-making process and absolute control in terms of the means and methods of their travel. And Arc is a utopian technocracy: over the course of the novel, they display advanced diving gear (30), books with shining, moving-picture pages (37), a zoo with artificial animals and massive elevators (53), round, glass globes that operate as their primary transportation mode (41), alongside pseudoscientific advancements such as telepathy. Despite this, Anna's focus is almost exclusively religious. Her curiosity is limited to the citizen's faith, and maintaining her own in the face of their spiritual beliefs.

On a Sunday morning, she, Charley, and Mae ask one of Arc's citizens where they can find a church. He replies, "What is a church?" They explain that it is "where we pray to God." The Arc citizen responds, "Oh we should do that everywhere" (20). Eventually, they take Mae into the building that seems the most likely suspect: a "large domed enclosure . . . [with] crystal doors" filled with people who are "standing or sitting, all look serene, as sacred dreamy notes of melody fill the air, flower perfumed" (20). She marvels at the simplicity of the service, which involves a lady and gentleman "passing among the people, speaking kind admonitions, solemn adoration, or cheering responses" (20). Part of the service features dancing, and Mae enthusiastically participates. Anna reflects approvingly: "Are not all church rites illustrative of adaptions of the one worship—Spirit and Truth?" (21). Anna is similarly approving when the church gives out food and drink to their members, wishing that all churches fed their flocks, particularly ones with poor members (21). Only further reflection leads her to suddenly gasp and reach for little Mae's hand with panic, exclaiming, "Child, this is a *saloon!*" (21).

Adolph draws humor from her narrator's shock, but also quickly gives the character deeper insight. Ultimately, the narrator realizes the "saloon" is church, courthouse, and tavern collectively: "I am quite converted and wish ours at home would become the same," she tells us (22). Despite her conventional morals, then, Anna is progressively minded and shows that, even before coming to Arc, she had her own opinions about the practice of popular Christianity in the United States. She isn't put off by the dancing in the church because, as a Methodist Episcopalian, she thinks "my M.E. founder, Asbury, was lame, so could not dance, therefore we preach it down" (21). She pointedly distinguishes between dogma and some kind of God-given truth, in this case contextualizing her church's rules with what she knows about Bishop Francis Asbury's biography and drawing a conclusion different from that church father. Similarly, when pondering if Arc is a perfect civilization brought about by Christ's return, Anna immediately contemplates her atheist father: "Where would be my father's place, as he is an infidel. . . . Would Jesus enfold him as a neighbor of kind heart? I think so" (24). In fact, she does not read the Bible literally at all. When her husband makes plans to harvest grapes and introduce Arc's citizens to wine, she convinces him to not do this: "I earnestly believe it was water and not wine that Jesus recommended. (That has been mistakenly translated.) That being plain God's design" (26). While internally compelled to evangelize to Arc's citizens, Anna also shows herself to be a critical thinker who relies on her internal logic as much or more than the Bible. *Arqtiq*'s narrator does not appeal to specific passages or dates from Scripture for facts, as Frank Reade Jr. does. If Reade is a secular, nominally Christian technocrat who nevertheless views the Bible as authoritative, Anna is the reverse. She is a devout, practicing Christian who reads the Bible without an expectation of literalism. Instead, materialist concepts, such as unreliable translations of Scripture or the influence of personal predilections of each denomination's founder, inform her faith.

A telling moment comes when Anna finally attempts to convert their host, Roban, to Christianity. Their discussion, as described by Anna, is nuanced in unexpected ways:

> "O dear, dear Roban, do you love God?" I am pleading for a soul.
> "That I do," is her positive confession.
> "Do you love His Son?" my hands clasped toward her.
> "Anything that belongs to Him," so beatifies me I spring to my feet and declare:
> "Then you will be saved, for love is the fulfilling law." (53)

How seriously is this conversion meant to be taken? Clearly, Roban has not changed her views on anything; she is simply affirming her existing beliefs about God. It is Anna who conforms her beliefs, bending over backward to prove to herself and her readers that Roban is, effectively, a Christian. From that perspective, her "conversion" of Roban fairly begs to be read as satire, if not outright commentary of the audience's expectation that a Western explorer would proselytize Christianity even when faced with a community that behaves more equitably and charitably—more Christian—than her own.

As the novel becomes increasingly surreal, it subverts another trope—the hollow-earth trope—to religious ends. Anna joins an expedition through the earth's core in one of the globe vehicles. "I am not the first who has thought the earth to be hollow and entered at the Arctics. Also that a rolling fire and open sea, are within" (70). In most other novels, this would be a scientific voyage in the Vernian manner. In Adolph's work, it is a surrealistic expression of religious cosmology. Her reason for joining the journey is not scientific, but due to an intuitive sense that "God of the universe, Creator of aurora has led me hither for that purpose" (69). Portions of the novel are deemed "exuberantly incoherent" by Bleiler, and the hollow-earth journey culminates the visionary tone.[12] She determines that Earth is like "a Chinese lantern; made by Deity's hand to revolve around the glowing sun" (72). She awakens and learns it was a dream, a technique frequently utilized by nineteenth-century feminist utopian novels.[13] Adolph uses polar exploration and hollow-earth motifs to express idiosyncratic views. Like Orion Clemens before her, however, the ultimate thrust is religious commentary of a particularly subversive nature. Despite her being an inventor with a fairly nonliteral take on scripture, *Arqtiq*'s protagonist conceptualizes her journey in evangelical, rather than technocratic, terms. The narrator's skepticism about dogma and her gradual approval of Arc's mode of worship suggest the utopian community is genuinely being portrayed as a better place.

Another polar exploration text satirizes conversion as well. Several years before he became Twain's official biographer, Albert Bigelow Paine wrote *The Great White Way*. The novel follows the path of *A Connecticut Yankee*, satirizing the expansionist impulse in terms of economic capital and Christian morals. As such, it is not truly a technocratic exploration novel as much as a utopian novel that satirizes technocrats.[14] The story is narrated by Nicholas Chase, a young man who has yearned to explore the South Pole his entire life. He holds the conviction that the Antarctic possesses a warmer, temperate world akin to "the verdant plains of California."[15] He imagines a populous society beyond its ice floes warmed by the "oblation of the earth, which brings the surface there sufficiently near the central heat to counteract the otherwise low temperature resulting from the oblique anger of the direct solar rays" (28). It is, essentially, the identical belief that Mary Shelley's frame narrator of *Frankenstein*—the explorer Walton—holds regarding the North Pole in the late seventeenth century, driving his journey to find a region where the continuous sunshine yields a habitable climate; a hundred years later, the concept has switched poles but has the same allure. Chase's dreams are realized when he meets a real estate tycoon named Chauncey Gale, a "self-made capitalist" who agrees to finance the arctic expedition and make the journey on his private yacht (24). The crew includes an Italian wireless radio engineer named Ferratoni and the yacht's steward, William Sturritt, himself a technocratic inventor of condensed food lozenges that make the journey possible. Gale's daughter, Edith, joins them and becomes Chase's mutual love interest early on. The elder Gale, then, is both Chase's financial backer and potential father-in-law.

While Chase is an idealist fascinated with exploration for its own sake, Gale is a technocrat and real estate mogul, as full of self-confidence as Hank Morgan. Twain's "Boss," however, reveals himself and his prejudices to readers directly, even to the point of audiences mistaking him as Twain's surrogate. Gale's opinions come filtered through Chase's milquetoast idealism and his love of Gale's adoring daughter. Still, Gale's true nature becomes clear. As they bide time during the journey, Gale begins citing his own list of "observations," a string of aphorisms reminiscent of Twain's character Pudd'nhead Wilson:

V. "It isn't hard work to judge human nature if you let the other man do the talking."
VI. "A man's word may be as good as his bond, but if it is he won't mind giving his bond, too."
VII. "The commuter who keeps his lawn mowed is a gentleman. If he mows the vacant lot next to him, he's fit for a better world." (164)

Such witticisms add to Gale's larger-than-life appeal, until he gets to his final observation (XVII): "Never laugh at a lunatic's plans. The biggest fool scheme to-day may be a sound business proposition to-morrow" (165). Chase immediately realizes that this comment encapsulates his and Gale's relationship—he is the lunatic whose dreams Gale hopes to cash in on—but decides that it is merely "uncomplimentary in form," and that he still admires, and even loves, Gale (165). His charitability comes in part because Chase loves Edith. Readers must suspect, however, that Chase matters to Gale only as much as potential profits are concerned.

Gale's pragmatism extends to his daughter's beliefs. "My daughter is a sort of missionary," he explains early on. "She makes people good and I sell 'em homes and firesides. Or maybe I sell 'em homes first and she makes 'em good afterwards, so they'll keep up their payments. Whichever way it is, we've been pretty good partners" (27). Gale convinces his daughter to join their party by telling her that Chase plans to "convert the heathen" at the South Pole. She tells Gale, "I'm not really a missionary. . . . I have just a little hobby—a very little one—of helping people to better ideals though a truer appreciation of the beautiful in nature" (39).

Gale and his daughter's relationship allows Paine to satirize capitalism and Christian liberalism. In Gale, we have the American imperialist who links his economic conquest to evangelical outreach. In Gale's view, the combination is so natural, so normalized, that he doesn't even recognize the nu-

ances of his daughter's faith. Edith's so-called missionary work is really benevolent charity, done at a time when Christian charity work and social uplift
were conflated.[16] Such a scenario grows from the kind of worldview examined by scholars such as Jill Bergman, Dorice Elliott, and Claudia Stokes, who
note the increasing opportunities for women in benevolence societies despite otherwise restricted roles in nineteenth-century culture.[17] Edith never
overtly identifies herself as Christian, and in many ways resembles what
Nancy T. Ammerman calls "Golden Rule Christianity": the liberal Christianity emphasizing good works over literal readings of the Bible. As Ammerman notes, such individuals have often been dismissed by both fundamentalist believers and by sociologists who each "tend to measure strength
of belief and commitment against a norm defined by evangelicalism . . .
painting these non-exclusivist, less involved practitioners as simply lower
on the scale."[18] To Edith's father, however, such distinctions mean little. She
tries to help people, and Gale simply equates that with missionary work. Tellingly, it is the businessman father, not his socially engaged daughter, who
conflates benevolent charity with Christianity, giving it a faith-based tinge
that Edith herself does not presume.

The novel's next major satirical element occurs when Edith is left behind
on the ship as the men take a balloon to the pole. Edith is removed from
the narrative when the crew's communications gear fails, but her presence
is constant in the conventional morality she represents. Barely surviving the
journey, the men discover a polar civilization and meet the local inhabitants.
Gale introduces himself by half-sarcastically saying, "We're from New York
City, United States of America—best town and biggest country on earth.
We've come down here to discover you, and take a look at your country to
see whether we want to annex it or not" (231). As with *Arqtiq*, the pleasant
land beyond the poles transforms the protagonists. The people communicate through "thought vibrations," although the visitors' minds are different enough from them to conceal their thoughts and vice-versa (246). As a
result of their mind-reading, almost no crime occurs between the natives;
they also seem able to communicate with the disembodied dead, which removes much fear from the citizens (255). Chase reports: "Like the people of
the Incas, the Antarcticans have no money and no need of it. The lands are
held in common, and the harvests yield more than enough for all" (255). He
goes on to say: "They are deeply opposed to what we know as progress, be-
lieving it conducive only to discontent and evils innumerable. They regard
with sorrowful distrust our various mechanical contrivances" (258). In short,
they are precisely the kind of utopian, pastoral society found in many lost-
race novels, spiritually evolved but opposed to technology. Under such cir-

cumstances, Gale falls into despair: "How is anybody going to do business here? Nobody wants any homes and firesides, or trolleys, or steamboats, and if they did, they haven't got any money to pay for anything with" (265).

The book's satire of genteel morality becomes clearest in its treatment of male sexuality. As Thomas Clareson has shown, veiled erotic content typified most lost-race novels, as their Western male protagonists met and wooed beautiful "pagan" women in the discovered country.[19] In pastoral lost-race novels, this imperialistic romantic subplot often culminated in marriage, with the Western man staying behind in the lost world rather than returning, due to the idyllic lifestyle and the charms of his chosen native girl. Paine seems quite aware of this convention, and he has the spiritually minded engineer Ferratoni find love with the princess and stay behind in the Antarctic, in the iconic manner detailed by Clareson. But Paine also skewers the implicit erotic content of the subgenre, forcing Gale and company to confront their own behavior. After some weeks pass, Gale perceives that his fellow travelers are paying a great deal of libidinous attention to the native girls. He chides the others: "By the way Nick, who is that yellow-haired girl that is setting up to you . . . and that other one, Bill, that dark-eyed one who walks about with you so much, holding hands" (267). While Bill stammers as he attempts to reply, Nick Chase reflects a moment and says, "I think . . . she is a cousin to that very delightful little auburn-haired creature, who sits all day at the feet of our Admiral" (267). Gale's follow-up is telling. "Nick," said Gale, "if anything should happen that we ever did get out of this snap, and back to— to people—the yacht, and Biff, and [Edith], I mean — I suppose it would be just as well not to mention some of the things that happen down here. They wouldn't quite understand the conditions, you see—the—the atmosphere, as the artists say. . . . You wouldn't want to say anything yourself—" (267). Paine renders the speech of the ordinarily loquacious, confident Gale as fragments, his dialogue suddenly and deliberately filled with dashes when confronted with the notion that his sexual behavior could be reported to his daughter. His final broken statement of "you wouldn't want to say anything yourself" carries an air of blackmail about it, suggesting that he is prepared to tell Edith of Nick's indiscretions should his would-be son-in-law reveal information about Chase's behavior.

Gale's true comeuppance happens when his overt technology use causes the technophobic Antarcticans to banish his party. When they see the protagonists using a telephone to reach Edith, the citizens lose faith in them. Chase notes: "They had witnessed our sudden transformation from people not greatly different to themselves into what must have appeared to them unholy barbarians—wild untamed savages, awakened to a fierce and to them brutal frenzy by the unseen electric summons. In their faces was a horror and condemnation never before written there" (273). It does not help that Gale explains his plans to his daughter on the phone: "We'll get franchises from the government for electric lights and trolley lines, and steamboat traffic, and we'll build some factories" (274). In fact, the inhabitants turn on them violently, sparing the engineer Ferratoni only because of his mutual love for the Princess (279). While the Princess is herself "not opposed to any appliance that would benefit her people without destroying their lives or repose of spirit," it becomes clear that "the radical changes contemplated in the mind of [Gale] were abhorrent to her" (276). Gale, Chase, and Sturritt flee quickly and return to the United States, neither richer nor more spiritually satisfied.

Paine satirizes the colonial impulse, both in terms of economic capital cultivation and morals, but he particularly pokes fun at the conversion impulse. Gale tells his daughter via a telephone, "They don't need any missionary work here, or homes, but they need everything else" (273). Like *Arqtiq*'s narrator, Gale is a product of nineteenth-century American society that presumes technocratic travel must some evangelical component. Gale, however, is simply going through the motions, treating evangelism as an unavoidable afterthought at best and outwardly mocking it at worst. In some ways, the approach prefigures (and contrasts) Paine's portrayal of Mark Twain in his three-volume biography of the author, particularly moments where he lauds Samuel Clemens's broad-mindedness and religious skepticism. Most notably, it appears in Paine's recounting of Clemens's admission in 1878 to his best friend and minister, Joe Twichell, that "I don't believe in your religion at all. I have been living a lie right straight along whenever I pretended to. I have been almost a believer, but it immediately drifts away from me again."[20] Paine presents this as a definitive moment, noting approvingly that Clemens's "philosophies were too wide and too deep for creeds and doctrines."[21] The same admiration is seen in Paine's endeavor to "make rather extended record" of Twain's late-life dinner conversations related to evolution and God.[22] If Paine portrays Gale's nods to evangelism as the hollow practices of a secular man, he portrays Twain's secular skepticism as engaged, honest, and deeply considered. Gale embodies unreflective secularism that nevertheless sees Christianity as an ordinary component of civilization, but little more.

Arqtiq and *The Great White Way* are both satires and somewhat atypical of technocratic adventures. *Arqtiq* culminates in Anna wishing to join a technocratic, spiritual society even at the expense of compromising the evangelical Christian beliefs she brings with her. *The Great White Way*'s denouement sends its heroes home without any transformation at all. Paine portrays Chauncey Gale as a secular extreme: the idea of Christian charity unmoored from technocracy and capital acquisition is unthinkable to him.

Uncovering the Past in Africa and Mars

Two novels from the same era demonstrate the more common approach of technocratic exploration novels. Garret P. Serviss's *Edison's Conquest of Mars* and Pauline Elizabeth Hopkins's *Of One Blood, or the Hidden Self* commingle Edisonade and lost-race conventions to create texts that portray technocratic exploration as a means to reestablish biblical authority in matters of history, engaging with literalism in much more direct, reflective ways than even the Frank Reade novels that precede them. Reading *Edison's Conquest of Mars* side by side with *Of One Blood* demonstrates how proto-science fiction exploration novels with dramatically dissimilar viewpoints towards empire and race arrive at similar assertions regarding technology and the Bible. *Edison's Conquest of Mars* is overtly militaristic, expansionist proto-science fiction that imagines an attack on the planet Mars; *Of One Blood*, in contrast, resists overt imperial themes by asserting the primacy of an African technocratic nation over the civilization of the American explorers who "discover" it. Both novels, however, prominently feature the by-now-common narrative shift when the protagonists reach their exotic destinations. At that point, each book proceeds to highlight uncovered historical evidence tied to race and identity. In creating stories that vindicate biblical history, Serviss and Hopkins are not necessarily arguing for a specific, literal reading of the book of Genesis. In fact, they do not undertake serious biblical exegesis. Rather, the Bible represents a cultural authority on history that provides certainty in the face of new discoveries. Their appeals to the Bible's presentation of race and history demonstrate an attempt to simultaneously reassert its position as a final arbiter in cultural issues and suggest that race—arguably the most fraught and contested issue in a deeply divided United States plagued by lynchings and race riots—was a clear, simple concept with easily resolved contradictions. If earlier technocratic protagonists such as Frank Reade Jr. were not above using religious superstition to get what they wanted, Twain's *A Connecticut Yankee* and *Tom Sawyer Abroad* further suggested that American technocrats would cling so tightly to their religiously informed identity that it would limit their ability to see possibilities. Serviss and Hopkins suggest more. As they engage with the established technocratic narrative, they ultimately promote a point of view that values established religious tradition over science by providing plots in which technologically enabled exploration produces discoveries that undermine the scientific theory of evolution. In *Edison's Conquest of Mars* and *Of One Blood*, biblical history does not merely need to be reconciled with the new horizons opened by science, but can actually be *recovered* and reestablished as authority through technologically enhanced exploration.

Serviss began his writing career by creating science essays for mass audiences. As a journalist, he produced a number of texts aimed at general readership, culminating in a two-year lecture tour and his most popular nonfiction book, *Astronomy with an Opera-Glass*, in 1888.[23] When the *New York Evening Journal* sought to capitalize on the success of H. G. Wells's *War of the Worlds*, Serviss's name recognition and writing experience made him a logical choice for them. In fact, the publication of *Edison's Conquest of Mars* shifted the trajectory of Serviss's writing career from nonfiction to fiction, and he subsequently began selling science-based novels to the slick, popular magazines of the time, including *A Columbus of Space*, serialized in 1909, and *The Second Deluge*, serialized from 1911 to 1912.[24] Readers taking up the original serialization of *Edison's Conquest* would likely have known that they were reading a story written by an individual with an encyclopedic knowledge of contemporary science and technology who had made a successful career out of his lucid explanations of their concepts.

Edison's Conquest of Mars is an Americanized sequel to Wells's *War of the Worlds*, appearing a mere six weeks after that story finished American serialization.[25] It recounts the aftermath of a Martian attack on Earth in which Thomas Alva Edison aids humanity by inventing spacecraft and weapons that enable a counterstrike against Mars. Eschewing the Darwinian underpinnings of Wells's tale, it instead focuses on the construction of new technology and the attack on Mars by an international force led by Edison and an array of other fictionalized versions of actual scientists, including Lord Kelvin, Sylvanus P. Thompson, and Wilhelm Roentgen.[26] Serviss uses the Edisonade formula of invention, travel, and conflict, and repackages it for the *New York Evening Journal*'s adult audience. With no little chutzpah, Serviss used the real-life inventor as his protagonist rather than a fictional young inventor of the type found in *The Steam Man of the Prairies* or Senarens's Frank Reade Jr. stories. This approach led John Clute to single out Serviss's novel as the work in which "the native Edisonade took its mature shape."[27] During their invasion of Mars, however, the scientists discover ties to an earlier civilization from Earth that confirms theories of human development tied more to the Bible than to evolutionary theory. Like the subgenre it epitomizes, *Edison's Conquest of Mars* establishes an imperial expansionist storyline that rather suddenly develops a religious subtext as it progresses.

The novel's technocratic approach is evident from the beginning. Its narrator discovers that Thomas Edison has studied the Martians' remaining war machines, as media outlets broadcast the news to a demolished but defiant Earth: "Suddenly from Mr. Edison's laboratory at Orange flashed the startling intelligence that he had not only discovered the manner in which the invaders had been able to produce the mighty energies which they employed with such terrible effect, but that, by going further, he had found a way to overcome them."[28] The narrator joins Edison on a test flight around the moon. Once Edison proves that he has mastered space flight and can reproduce his ship to create a fleet, humankind agrees to a strategy: "Let us go to Mars. We have the means. Let us beard the lion in his den. Let us ourselves turn conquerors" (18). While the heroes of Serviss's novel do not actually engage in imperial control of the distant territory they conquer, the philosophy behind their invasion mirrors the pervasive imperialist themes in scientific romances of the era. Noting that it was published shortly after the Spanish-American War, John Rieder finds that "Serviss's nationalism . . . is that of a new imperial competitor bristling with eagerness to reshape the international order of things."[29] Subsequent chapters recount the creation of space suits and "disintegrator" guns, the eventual cooperation of nations to back the endeavor, and the creation of an international strike force led by Edison. Substantial portions of the early narrative address the logistics of space flight, including an encounter with a comet's gravitational pull that almost dooms the expedition (71–75). Space suits are described, including methods for communication between suits via telephone in an airless environment (49–50). One line late in the novel embodies the book's worldview: "But the genius of one man [Edison] had suddenly put us on the level of our enemies in regard to fighting capacity" (132). The machines and weapons created by Edison and his followers serve the practical purpose of evening the odds against a foe that was originally seen as overwhelming.

If the novel's contents seem driven by contemporary science fiction's naturalistic portrayal of fanciful technology, its tone positions it elsewhere. Unlike Wells's narrator, who explicitly reports bacteria as the cause for the Martians' withdrawal, Serviss portrays President McKinley speaking to the collected nations about the invasion: "It was through the entirely unexpected succor which Providence sent us that we were suddenly and effectually freed from the invaders" (32). Supernatural Providence, rather than an evolutionary process that made humans immune to the same bacteria that killed the Martians, receives the credit for the Martian retreat. References to events or artifacts of biblical history, such as the Tower of Babel, are offered as factual, historical occurrences (189). The explorers are called "descendants of Adam" on two occasions (69, 165). When the astronauts discover remnants of a civilization on the moon, Serviss describes the lost culture as having "vanished probably ages before Adam and Eve appeared in Paradise"—a sign Serviss's science fiction operates within the popular, post-Darwinian framework that takes Genesis as fact, but reads the "days" of creation as metaphor (64). Similarly, Serviss portrays the Martians using a blend of science and the Bible.

Serviss likens the protagonists' first encounter with a Martian to standing "face to face with Satan, when he was driven from the battlements of heaven by the swords of his fellow archangels, and . . . transformed from Lucifer, the Son of Morning, into the Prince of Night and Hell" (89). Tellingly, the Martians are not portrayed as the evolved brain-on-tentacles combination described by Wells's narrator in book 2, chapter 2 of *War of the Worlds*, but rather as intimidating, giant humanoids. Doing so, Serviss once again removes an overt, evolutionary component of Wells's original text. The book describes a captured Martian as "a personage who had presumably inherited from hundreds of generations the results of a civilization, and an intellectual advance, measured by the constant progress of millions of years" (123). Such a description seems congruent with the earlier, nebular view of the universe described by antebellum American scientists, such as James Dana. Essentially, Serviss uses the language of the pre-Darwinian evolutionist, dealing with epochs of time and biblical history simultaneously.

The combination becomes more intriguing because of the major narrative shift in the latter third of the story, when the story begins to explicitly focus on concepts of race and history. Once the expedition reaches Mars, the character Edison moves to the plot's background and the novel begins to focus on the narrator's adventures with crew members who are stock fictional characters, rather than fictionalized portrayals of actual scientific personages. These include Colonel Alonzo Jefferson Smith, an army veteran of "many wars against the cunning Indians of the West" (162), and a "handsome young fellow in the flagship" named Sydney Phillips (190). The two men become embroiled in a love triangle after a shocking discovery: a human woman is a captive on Mars. While engaged in reconnaissance in a Martian palace, Smith, Phillips, and the narrator hear "music of the earth" coming from a room (168). They find the woman playing music for the Martians. When she sees the humans spying on her, she cries out to them, alerting the Martians to the humans' presence:

> The girl sprang to my side and grasped my arm with a cry of fear. This seemed to throw the Martian into a sudden frenzy, and he raised his arms to strike.
>
> But the disintegrator was in my hand. My rage was equal to his. I felt the concentrated vengeance of the earth quivering through me as I pressed the button of the disintegrator and . . . saw the gigantic form that confronted me melt into nothingness. (172–73)

Clearly, Serviss presents the woman as a damsel in distress to be saved by the technological prowess of the earthmen, an attempt to inject romance and melodrama into his tale. Her appearance, however, signals a transition in the story. Once the adventurers are able to communicate with her, they learn that she is the last surviving member of a race of humans who were captured during a Martian invasion centuries earlier and taken back to Mars as slaves, many of whom were recently murdered when Edison's spaceships appeared. The girl, Aina, described as "a beautiful daughter of our common mother, Eve," becomes a living link to Earth's past (188).

In the process of striking against the Martians, the heroes come into contact with a member of a lost race who rewrites, or confirms, one existing theory about the Earthlings' own past. Aina's story provides the solution to a seemingly unrelated Earth mystery, one that becomes foregrounded by the narrative as the final battle with the Martians looms. Among the scientists is a linguist from the University of Heidelberg who determines that Aina's language has "the roots of the great Indo-European, or Aryan stock. . . . Her language every tongue that now upon the earth is spoken antedates" (180–81). The professor teaches her English and slowly reveals her story. Her people came from the Vale of Cashmere and were taken to a "Land of Sand" where they were forced to build mountains of stone and statues of the Martian leader; the professor immediately identifies this with Egypt's pyramids and Sphinx. "It was not," the narrator concludes, "the work of puny man, as many an engineer had declared that it could not be, but the work of these giants of Mars" (197). Based on Aina's people's estimation of the number of Martian days since they were taken from Earth, the scientists calculate that the Martians visited Earth and captured Aina's people "more than 9,000 years" in the past (200). Serviss's narrator ties this to actual theories of eighteenth-century German philologist Johann Adelung, which referred to biblical history. The narrator states,

> Now on Mars, we had put to rest no less mysterious questions relating to the past history of our own planet. Adelung, as the Heidelberg professor asserted, had named the Vale of Cashmere, as the probable site of the Garden of Eden, and the place of origin of the human race, but later investigators had taken issue with this opinion and the question where the Aryans originated on the earth had long been one of the most puzzling that science presented.
>
> This question seemed now to have been settled. (200)

So, Aina's story provides scientific certitude of the past, confirming at once philological theory, Western concepts of racial identity tied to an "Aryan" cultural origin, and biblical history. This passage's language further demonstrates the technocratic exploration novel's ability to provide definitive proof in historical matters. While the text's language grounds itself in referents such as Adam and Eve, Babel, and Lucifer, the explorers' discoveries are also phrased in the language of scientific theory backed by conclusive evidence. The discovery of Aina has "put to rest" the issue of the origin of the human race; the issue is "settled." The novel ultimately values the expedition less for its military success or its scientific endeavor than for its ability to uncover mysteries of the Earth's past related to biblically based history and the certainty that it offers in matters of racial identity and cultural authority.

African American activist and editor Pauline Elizabeth Hopkins used her novel *Of One Blood* to reconsider elements of earlier lost-race adventures, foregrounding issues of race and history that appear quite suddenly in Serviss's adventure tale. Serialized in the *Colored American Review* between 1902 and 1903 during Hopkins's tenure as its editor, the novel features a light-skinned, African American scientist passing for white in order to study medicine who journeys to a hidden African city where he finds a technologically advanced civilization whose existence undermines notions of white Western superiority.[30] Despite its different approach to racial history, *Of One Blood* demonstrates the same kind of exuberance for technology and appeal to biblical authority on matters of race and history found in Serviss's novel.[31] In Hopkins, we find the references to Egypt as a cradle of civilization and to the Bible as a legitimate source of scientific knowledge that can be confirmed under the right set of circumstances, often using the same language of certitude used in Serviss's work. Hopkins calculatedly adapts popular literary form, using the lost-race story's features to reinterpret and reinvigorate discussion of African American history.[32]

Hopkins's approach to science and the Bible can be seen in the novel's full title: *Of One Blood, or the Hidden Self*. The main title, *Of One Blood*, comes from the book of Acts 17:26, which states that God "hath made of one blood all nations of men for to dwell on all the face of the earth." The phrase had a long history in racial debates before Hopkins adopted it, and Hopkins uses its appeal to biblical authority to counter-assert a common human ancestry against prevailing racist ideologies that used the Bible to justify racial subordination and white supremacy. In contrast, her subtitle, *The Hidden Self*, comes from an 1890 article by philosopher William James in *Scribner's Magazine* in which he calls for scientific examination of mental perception.[33] The book's title, then, signals the novel's attempt to find authority in both the Bible and the then-cutting-edge science of psychology, as Hopkins—taking her cue from James—simultaneously valorizes exploration while questioning the authority of established scientific fact. James wryly notes, "The ideal of every science is that of a closed and completed system of truth. The charm of most sciences to their more passive disciples consists in their appearing, in fact, to wear just this ideal form."[34] James asserts that science's practitioners and its public both overemphasize science's ability to settle disputed matters conclusively through investigation and proof. Instead, James emphasizes science's unfinished nature, holding out the possibility that further research in one area could validate ideas that have been dismissed or relegated to the periphery. James advocates closer examination of the "unexamined residuum" that does not so closely fit the parameters of science, including "phenomena generally called mystical."[35] Such a viewpoint pervades *Of One Blood*, providing it with an explicit theoretical basis that many lost-race novels lack but also with a willingness to place the boundaries of science in the same location where they began, in an age before Darwin.[36] Both James and lost-race novels imply that further scientific research could confirm the very supernatural or superstitious concepts that existing science has undermined.

Of One Blood features multiple, overlapping plot lines, many of which offer sustained critique of Americans' opinions about race.[37] The novel introduces Reüel Briggs, a light-skinned African American passing for white in order to study medicine. Briggs is also, however, the character in the novel who most closely resembles the kind of theatrical scientific genius found in the Edisonades. As a doctor, Briggs immerses himself in the kind of scientific "residuum" that James advocated, blending established chemistry with studies in "volatile magnetism" (468). He produces a powder containing an artificial version of this magnetism that can restore life to individuals on the brink of death. He explains it to his peers:

> This subtle magnetic agent is constantly drawn into the body through the lungs. . . . When respiration ceases this magnetism cannot be drawn into the lungs. It must be artificially supplied. . . .
>
> This compound, gentlemen, is the exact reproduction of the conditions existing in the human body. . . . The product becomes a powder, and *that* brings back the seeming dead to life.[38]

Briggs establishes his scientific prowess by restoring life to Dianthe Lusk, an African American member of Fisk University's singers, who was thought dead by her doctors. While Briggs's scientific work gains renown, pervasive racial intolerance in the United States exerts pressure on him. He falls in love with Lusk and marries her secretly despite the fact that this means she will have to pass for white as well. When medical and academic jobs do not pan out, Briggs fears that his ethnicity has been revealed and joins an expedition to Africa in hopes of making a fortune there. In Africa, he encounters the hidden, technologically advanced city of Telessar, where he learns he is descended from their lineage of Ethiopian kings and that it is his destiny to lead their African civilization.

The most revealing moments in terms of the novel's approach to history come in its exploration portions. Briggs's expedition is led by Professor Stone, an Englishman who insists that his excavation of the Ethiopian city of Meroe will reveal "invaluable records and immense treasure" (520). Perhaps surprisingly, Stone articulates much of the Africa-centric view of the book. Briggs, whose own passing stems from fear of lost opportunities in the face of American racism, expresses concern over Stone's radical ideas:

> "Your theories may be true, Professor, but if so, your discoveries will establish the primal existence of the Negro as the most ancient source of all that you value in modern life, even antedating Egypt. How can the Anglo-Saxon world bear the establishment of such a theory?"
>
> The learned savan settled his glasses and threw back his head.
>
> "You and I, Briggs, know that the theories of prejudice are swept away by the great tide of facts. It is a *fact* that Egypt drew from Ethiopia all the arts, sciences and knowledge of which she was mistress. . . . I have even thought . . . that black was the original color of man in prehistoric times. You remember that Adam was made from the earth; what more natural than that he should have retained the color of the earth? What puzzles me is not the origin of the Blacks, but of the Whites." (520–21)

In the single comment, Hopkins's character articulates a progressivist view of science, in which researched "facts" establish paradigmatic truths, and inverts racial hierarchies by tying his claims to a pro-African version of the biblical creation narrative. As Stone later states, "The Biblical tradition is paramount to all. In it lies the greatest authority that we have for the affiliation of nations" (533).

Ultimately, Stone's blend of Old Testament history with an evolutionary time frame appears similar to the views in *Adamites and Pre-Adamites* that resulted in Alexander Winchell's firing from Vanderbilt in 1878, albeit without Winchell's assertions of black inferiority. While Winchell stated Adam had "descended from a common stock with the Negro," he proclaimed that "the inferiority of the Negro is a fact everywhere patent."[39] Winchell, then, had embraced a nonliteral interpretation of Genesis at least in part because the "degeneracy" of Adamic whites into blacks could not have occurred in the scale of time allowed by the Bible. Instead of asserting a long span of time to explain the transformation of Adamic whites to blacks, Hopkins holds out Africans as the original Edenic civilization that degenerates into whiteness. Events in the novel bear Stone's comment out; Hopkins distinctly ensures that her scientific expedition's findings will vindicate both African superiority and the "Biblical tradition."

Most of Stone's historical hypotheses are confirmed when Briggs is taken to Telessar, where he finds a lost city that would have been familiar to any readers of lost-world utopias who stumbled upon Hopkins's novel. The citizens wear garments of "golden clasps and belts," and Briggs is gifted by the citizens with a "jeweled dagger literally encrusted with gems" (549). Such wealth displays the kind of conspicuous consumption Khouri finds as pervasive in lost-race novels.[40] Hopkins's story, however, is adamantly pro-technology; her narrative never lapses into the ambivalence about technological advance that Khouri finds to be a hallmark of lost-race utopias. Telessar has technological wonders, among them a disc that allows remote viewing. This extraordinary device enables Briggs to learn of his wife's abduction and forced marriage to his scientific partner, Aubrey Livingston, back in America (575–78). Telessar also seems to bring out Briggs's previously established abilities as a telepath and mesmerist. Briggs notes: "In the heart of Africa was a knowledge of science that all the wealth and learning of modern times could not emulate" (576). Even as it deals with the kind of pseudoscientific endeavors promoted by William James, the positive portrayal of science and technology defines the narrative.

Hopkins's approach to Telessar's technology has elicited commentary from many scholars analyzing the novel's relationship with American imperialism. While the technocracy of Hopkins's vision connects her work to the Edisonade, it arguably problematizes her other, more culturally explicit goals involving her attempt to, as Lois Brown puts it, "enact a corrective and more expansive African history."[41] Martin Japtok asserts that these elements of African technology undermine Hopkins's attempt to vindicate African culture and values by making "material, technological accomplishments the standard by which any people should be measured."[42] Similarly, Kevin Gaines has argued that the novel builds African identity on an existing Western "civilizationist ideology" that by its very nature is pro-imperialist.[43] Hopkins's Ethiopian lost city intertwines advanced technology and the right to lead in a manner similar to imperialist America at the turn of the twentieth century.[44] In order to resist the prevailing American conception of race, *Of One Blood* draws from the existing American imperial imaginary by blending a technocratic viewpoint and a Protestant Christian appeal.

The novel also presents an incident of mass conversion that is nearly identical in tone to the conversion of Granville's *The Fallen Race*. The natives of Telessar are more than willing to adopt Briggs's Protestant faith when he becomes King Ergamenes. He questions Telessar's wise man, Ai, about the people's faith and is told, "Our religion is a belief in One Supreme Being, the center of action in all nature" (562). After hearing a full explanation that incorporates reincarnation and other less-than-fundamental beliefs, Briggs expresses a single concern:

> "What of the Son of man? Do you not know the necessity of belief in the Holy Trinity? Have not your Sages brought you the need of belief in God's son?" Ai looked somewhat puzzled.
> "We have heard of such a God, but have not paid much attention to it. How believe you, Ergamenes?"
> "In Jesus Christ, the Son of God," replied Reuel solemnly.
> "O Ergamenes, your belief shall be ours; we have no will but yours. Deign to teach your subjects." (562–63)

Despite the lost city's vast social and technological advancements and the fact that it is an improvement upon turn-of-the-century America in nearly every scientific and sociopolitically possible way, Protestant Christianity finds a welcome reception in Telessar. The prevailing American religiosity is the only thing Briggs can offer the African utopia, and the narrative stacks the odds toward his faith. Hopkins presents this at face value, resulting in a narrative as weighted in favor of Western religion as it is weighted in favor of African technology.

As in Serviss, the scientific discoveries in Hopkins's novel become secondary to the confirmation about pre-Darwinian history and the clarification of human racial identity that results. *Of One Blood*'s portrayal of race is at once complex and simplified—particularly as it deals with "passing" and the inadvertent incest that occurs in the novel. By the conclusion, it is revealed that Dianthe Lusk, Reuel Briggs, and Aubrey Livingston are all half-siblings with African blood, although Briggs and Lusk are married and the villainous Livingston essentially kidnaps Lusk to marry her after Briggs is declared missing in Africa. Despite these nuances, the novel's approach to race becomes clear when Briggs, after a failed attempt to save Lusk from death, returns to Telessar to marry the queen and become its legitimate ruler. As Walter Benn Michaels demonstrates, the book ultimately claims that Briggs's lineage from the Ethiopian dynasty of kings "guarantees a racial identity no amount of miscegenation can obscure."[45] Similarly, Telessar's history confirms the biblical tradition's truth, resulting in what Jennie Kassanoff calls Hopkins's "own elaborately wrought brand of monogenist creationism."[46] The biblical tradition allows for the single heritage from black ancestors described by Professor Stone earlier in the book. Hopkins asserts that scientific exploration will enable verification not just of biblical history, but her interpretation of the Bible's view of race.

In many ways, then, race becomes the vehicle in which earlier history is embodied and held up to counter the prevailing scientific worldview by both Serviss and Hopkins. Both novels end with male explorers joining by marriage the pure bloodlines of the discovered other. When Briggs's first wife dies, he becomes Telessar's ruler, "teaching his people all that he has learned in years of contact with modern culture" and marries Candace, the city's virgin queen (621). Similarly, Serviss's tale ends in marriage. Upon returning to Earth, Sydney Phillips weds Aina. The novel's final lines express concepts of race and history in a confident tone, revealing just how much emphasis the text places on racial certainties. "And thus was united, for all future time, the first stem of the Aryan race, which had been long lost, but not destroyed, with the latest offspring of that great family, and the link which had served to bring them together was the far-away planet of Mars" (254).

Marriage to a "pure" bloodline becomes the connection between a character from the modern world and the prehistory the woman represents. Kassanoff notes this same element in *Of One Blood*, finding in Candace's dark-skinned appearance a tie to "pointedly visible" African blood and in her name a tie to a long Ethiopian tradition of queens.[47] Such a wedding validates Briggs's ascension to Telessar's throne and his own African heritage. Moreover, in both works, the biblical references to history represent the system of preexisting thought that will be vindicated by these later scientific expeditions. These are the "facts" that Professor Brown hopes to find in Telessar and that seem "settled" by Edison's expedition to Mars. During a period when race was a key factor used to justify imperial endeavors, these works appeal to a concrete interpretation of race tied to both scientific discovery and the Bible.

While both stories valorize technological achievement and exploration founded on scientific principles, their approach to actual scientific discoveries is ambivalent because both texts find authority centered in earlier understandings of the world. Like the scientists debating human origins and Darwinian evolution in the latter half of the nineteenth century, both texts struggle to find ways to be both progressively scientific and to accommodate or utilize an existing, biblical paradigm. By injecting elements of a contemporary scientific debate into a lost-race adventure, Hopkins critiques the ethnocentric elements of the genre. Serviss, in contrast, brings those very elements into a tale that otherwise would be a straightforward adventure, much the way Senarens did in the Frank Reade series. Both works, however, find in their resolutions an affirmation of technology in the service of exploration and racial identity construction. The adventures clarify the past, rewriting it to create solid and certain versions of race and history. In Serviss and Hopkins, technocratic expansion becomes the stage on which contradictions between Darwinian evolution and traditional Christianity are reconciled. The very ideas that post-Darwinian science necessarily complicates—race and identity, religion and history—become concepts that can be clarified and re-simplified through technocratic exploration, holding out the possibility that scientific revisionism could be instigated by the revelations discovered in some far-off destination.

1910: Endings and Beginnings

By 1910, the heyday of dime novels had passed. The technocratic exploration narrative that they had played such a central role in developing, however, had pervaded the American imagination enough to be used frequently by writers such as the ones covered in this chapter. As the twentieth century's first decade ended, some additional developments occurred that help put the genre into perspective.

During the last years of his life, Samuel Clemens finally wrote a religious satire that engaged directly with evolutionary science and time—though it wouldn't see publication in his lifetime. *Letters from the Earth* begins with God discussing the possibility of creating life with his angels. Twain then inserts a parenthetical stage direction, "Interval of three centuries, celestial time—the equivalent of a hundred million years, earthly time," before restarting the action with the birth of life on Earth.[48] If that weren't enough of a poke at literal readings of Genesis, he later presents the angel Satan sending dispatches to Heaven reporting on his observations of life on Earth, much like young Mark Twain reporting from the Sandwich Islands or the Holy Land in the early stages of his career. Satan finds much to mock about humans, particularly the idea expressed in their Bible that the universe was made in six days. Satan notes: "For three hundred years, now, the Christian astronomer has known that his Deity didn't make the stars in those tremendous six days, but the Christian astronomer does not enlarge upon that detail. Neither does the priest. . . . According to the Book and its servants the universe is only six thousand years old. It is only within the last hundred years that studious, inquiring minds have found out that it is nearer to a hundred million."[49] It seems, in the end, Samuel Clemens couldn't resist writing a work that did many of the things he had warned Orion against in 1878, but he had retained at least some sense of propriety about appropriate ways to express religious anger and doubt. He did not attempt to publish it, and it remained unpublished until 1962.

At least some of the impetus to leaving *Letters from the Earth* unpublished came from Albert Bigelow Paine.[50] After publishing *The Great White Way* in 1901, he continued magazine editing and writing, producing more novels and a biography of political cartoonist Thomas Nast. In January 1906, based on favorable reviews of his work on Nast, he reached out to Samuel Clemens.[51] From that point forward, he was Mark Twain's official biographer, a position that ultimately gave him more fame than his fiction. The job evolved into a literary executorship, as he and Clemens's daughter Clara determined when and how to release Twain's unpublished manuscripts and memoirs, doing what they saw necessary in order to protect the Twain "brand."[52] Paine's work with Clara was preceded by lengthy discussions with Clemens himself while he lived. For over four years, Paine regularly met with the author to document his memories, opinions, and intellectual obsessions.

In July 1909, Clemens famously predicted the general time of his death by reminding Paine that Halley's comet had last passed the same year as his birth in 1835, and stating he expected to die when it returned in 1910. The author couldn't resist adding a bit of dark, mock religiosity to his pronouncement: "The Almighty has said, no doubt: 'Now here are these two unaccountable freaks; they came in together, they must go out together.'"[53] Clemens, however, did not sit around waiting for the comet to arrive; despite an ongoing battle with angina, he wrote, socialized, and traveled during the last year of his life. He accompanied friends to Bermuda in 1909, then returned home to Stormfield, his Redding, Connecticut mansion, for the holidays. During this time, his adult daughter Jean drowned in the bathtub. Early 1910 found Clemens embarking for Bermuda again while still in mourning.[54] He suffered chest pains on and off for three months before telling Paine via letter that he didn't want to die in Bermuda. Paine arrived on the island on April 4, 1910, to accompany the author on a voyage home. Clemens returned to Redding and waited under Paine's care until Clara arrived to see him.[55] He died on April 20, 1910. The man who wrote nineteenth-century America's two greatest technocratic exploration tales was gone.

While Twain attempted to convalesce in Bermuda, developments in publishing took place that further changed the technocratic exploration subgenre. Hardback novel series eventually eclipsed weekly dime-novel serials. After developing a career writing and editing for Street and Smith and other dime novel companies, publisher Edward Stratemeyer began publishing book series aimed at juvenile readers; his business eventually brought the world still-famous children's literature series such as the Hardy Boys and Nancy Drew.[56] Such series flourished as dime novels waned, making them the delivery method du jour for pre-adolescent adventure fiction. Stratemeyer commissioned four novels about Tom Swift, a boy from a mythical town of Shopton, New York, who had a knack for invention. Under the pseudonym Victor Appleton, established children's author Howard R. Garis wrote these based on story outlines written between February and April 1910. They were composed with a rapidity similar to dime novel production: Stratemeyer delivered the first three books to publisher Grosset and Dunlap on February 23, March 21, and April 27, respectively.[57] The first four were released in that single year. From their first conceptualization, then, the Tom Swift novels were designed to be an ongoing series focused on an adolescent hero whose signature trait was engineering ability.

The Tom Swift novels' impact is undeniable. As Bleiler has noted, the books sold over six million copies in twenty years and were "a major part of the cultural background when American science fiction burst forth in the genre magazines in the 1920s and 1930s."[58] They were, then, one of the primary referents for authors writing during the "Golden Age" of science fiction and were name-dropped by writers such as Isaac Asimov (who, nevertheless, expressed a preference for Stratemeyer's Rover Boys series over Swift).[59] Stratemeyer and Garis, however, clearly knew they were not creating the "boy inventor" from scratch, and the series' links to earlier Edisonades reveal their take on the tradition. Like Frank Reade Jr., Tom is the son of a successful inventor with an established shop that provides him access to tools and materials. Like Edisonade dime novels, the titles all mention the primary invention, which is almost always a vehicle. In the first book, *Tom Swift and his Motor-Cycle, or Fun and Adventures on the Road* (1910), Tom rides back and forth through New York's roadways attempting to deliver his father's engineering model to a potential investor. While some actual New York cities are mentioned, at least two fictional towns—"Reedville" and "Pompville"— suggest a tip of the hat to Senarens's boy hero and his best-known sidekick.[60] Tom's ability to repair mechanisms, from lawnmowers to butter churns, is frequently displayed.[61] The earliest Swift stories, however, differ from dime-novel Edisonades in unusual ways. Tom produces uncommon—or at least slighted augmented—vehicles, but never leaves the eastern United States, traveling only as far as North Carolina in his airship.[62] Not until the fourth novel, *Tom Swift and His Submarine Boat; or, Under the Ocean for Sunken Treasure*, do Swift and company go outside US borders. The first three Swift novels, that is to say, are technocratic novels but not *exploration* novels. The series eventually developed an exploratory bent, with Tom traveling to— and even bringing back a sidekick from—a lost city.[63] But the original 1910 novels focus mostly on life around Shopton, New York, without the international escapades of dime novels from two decades earlier. Even the technology seems strangely backward, particularly in a post–Wright Brothers world where rapid air travel is no longer a fantasy. The airship featured in the third novel is described as "that of the familiar aeroplane, but in addition to the sustaining surfaces of the planes, there was an aluminum, cigar-shaped tank . . . that would serve to keep the ship afloat even when not in motion" (27). The text not only acknowledges airplanes' ubiquity in the early twentieth century, but also passingly mentions biplanes, monoplanes, and other types of then-cutting-edge aircraft, including a race between Tom and a French monoplane pilot (80–85). Swift's part-balloon airship seems a throwback to Frank Reade or Tom Sawyer's ostentatious, intricate craft. In this, it is possible to read the earliest books in the series as a nostalgic reflection of the Reade novels rather than a refinement on Edisonade tropes.

With Twain's death and Swift's creation, the technocratic exploration subgenre opens a new chapter. The first wave of Swift stories, with their less far-flung, more secular storylines, leaves behind the kind of religious commentary that had been in Twain's work. Gernsback's *Amazing Stories* would not appear to revolutionize and codify science fiction until 1926. A year prior to that, the state of Tennessee passed a law that prohibited the teaching of evolution in science classes, resulting in the much-publicized, now-legendary trial against instructor John Thomas Scopes.[64] Ultimately, American technocratic fiction and American biblical literalism each became more pronounced and readily identifiable in the public mind, while they diverged from each other somewhat. In some moments, such as Gernsback's 1920 attempt to explain Noah's Flood in *Science and Invention*, the two would be addressed together. In popular fiction, however, the comingling became less pronounced. Instead, the technocratic exploration narrative's scientific revisionism was incorporated into the larger culture, becoming part of the common American parlance.

Conclusion

Technocratic Exploration's Legacy

Technocratic exploration stories provided Americans with one of the earliest post-Darwinian drafts of a still-influential cultural narrative. They posited that access to remote locations could produce discoveries with religious implications, that discoveries made there might result in spiritual certainty. Even variants such as Orion Clemens's *John Franklin* manuscript and Anna Adolph's *Arqtiq*, which counter rather than embrace the popular Judeo-Christian narratives of the postbellum United States, are ultimately more about resolving their characters' religious doubts than showcasing flying machines or polar exploration.

Prior to the zenith of technocratic exploration novels' popularity, many public thinkers expected outright reconciliation of religious tradition and scientific findings, including scientists like Asa Gray, ministers like Henry Ward Beecher, and academics like Princeton's James McCosh. By the turn of the century, concurrent with the development of Christian fundamentalism, the sciences most primed to mimic the approach found in technocratic exploration novels were struggling to maintain neutrality. In 1910, for example, Rudolf Kittel's lecture series, published as *The Scientific Study of the Old Testament*, considered the perceived impact of science and archaeology on biblical study. Outright asserting that "History, in the modern sense of the term, cannot be looked for in the Old Testament," he nevertheless concluded that studying conflicting evidence or "immature ideas" unsupported by science would "assist us onwards toward the correct understanding of Christianity— to understand the genesis of the perfect revelation of God in Christ."[1] Tellingly, the book includes questions from lecture attendees in a supplement at its end; the first two questions directly ask for more information on the impact of science on the creation narrative from Genesis. Kittel's replies invoke the theory of evolution and Laplace's nebular hypothesis, asserting that scientific understanding of human origins aligned with the Bible's creation story if one assumed that the six days mentioned in Genesis were not literal twenty-four-hour periods.[2] In 1910, then, Kittel reiterates the old paradigm popular with mid-nineteenth-century American theologians and found in the fiction of Verne and Serviss. In perhaps the uncanniest example of Kittel's approach, the scholar foregrounds his study with an explanation of the scientific process, explaining how hypotheses and theories develop. When he asserts, "The Copernican theory is only a hypothesis!" he does so not to undermine the scientific method in favor of biblical literalism, but to contextualize the use of the scientific method in interpreting the Bible.[3]

Today's readers are no doubt more familiar with a different approach to a similar assertion. Virtually everyone knows of the back-and-forth arguments about the teaching of evolution in US public schools, where creationists' claim against evolution frequently comes down to the oft-repeated claim that it is merely a "theory."[4] Such an argument hinges on the same concept articulated in technocratic exploration stories—that historical details presented in the Bible can and will be verified. The novels' narrative enables a pro-science, pro-technology, and pro-literalist reading of the Bible. That same promise fuels the contemporary debate. As Jeffrey P. Moran notes in his study of religious debate over the teaching of evolution, "antievolutionists have never seen themselves as antiscience."[5] In 2016, a school board in Georgia required a school to put stickers on biology textbooks, explaining to students that evolution is a "theory" rather than a fact.[6] On the Institute of Creation Research's web site, creationist John D. Morris presents an essay arguing for the validity of James Ussher's young-earth chronology—the same one Senarens used for dates in his 1893 Frank Reade Jr. story. The site notes that "numerous discoveries have come to light since Ussher. . . . But none of them change his conclusions to any great extent"; it concludes by hoping that the institute's "new work will reestablish Ussher's chronology as a standard research tool."[7] "New work" is frequently the key. When intelligent design proponents attempt to introduce concepts in public schools, as they did in Pennsylvania's Dover school district, it is couched in terms that highlight the need for more information and evolution's incomplete nature.[8] The textbook in that case, *Of Pandas and People*, provides a quintessential example of creationist science rhetoric. Each chapter ends with an assertion that current scientific understanding is inconclusive. A chapter considering gaps in the fossil record notes: "Who, or what were man's ancestors? The fossils surely don't give us any conclusive answer."[9] Discussing human development, the book states, "Darwinian scientists have sought to trace evolutionary relationships between organisms based in some principled way on similarities. But clear principles have been elusive."[10] Behind all these articulations is a variant of the ideas in technocratic exploration novels of the 1800s: more evidence will come if we keep exploring, and it will reaffirm an older viewpoint threatened by findings of contemporary science.

Of course, creationist writers' views differ in degrees; young-earth creationists, for example, tend to resent intelligent design proponents' willingness to concede the possibility of longer epochs of time and to emphasize a general creator rather than the literal God portrayed in Genesis.[11] The narrative, however, pervades larger American popular culture. Witness the multitude of documentaries on basic cable television dealing with biblical history. The History Channel's *Bible Secrets Revealed*, for example, states that it considers "a variety of historical and theological perspectives" as it discusses stories from the Bible and the scientific evidence for or against them.[12] In "The Promised Land," an episode that aired in November 2013, archaeologists and religious studies scholars are interviewed about historical evidence supporting the book of Exodus. The show features a number of scholars who claim that there is no archeological evidence to support this key biblical event. At that point, however, the narrator intercedes and poses a question: "But even if there are those who believe that the story of the Exodus might have been exaggerated, wouldn't the discovery of a piece of physical evidence prove them wrong?"[13] The series then discusses searches for the Ark of the Covenant, holding it out an object whose discovery could validate scriptural history. Why does this rhetorical question occur? Perhaps the continued popularity of the Indiana Jones films have made the "lost ark" an immediately accessible symbol for religious certainty. (What is *Raiders of the Lost Ark*, after all, if not a continuation of the technocratic exploration narrative in its episodic adventure? While it has no steam-driven robots or large flying machines, it certainly follows the template of Haggard's American lost-race imitators, commingling science and religion into a single, palatable package.)[14] The question posed by the History Channel's series, however, has a more serious goal, provoking the viewer to consider the comforting possibility of a definitive answer.

If creationist rhetoric emphasizes scientific gaps, the rhetoric of Bible history documentaries often tends to state possibilities or pose questions, suggesting scientific confirmation of biblical content without asserting it outright. Like the 1920 "What Caused the Great Flood?" from *Science and Invention*, they report scientific or historical facts, but also pose hypothetical scenarios where science, history, and the Bible align. *Mysteries of the Bible: Cain and Abel* investigates the Book of Genesis, using the same type of language Gernsback did in 1920, conflating history and religious tradition by presenting biblical figures as historical personages and biblical narratives as though they constitute attested historical data. *Decoding the Past*'s "Mysteries of the Garden of Eden," similarly, posits the evidence for the garden's location in a manner similar to the professor from *Edison's Conquest of Mars*. The research begins with pieces of scriptural information that hint at Eden's location and discusses various attempts to confirm that information. The documentary showcases exploration of targeted Middle Eastern sites, from discoveries by translator Henry Rawlinson (described as "very much an Indiana Jones-type") in the 1830s to modern use of satellite imagery to determine the possible location of the extinct rivers Pison and Gihon mentioned as adjacent to Eden in the second chapter of Genesis.[15] The documentary begins with narration that attempts to be even-handed and informative, while suggesting provocative questions. "To a literal believer in the Bible, [the Garden of Eden] is the place where God created Man. To a secular scientist, Eden is a metaphor for the origins of humanity. Either way, the first chapters of the Bible affect every person in Western civilization. . . . And now Mankind may be closer than ever to finding the Garden itself."[16] While it begins with context, the narration quickly moves into possibility, suggesting that the Garden of Eden is an actual location to be found.

These modern variants follow the line of thought established in part by technocratic exploration novels, but they also lack something: directness. Unlike variants of modern Christian literalism, nineteenth-century technocratic exploration fiction provided moments of precise affirmation. Obviously, as imaginative works, they can explicitly portray what non-fiction narratives can only suggest. Read in contrast to their modern legacy, what stands out is the unbridled enthusiasm with which technocratic exploration novels assert their religious implications. Consider Frank Reade Jr.'s exuberance at finding "God's chosen people" in *The Mysterious Mirage* (11). Or Frank's companion Whitwell's realization that "the religious and scientific world will be electrified" by their discovery of the Malakites in *Sea of Sand* (18). A Martian woman gives Professor Adelung the linguistic evidence he needs to confirm the location of the Garden of Eden, and the matter is "settled" (200). Reuel Briggs's adventures confirm human origins in precisely the manner Professor Stone promised, and "theories of prejudice are swept away by the great tide of facts" (520). Reading these tales in light of their contemporary descendants highlights just how much the technocratic exploration novel revels in portrayals of unambiguous, literal truth. These narrative moments portray the joy of discovery—and of absolute certainty. Behind all these contemporary narratives we find a longing for that kind of decisive, cathartic realization.

Where does this leave the Americanist literary scholar interested in religion and science? First, it demonstrates that the cultural conversation regarding evolution and the Bible was not limited to realist novels, religious essays, or sermons. Some of that conversation happened in books aimed at young adults, written by individuals whose true identities were hidden behind pseudonyms and whose detailed biographies are probably lost to scholars today. Despite the pervasiveness of modern cultural studies, and a tradition of examining the interplay of a broad range of cultural sources that goes back to American literary scholarship of the 1980s, we are still often slow to acknowledge the deep cultural conversation that cheap, ephemeral, "pulp" subgenres have with American faith.[17] Second, as we attempt to avoid the pitfalls of secularism in literary study, we must acknowledge the long-term allure that such narratives hold. We should continue to locate cultural conversations where American enthusiasm for science and technology overlaps with conservative religious views. Too often, they are presented as opponents when they have frequently been uneasy allies. This is not to say we need give credence to disingenuous claims to scientific impartiality, but we must consider the implications. A 2014 Gallup survey finds that 42 percent of Americans are creationists who believe God created humans in their present form, while another 31 percent believe God "guided" the evolutionary process.[18] And recent studies by O'Brien and Noy et al. suggest that many of these believers do not view themselves as anti-science. The fact remains: a large portion of nineteenth-century Americans clearly relished stories that were pro-technology and pro-Christian literalism, and many contemporary Americans still long for these kinds of narratives, something we must keep in view as we continue to reexamine the roles technocracy and religion have played in America's national identity. Only then can we really assess how far modern America has progressed from Mark Twain's era.

Notes

Introduction

1. Twain, *Tom Sawyer Abroad*, 21 (hereafter cited parenthetically).

2. See Gernsback, "A New Kind of Magazine," 3, the genre-defining editorial that described the type of stories he hoped to publish: "I mean the Jules Verne, H. G. Wells, and Edgar Allan Poe type of story—a charming romance intermingled with scientific fact and prophetic vision." Gernsback's role as the market-conscious publisher of an exclusively science-fiction magazine has traditionally led SF historians to single him out as a key figure in twentieth-century science fiction's definition. See also Moskowitz, *Explorers of the Infinite*, 11; and Ashley, *The Time Machines*, 45.

3. "What Caused the Great Flood?," 667–68.

4. See Gunn, *Alternate Worlds*, 124. *Science and Invention* had been titled *Electrical Experimenter* until August 1920. The new title signified a broader approach that ultimately included, among other things, fiction about scientists and engineers. No less a personage than inventor Alexander Graham Bell wrote the publication a letter, published in October 1920, commending them on their new title and expanded focus. See Bell, "From the Inventor of the Telephone," 609.

5. See, for example, Gunn, *Road to Science Fiction, Volume I*, xviii, and *Volume II*, ix–xiii. The Science Fiction Research Association's anthology has only two pre-1900 works: Hawthorne's "The Birth-Mark" (1843) and Wells's "The Star" (1897). See Warrick, Waugh, and Greenberg, *Science Fiction*, v–ix.

6. Landon, "Dime Novels," 198.

7. Hanson, "Lost among White Others," 523.

8. Coleman, *Preaching and the Rise of the American Novel*, 4.

9. Fessenden, "The Problem of the Postsecular," 164–65.

Chapter 1

1. See Stross, *The Wizard of Menlo Park*, 14, 30–37.

2. For a historical overview, see Landon, *Science Fiction after 1900*, 40–50; and Bleiler, "From the Newark Steam Man," 101–16.

3. Clute, "Edisonade," 368.

4. Bleiler, "Dime-Novel SF," 335.

5. Brown, *Reading the West*, 360.

6. Clute, "Edisonade," 370.

7. Portions of *The Wizard of Oz*, particularly its "Dainty China Country" chapter, have been read as a satire of US imperialism's destructive power. For more on anti-imperialist, allegorical readings of *The Wizard of Oz*, see Dighe, *The Historian's Wizard of Oz*, 37–38, and 122–23.

8. Marx, *Machine*, 29. Indeed, Marx argues that this "trope of the interrupted idyll" is a major feature of nineteenth-century American pastoralism (27). Marx's most famous examples include the locomotive whistle that interrupts Nathaniel Hawthorne's reverie in his notebooks of 1844 (12–13) and the steamboat that overruns and destroys Huck and Jim's raft in *Adventures of Huckleberry Finn* (330).

9. For catalogues of these tales, see Bleiler, *Science-Fiction*; Clareson, *Science Fiction in America*; and Nevins, *Encyclopedia of Fantastic Victoriana*.

10. See Clareson, "Lost Lands, Lost Races," 121; and Khouri, "Lost Worlds," 172.

11. Such works include the futuristic nationalist utopia of Edward Bellamy's *Looking Backward: 2000–1887* (1887), Ignatius Donnelly's futuristic dystopia *Caesar's Column* (1890), and Alvarado M. Fuller's *A.D. 2000* (1890). Again, such stories are catalogued in Bleiler, *Science-Fiction: The Early Years*, and Clareson, *Science Fiction in America*.

12. For more on the wider spectrum of pre-twentieth-century science fiction, see Aldiss, *Trillion Year Spree*; Gunn *Alternate Worlds*; and Suvin, *Victorian Science Fiction*. The term "science fiction" was coined in the twentieth century, so the nineteenth-century works addressed here were labeled in multiple ways during their era, including "scientific romance."

13. This definition of technocracy, then, does not refer solely to the idea that society-at-large should be run by engineers. It also differs from the idea of the technocracy movement that existed in the United States during the early twentieth century. In fact, the majority of Edisonade dime novels predate this specific sociopolitical movement. See Akin, *Technocracy and the American Dream*, for an articulation of the development of the Technocrat Movement.

14. For information about the rise of technocratic governments in Europe, see Bucchi, *Beyond Technocracy*.

15. For more on elements of this oft-discussed but unrealized "thoroughly technocratic vision," see Martin, "Strategies for Alternative Science," 278–86.

16. Wyatt, "Technological Determinism Is Dead," 168. See also Heilbroner, "Do Machines Make History?," 53–65, a foundational essay from 1967.

17. Said, *Culture and Imperialism*, 9.

18. Alemán and Streeby, *Empire and the Literature of Sensation*, xiv.

19. Nugent, *Habits of Empire*, 304.

20. For detailed examinations of postbellum Americans' tendency to align the concept of "American" with an exclusively Northern European–descended, Protestant identity, see Fessenden, *Culture and Redemption*, 6; Blum, *Reforging the White Republic*, 7; and Lears, *Rebirth of a Nation*, 285–91. For consideration of this identity's role in facilitating—and often hindering—US imperial expansion, see Harris, *God's Arbiters*, 23; and Love, *Race over Empire*, 7.

21. Anderson, *Imagined Communities*, 6.

22. Ibid., 25.

23. Ibid., 35.

24. Obviously, my argument rests on the fundamental assumption that texts are shaped by their culture and in turn shape it. By now, it is a well-established trope to consider the "cultural work" of specific types of fiction. See, for example, foundational work in this approach in Tompkins, *Sensational Designs*, 125–30, particularly her work on *Uncle Tom's Cabin*—a book designed to change the landscape of American hearts and minds—which simultaneously values the book's ability to clearly reflect popular women's values from its era in a manner that is "not exceptional but representative" and the book's success at proselytizing readers by presenting a narrative with the "power to work in, and change, the world."

25. Latour, *Science in Action*, 174.

26. Bruce, *The Launching of Modern American Science*, 135.

27. Ibid., 155.

28. Latour states "when one accepts the notion of 'science and technology' one accepts a package made by a few scientists to settle responsibilities, to exclude the work of the outsiders, and to keep a few leaders." Latour, *Science in Action*, 174. For more on Actor-Network Theory's ability to deemphasize this individualized view and complicate how we view such groups, see Latour, *Reassembling the Social*, 27–42. See also Sergio Sismondo, who notes that modern STS encompasses two different approaches to technology's role in knowledge-making: one that investigates technology's unique traditions and social structures that make it "autonomous" from science, and another (Latour's view) that comes from the "opposite direction" by emphasizing overlapping methodologies that blur clear boundaries between the two. Sismondo, *An Introduction*, 95.

29. Bruce, *The Launching of Modern American Science*, 128.

30. For an overview, see Godin, "The Linear Model," 635, which cites a 1959 National Science Foundation report that provides a representative definition of the linear model as understood by American industry. As Godin notes, such ideas present "a one-way cooperation" in which "pure" science begets technology's applied research and development. Godin, "The Linear Model," 642.

31. See Sismondo, *An Introduction*, 93–96.

32. Rosenberg, *Exploring the Black Box*, 139.

33. MacLeod, "Concepts of Invention," 138.

34. Bruce, *The Launching of American Science*, 130.

35. For a contrasting view to the heroic ideology that stresses "community and tradition," see Constant, "Communities and Hierarchies," 29–31.

36. De Solla Price, *Little Science, Big Science*, 3.

37. Hobsbawm, *The Age of Capital*, 271.

38. O'Brien and Noy, "Traditional, Modern, and Post-Secular," 103. They cite a 2012 finding that only 17 percent of Americans believe that "religion and science are incompatible." See Baker, "Public Perceptions of Incompatibility," 344. They also build from a 2012 survey that showed the majority of the US public has had consistently favorable attitudes about science since 1974, "except among conservatives and those who regularly attend church." See Gauchat, "Politicization of Science," 95.

39. O'Brien and Noy, "Traditional, Modern, and Post-Secular," 93.

40. Ibid., 94.

41. Asad, *Formations of the Secular*, 15.

42. Numbers, *Creation by Natural Law*, 89.

43. Ibid., 117.

44. Verne, *20,000 Leagues under the Sea*, 147.

45. Bruce, *The Launching of American Science*, 123. For more on Chambers's influence in America, see Ruse, *The Evolution-Creation Struggle*, 47–54.

46. Bruce, *The Launching of American Science*, 124; and Rossi, "Emerson, Nature and Natural Science," 127–29.

47. Numbers, *Darwinism Comes to America*, 28–29, and Numbers, *Creation by Natural Law*, 98–100.

48. Bruce, *The Launching of American Science*, 126.

49. Beecher, "Progress of Thought," 109.

50. Ruse, *The Evolution-Creation Struggle*, 137.

51. See Webb, *The Evolution Controversy in America*, 18; and Ruse, *The Evolution-Creation Struggle*, 155.

52. Hodge, *What Is Darwinism?*, 70.

53. Ibid., 26–27.

54. Ibid., 177.

55. Webb, *The Evolution Controversy in America*, 20–21.

56. For more on Gray's approach to Darwinism and his debates with Agassiz, see Croce, *Science and Religion*, 112–34.

57. Moody, *Moody's Latest Sermons*, 59.

58. Webb, *The Evolution Controversy in America*, 48.

59. Marsden, *Fundamentalism and American Culture*, 102.

60. Fundamentalism proper did not begin in America until after World War I. For more on Moody, Hodge, and the development of fundamentalism, see Butler, Wacker, and Balmer, *Religion in American Life*, 292–301. For overviews of the beginnings of fundamentalism, the Niagara Conference, and Billy Sunday, see Schlereth, *Victorian America*, 260–64.

61. Webb, *The Evolution Controversy in America*, 34. See also Roberts, *Darwinism and the Divine*, 223–27.

62. Webb, *The Evolution Controversy in America*, 33–34.

63. Ibid., 35.

64. See Dodel, *Moses or Darwin?*, 23–27. The introduction also complained about a number of larger issues causing the gap in science education in 1890s America, many of them remarkably similar to ideas voiced about modern education, including the use of "surreptitiously" religious textbooks as reading in secular schools, the lack of rigorous science courses, and the low pay of teachers (27). A short contemporary review in *Popular Science Monthly* noted that the translator's preface included "a disquisition on School Reform in the West, the burden of which is the installation of science and the elimination of all religious teaching in all the school." See "Literary Notices," 274–75. For an anecdote portraying the influence of Dodel's book in Europe, see the autobiography of German clay miner Nikolaus Osterroth in Kelly, *The German Worker*, 185–87.

Chapter 2

1. See Brown, "Science Fiction," 133; Bleiler, "Dime-Novel SF," 335; and Clute, "Edisonade," 369. Because of the reprinting, different scholars engaging with variants of the text refer to it by different titles. After its 1868 release as number 45 in *Beadle's American Novel* series, *The Steam Man of the Prairies* was reprinted under the same title as *Frank Starr's American Novels* 14 in 1869. The Beadle's publishing company then reprinted Ellis's text in 1876, retitled *The Huge Hunter; or, The Steam Man of the Prairies*, in *Beadle's Half Dime Library* 271. Gregory Pfitzer calls it *The Huge Hunter* in his scholarship, while Brown calls it *The Steam-Man of the Prairies*. I have chosen to refer to the text using its original title, rather than *The Huge Hunter*, although I acknowledge that the work's popularity was achieved under that latter title in 1876 and thereafter.

2. See Pfitzer, "Iron Dudes," 42–58.

3. Ellis, *The Steam Man of the Prairies*, 18 (hereafter cited parenthetically).

4. Brown, "Science Fiction," 132.

5. Perhaps the most famous science-fiction portrayal of the post–Civil War prosthesis comes in Jules *Verne's De la Terre á la Lune*, published in 1865 and translated as *From the Earth to the Moon* in 1873. Verne's main characters are a "Gun Club" of American munitions designers who find their lives boring when the war ends, nearly all of them in some way disfigured from their work with explosives: "Crutches, wooden legs, artificial arms with iron hooks at the wrist, rubber jaws, silver skill, platinum noses—nothing was lacking in the collection. . . . Not quite one arm for every four men, and only one leg for every three." See Verne, *From the Earth to the Moon*, 4. For overviews of Poe's influence on Verne in the context of science-fiction genre development, see Aldiss, *Trillion Year Spree*, 103; and Gunn, *Alternate Worlds*, 66.

6. Irving, *A History of New York*, 412 (hereafter cited parenthetically). For more on Irving's engagement with expansionism in *A History of New York*, see McGann, "Washington Irving," 354–55. For Irving's later skeptical views of Jacksonian Indian removal, see Antelyes, *Tales of Adventurous Enterprise*, 51–58.

7. For more on Wells and his "motive of humiliating imperial pride," see Rieder, *Colonialism*, 133.

8. Jones notes, "Just as modern readers would recognize references to Bill Clinton's libido or George W. Bush's garbled syntax, so 1809 readers picked up on the distinctly Jeffersonian traits displayed by Kieft: his red stockings, his penchant for waging war by proclamation, and his unusual scientific experiments." See Jones, *Washington Irving*, 96.

9. "Review of Knickerbocker's History," 35–36.

10. For more on Irving's similarities to Twain, see Rust, "Irving Rediscovers the Frontier," 156–63.

11. For significant historical overviews of Poe's influence on the development of SF, see Aldiss, *Trillion Year Spree*, 53–65; Gunn, *Alternate Worlds*, 55–58; Moskowitz, *Explorers of the Infinite*, 46–61; and Suvin, *Metamorphoses of Science Fiction*, 312–15. Author Damon Knight has singled out Poe's short story "Mellonta Tauta" (published in *Godey's Lady's Book* in 1849) as the earliest articulation of modern science fiction: "The first unequivocal appearance of the idea that the future will be essentially different from the past, the idea of irreversible social changes brought about by technology." See Knight, "The Early History." See also Beaver, "Introduction," vii–xxi; and Tresch, "Extra! Extra!"

12. Franklin, *Future Perfect*, 87.

13. For Poe's use of journalistic accounts regarding 1839s Indian conflicts in Florida, such as the Second Seminole War, see Silverman, *Edgar A. Poe*, 148. A number of scholars have attempted to identify a specific politician that Poe is satirizing. Daniel Hoffman names General Winfield Scott as the "real identity" of Smith. Hoffman, *Poe Poe Poe*, 197. William Whipple contends that Richard M. Johnson, then vice president and wounded veteran of the 1813 Battle of the Thames against Tecumseh, was the target of Poe's satire. See Levine and Levine, *Short Fiction*, 438. See also Warne, "If You Should Ever," 95; and Hutchisson, *Poe*, 90.

14. See Benesch, *Romantic Cyborgs*, 125, which draws its title from the author's assessment of "The Man That Was Used Up": "Its protagonist is literally a product of the wonder-working agency of modern technology, a Romantic cyborg wholly dependent on its exquisitely manufactured replacement parts." See also Marsh, "Stealing Time," 274, and Berkley, "Post-Human Mimesis," 366.

15. Haraway, "A Cyborg Manifesto," 272.

16. Ibid., 281.

17. Ibid., 273.

18. Poe, "The Man That Was Used Up," 386 (hereafter cited parenthetically).

19. Studies considering the "debunked hoax" motif in Poe's treatment of nineteenth-century science include Hoffman, *Poe Poe Poe*, 155–56, and Lee, "Probably Poe," 226.

20. Elmer, *Reading at the Social Limit*, 48–50.

21. See Willis, *Mesmerists, Monsters, & Machines*, 106; and Mead, "Poe's 'The Man That Was Used Up,'" 283–86.

22. See Benesch, *Romantic Cyborgs*, 120. See also Beuka, "Jacksonian Man of Parts," 28.

23. For more on Poe's satirical use of frontier violence, Reynolds, *Beneath the American Renaissance*, 527.

24. Whalen, *Edgar Allan Poe and the Masses*, 76.

25. Regarding these interruptions and their implications regarding the nature of human-machine hybridity, see Mieszkowski, "Exhaustible Humanity," 124; Berkley, "Post-Human Mimesis," 370; and Elmer, *Reading at the Social Limit*, 49.

26. See Poe, *Eureka*, 117, 139.

27. Recent scholarship from the field of disability studies tends to view the story in this way. See Warne, "'If You Should Ever,'" 98; Etter, "Teaching Poe," 180; and Behling, "Replacing the Patient," 58.

28. See Poe, *The Collected Works*, 391.

29. Cox, *Dime Novel Companion*, 96.

30. Johannsen, *House of Beadle and Adams*, 31, 33.

31. Brown, *Reading the West*, 165.

32. See Bleiler, "From the Newark Steam Man," for a full account of the Newark Steam Man's short-lived notoriety in the local press and its connection to the "boy inventor" genre's development. See also Landon, *Science Fiction after 1900*, 44.

33. Brown, "Science Fiction," 130.

34. Beadle's subsequent retitling of the novel as *The Huge Hunter, or the Steam Man of the Prairies* in 1876 is inexplicable, given that the Huge Hunter character appears in only a single chapter before Johnny eludes him. The decision is likely more indicative of the dime-novel publishing strategy of making old material seem new rather than an actual comment on the story's content.

35. See Pfitzer, "Iron Dudes," 52–53.

36. For a contrasting reading of the ending, which likens it to the catastrophic battle at the end of Twain's *A Connecticut Yankee in King Arthur's Court*, see Pfitzer, "Iron Dudes."

37. Bleiler calls the Tousey's first Frank Reade steam man novel a "near plagiarism" of Ellis's work. Bleiler, "From the Newark Steam Man," 105.

Chapter 3

1. See Ashley, *The Time Machines*, 21; Bleiler, *Science-Fiction*, 549; and Bleiler, "Introduction," vii. Determining the exact number of individual Reade stories is difficult due to the dime-novel publishing process of retitling/reprinting stories in multiple periodicals and missing issues in library collections.

2. Ashley, *The Time Machines*, 21. See also Moskowitz, *Explorers of the Infinite*, 120.

3. See Clute, "Edisonade," 370; and Brown, *Reading the West*, 360.

4. "Biography of Lu Senarens," 10. For a list of Senarens's other pseudonyms, see Cox, *Dime Novel Companion*, 237.

5. "L. P. Senarens Dies," 21.

6. See Gunn, *Alternate Worlds*, 74; Landon, *Science Fiction after 1900*, 40–50; and Moskowitz, *Explorers of the Infinite*, 106–27.

7. See "An American Jules Verne," *Science and Invention*, 622–23, 665; and "An American Jules Verne," *Amazing Stories*, 270–72. Both profiles were published by

Hugo Gernsback. Earlier association between Senarens and Verne occurred when Aldine Publishing Company reprinted the series in Britain between 1894 and 1906 with the heading "Jules Verne Outdone!!!" emblazoned on each cover. See Noname, *Frank Reade's Search for the Isle of Diamonds*, 1.

8. See Moskowitz, *Explorers of the Infinite*, 109; and "An American Jules Verne," *Science and Invention*, 623.

9. See Anderson, *Imagined Communities*, 37. Benedict Anderson's concept of "imagined communities" facilitates the concept of an imperial imaginary, particularly his assertion that print culture enabled a collective conceptual "simultaneity" that facilitated national consciousness.

10. Williams, "Utopia and Science Fiction," 53–54.

11. Bleiler, *Science-Fiction*, 548.

12. For anecdotal examples of written feedback from readers of Senarens's stories, see Alden, "A Writer of a Thousand Thrillers," 57; and Moskowitz, *Explorers of the Infinite*, 125. Additional information can be gleaned from unreprinted letter columns of original issues held in dime novel collections at research libraries. See Lindey, "Boys Write Back," 72–88.

13. See Landon, "Dime Novels," 198.

14. Denning, *Mechanic Accents*, 72.

15. Brown, *Reading the West*, 360.

16. Denning, *Mechanic Accents*, 72–73.

17. Ibid., 212.

18. A list of the pre-Senarens Reade stories (all of which appear in *Boys of New York* and feature Frank Reade Jr.'s father) is as follows:

> *The Steam Man of the Plains; or, the Terror of the West* (serialized from February 28 to April 24, 1876, reprinted from January 13 to March 31, 1879, and later retitled *Frank Reade and His Steam Man of the Plains; or, the Terror of the West*).
>
> *Frank Reade and His Steam Horse* (serialized from July 17 to September 25, 1876, and reprinted from July 21 to October 20, 1879).
>
> *Frank Reade and His Steam Team* (serialized from January 13 to March 31, 1880).
>
> *Frank Reade and His Steam Tally-Ho* (serialized from January 10 to April 4, 1882).

For more on elder Reade stories, see Moskowitz, *Explorers of the Infinite*, 114, who wryly notes that author "Enton was confusing numbers with originality" by simply adding to the number of steam-driven horses in each subsequent issue, a trend that ended once Senarens took over writing Reade stories.

19. See Brown, "Science Fiction," for more on the evolution of American SF from narratives such as Ellis's, in which technology normalizes the physically different body, to narratives like the Frank Reade stories that celebrate their protagonists' naturalized physicality.

20. Noname, *Frank Reade, Jr. and His Steam Wonder*, 2 (hereafter cited parenthetically as *Steam Wonder*).

21. Denning, *Mechanic Accents*, 205.

22. Bruce, *The Launching of Modern American Science*, 151.

23. Slotkin, *The Fatal Environment*, 501.

24. Noname, *Over the Andes*, 73 (hereafter cited parenthetically).

25. Clute, "Edisonade," 368.

26. Lévi-Strauss, "The Structural Study of Myth," 114.

27. Moretti, "Conjectures," 57.

28. Moretti, *Graphs, Maps, Trees*, 13.

29. See Bleiler, *Science-Fiction*, 549–50, which notes the series' frequent "clichéd incidents, often most inappropriately used, involving Indians, Western badmen, giant serpents, and bears; ethnic rancor and teasing." Bleiler sees these elements as hallmarks of Senarens's authorship.

30. See Bleiler, "A Chronological Note"; and LeBlanc, *Bibliographic Listing of the Boys of New York* and *Bibliographic Listing of Wide Awake Library*.

31. See Berrey, "Frank Reade, Jr.'s Dirigibles," 121.

32. Noname, *Frank Reade, Jr. and His Electric Boat*, 10 (hereafter cited parenthetically as *Electric Boat*).

33. Noname, *Frank Reade, Jr., Exploring a Submarine Mountain*, 3.

34. Bleiler, *Science-Fiction*, 550.

35. Senarens, *Ralph the Rover*, 20.

36. Cox, *Dime Novel Companion*, 236. See also "Biography of Lu Senarens," 11.

37. See, for example, Spencer, *The Yellow Journalism*, 123–51, and Kobre, *The Yellow Press and Gilded Age Journalism*, 118, 279–94.

38. Whitson, *Fighting for Cuba's Freedom*, 2.

39. Raymond, *Two Yankee Boys in Cuba*, in *Happy Days* 47 (September 7, 1895): 12.

40. Ibid.

41. Harris, *God's Arbiters*, 9. Such analogies persisted even after the Spanish-American War ended and Cuban self-rule was established. In 1913, for example, the Cuban government contemplated building a memorial to the US battleship Maine featuring George Washington and José Martí. See Iglesias Utset, "A Sunken Ship," 42–43.

42. Martí, *Selected Writings*, 267.

43. Raymond, *Two Yankee Boys in Cuba*, in *Happy Days* 44 (August 17, 1895): 2.

44. Ibid.

45. Raymond, *Two Yankee Boys*, in *Happy Days* 47 (September 7, 1895): 12.

46. Garne, *Maceo's Boy Guerillas*, in *Happy Days* 80 (April 25, 1896): 2.

47. See Denning, *Mechanic Accents*, 24.

48. An additional story appeared in *The Frank Reade Library* on April 15, 1898—*Six Days under Havana Harbor; or, Frank Reade, Jr.'s Secret Service Work for Uncle Sam*—after the sinking of the Maine, when war between the United States and Spain was presumed inevitable.

49. See Cox, *Dime Novel Companion*, 128–30, 132–33. Cox notes: "There is some

dispute about the number of years Hemyng spent in the United States and the authorship of some of the later Harkaway stories"; thus, it is possible the stories were written by one of the Tousey staff or Senarens himself. See Cox, *Dime Novel Companion*, 132.

50. Hemyng, "Young Jack Harkaway," 2.

51. For more on dime-novel correspondence standards and letters to Frank Reade's author, see Lindey, "Boys Write Back," 78–83.

52. "Answers to Correspondents," *Happy Days* 123 (February 20, 1897): 7.

53. "Answers to Correspondents," *Happy Days* 90 (July 4, 1896): 3.

54. Noname, *Running the Blockade*, 14.

55. Noname, *Frank Reade, Jr. in Cuba; or, Helping the Patriots with His Latest Air-Ship*, 2 (hereafter cited parenthetically).

56. "Weyler's Draconian Laws," 5. For more information, see Tone, *War and Genocide in Cuba*, 195, who notes that the decree has been sometimes ignored by present historians, partly because it was only the beginning of the brutal reconcentration policies that followed. For more information about the Cuban revolution before US intervention, see Ferrer, *Insurgent Cuba*, and Pérez, *The War of 1898*.

57. "Weyler Rules Like a Despot," 1. Weyler's reputation led to the moniker "Butcher Weyler," commonly used in the US press. See also "Editorial," 4, in the April 2, 1896, *New York Times*, which countered Weyler's claims that the insurgents were "simple bandits" rather than patriots.

58. "American Newspaper Man Liberated," *New York Times*, February 27, 1896.

59. See White, *Our War with Spain*, 245, 251.

60. "Rumor that W.G. Dygert Is Dead," *The Daily Inter-Ocean*, March 26, 1896.

61. "Must Tell Why Dygert Is Held," *Chicago Daily Tribune*, March 26, 1896.

62. Wisan, *The Cuban Crisis*, 151.

63. See Gillman, "*Ramona* in 'Our America,'" 91–94.

64. Martí, *Selected Writings*, 295.

65. Lomas, *Translating Empire*, 221–24. For a more detailed contrast of Frederick Jackson Tuner and Martí, see Thomas, "Frederick Jackson Turner," 275–92.

66. Qtd. in Lomas, *Translating Empire*, 221.

67. See White, *Our War with Spain*, 207–8, for reports of Gómez's guerilla tactics and his ability to "disappear, followed by his entire force, into the tropical underbrush."

68. See Blum, *Reforging the White Republic*, 3–19 and 91–95; and Michaels, *Our America*, 23–24. See also Love, *Race over Empire*, 1–25.

69. Harris, *God's Arbiters*, 71; see also 143–44.

70. Bleiler, *Science-Fiction*, 549. See also Bleiler, "Introduction," x, which argues that the racial tone is "somewhat softened" as the *Frank Reade Library* continued publication.

71. Slotkin, *The Fatal Environment*, 15.

72. Drinnon, *Facing West*, 50.

73. Noname, *Frank Reade and His Adventures with His Latest Invention*, 3 (hereafter cited parenthetically as *Latest Invention*).

74. Mark Twain famously uses mass electrocution to the same effect six years later

in the final battle of *A Connecticut Yankee in King Arthur's Court* (1889). See Twain, *A Connecticut Yankee*, 437–38.

75. Noname, *Frank Reade, Jr. and His Air-Ship*, 10 (hereafter cited parenthetically as *Air-Ship*).

76. Mielke, *Moving Encounters*, 2.

77. Bleiler, "Introduction," x. See also Bleiler, *Science-Fiction*, 550.

78. For a contrasting study of portrayals of African Americans in other dime novels, see Dobkin, "Treatment of Blacks," 50–56.

79. Twain, *Adventures of Huckleberry Finn*, 305.

80. Mailloux, *Rhetorical Power*, 117. See also Levy, *Huck Finn's America*, 50–62.

81. Mailloux, *Rhetorical Power*, 103–4.

82. Marx, *The Machine in the Garden*, 93, and Ellison, *Shadow and Act*, 50–52.

83. Senarens's portrayal of Maceo as a thoughtful, compassionate general continues the trend from his earlier Jack Wright storylines. For example, when Jack presents him with Spanish soldiers he has captured, Maceo replies that they must merely make an oath "not to take up arms against the Cubans again," and then should be released. When Jack asks why that is his policy, Maceo replies "We are carrying on a humane war." See Noname, *The Flying Avenger*, 15.

84. Maceo was killed on December 7, 1896. When *Frank Reade, Jr. in Cuba* was reprinted in the *Frank Reade Library* on May 14, 1897 (less than a year after it finished serialization in *Happy Days*), Maceo had already died in action and the subsequent reprinting would have no doubt taken on an elegiac quality to informed readers.

Chapter 4

1. Qtd. in Schirmer and Shalom, *The Philippines Reader*, 22–23. For more on the attribution of McKinley's quote, see Harris, *God's Arbiters*, 206–7.

2. See Nugent, *Habits of Empire*, 204. See also Love, *Race over Empire*, 7; and Harris, *God's Arbiters*, 25–30.

3. Pizer, "Evolution and American Fiction," 204.

4. Hamlin, "Sexual Selection and the Economics of Marriage," 151–52.

5. See Roberts, *Darwinism and the Divine in America*, 120.

6. O'Brien and Noy, "Traditional, Modern, and Post-Secular," 103–4.

7. "A Dime Novelist," 14.

8. Moskowitz, *Explorers of the Infinite*, 122.

9. See, for example, Noname, *Over the Andes with Frank Reade, Jr.*, 97.

10. Noname, *Across the Continent on Wings*, 19.

11. Ibid.

12. Noname, *Frank Reade, Jr., in the Sea of Sand*, 3 (hereafter cited parenthetically as *Sea of Sand*).

13. See Rieder, *Colonialism*, 21–24; and Clareson, "Lost Lands, Lost Races," 122–26.

14. Hanson, "Lost among White Others," 499.

15. See the description of Kukuanaland's history in chapter 8. Haggard, *King Solomon's Mines*, 116. See also Rieder, *Colonialism*, 22–23.

16. Rieder, *Colonialism*, 42–43.

17. The biblical connection varies depending on which contemporary translation Senarens read. The giant, seen at a distance tending a flock of mastodons, is called "ce berger antédiluvien" in Verne's text. English editions of Verne from the 1870s translate his phrase differently. The 1877 translation by Malleson, for example, calls him "this shepherd of the geologic period." See, for comparison, Verne, *Voyage au Centre de la Terre*, chap. 39; Verne, *Journey to the Interior of the Earth*, chap. 39; and Verne, *A Journey to the Center of the Earth*, chap. 36. See also Butcher, "Journey without End: On Translating Verne," n. pag.

18. Gen. 6:1; Deut. 3:1–15 (AV).

19. "The Revised New Testament," *Boston Daily Advertiser*, May 17, 1881.

20. Dana, "New Version Analyzed," 12.

21. Hendel, "Of Demigods," 21.

22. Noname, *Frank Reade, Jr., and His Electric Coach; or, the Search for the Isle of Diamonds*, I:10 (hereafter cited parenthetically as *Electric Coach*).

23. Bleiler, *Science-Fiction*, 552.

24. Deut. 3:3.

25. Deut. 3:11.

26. Deut. 3:16, 4:48.

27. Lindey, "Boys Write Back," 82–83.

28. Sarfati, "Archbishop's Achievement," n. pag.

29. Noname, *The Mysterious Mirage*, 3 (hereafter cited parenthetically).

30. 2 Chron. 9:11.

31. Haggard, *King Solomon's Mines*, 51. See also editorial notes on 287–90.

32. Bleiler notes the similarity between "Habana" and the Cuban capital city, Havana, suggesting that Senarens may be making a veiled reference to his father's homeland. See Bleiler, *Science-Fiction*, 555.

33. Rieder, *Colonialism*, 52.

34. For more on Wertham, including similarities between his work and *Traps for the Young*, see Hajdu, *The Ten-Cent Plague*, 229–39.

35. Comstock, *Traps for the Young*, 20.

36. Ibid., 25.

37. Bleiler, "Introduction," x.

Chapter 5

1. See Ketterer, *Science Fiction*, xx; Franklin, *Future Perfect*, 370; Clute, *Encyclopedia*, 368–9; and Powers, *Mark Twain*, 523. See also Lerer, "Hello, Dude," 474, which describes Hank Morgan's behavior as "Edisonian performativity" that values "stagecraft" as much as actual knowledge.

2. Sources that connect Twain to dime novels include Levy, *Huck Finn's America*, 50–63; Mailloux, *Rhetorical Power*, 100–129; Stone, *The Innocent Eye*, 159; Abate, "Bury My Heart," 115–20; and Pfitzer, "Iron Dudes," 45–50. Also note, Alan Gribben's reconstruction of Twain's library does not include any of the Tousey proto-SF dime novels.

3. Weldon, "Ned Buntline," 107. One of the first things Clemens ever printed—an 1852 satirical newspaper piece mocking the rival newspaper publisher in Hannibal—was compared to Ned Buntline's work in a printed rebuttal by the target of Clemens's satire, likely indicative of the low regard held by "serious" journalists for dime novelists. See Powers, *Mark Twain*, 54.

4. See *Mark Twain's Letters to His Publishers*, 136–37; and *Mark Twain's Notebooks and Journals, Vol. II*, 393–95.

5. For more on *Harper's Franklin Square Library* and distinctions between libraries and dime novels, see Schurman, "Nineteenth-Century Reprint Libraries," 81–87.

6. Berkove and Csicilla, *Heretical Fictions*, 14–17.

7. Fessenden, *Culture and Redemption*, 141.

8. Fulton, *The Reverend Mark Twain*, 19.

9. Bush, *Mark Twain and the Spiritual Crisis of His Age*, 13.

10. To avoid confusion, I refer to each of the Clemens brothers by first name. Following the lead of biographers such as Ron Powers, I reserve the name "Mark Twain" for use when dealing with Sam Clemens's literary output and public persona.

11. Fanning, *Mark Twain and Orion Clemens*, 170.

12. Qtd. in Fanning, *Mark Twain and Orion Clemens*, 170.

13. Fitting, *Subterranean Worlds*, 95–97.

14. See Frank and Hoeveler, "Appendix A," 251–2.

15. Samuel Langhorne Clemens to Orion Clemens, December 19, 1877 (*UCCL 01512*), Mark Twain Papers, University of California, Berkeley (hereafter cited as MTP).

16. Orion Clemens to Samuel Langhorne Clemens, December 9, 1877, MTP.

17. Orion Clemens to Samuel Langhorne Clemens, January 24, 1878, MTP.

18. Orion Clemens to Samuel Langhorne Clemens, February 5, 1878, MTP.

19. Ibid.

20. Lofficier and Lofficier, *French Science Fiction*, 736.

21. Evans, "Jules Verne's English Translations," 80.

22. Miller, "Afterword," 458–59. Also of note are the two "redactions" on Project Gutenberg's versions of *A Journey to the Center of the Earth*. The 1871 translation with added and excised material comes with a note that it is "the most reprinted version" but that another translation, also on Gutenberg, has been deemed more accurate. That other translation, from 1877 by Reverend Frederick Malleson and entitled *Journey to the Interior of the Earth*, contains a redaction noting that the clergyman/translator rephrased material when dealing with epochs of time and the biblical deluge. Arthur Evans has voiced concerns that free, downloadable versions of Verne's early translations are "giving a second—electronic—life to these Verne travesties." See Evans, "Jules Verne's English Translations," 82.

23. Evans, "Jules Verne's English Translations," 89.

24. Blount, "Afterword," 76.

25. Twain, *A Murder, a Mystery*, 62. See also Barber, "A Mysterious Manuscript." Twain attempted to sell the idea to Howells again in April 1879, and in 1884 tried "shopping the idea to other publications."

26. Samuel Langhorne Clemens to Jane Lampton Clemens, February 23, 1878 (*UCCL 01535*), *Mark Twain's Letters, 1876–80, Mark Twain Project Online.*

27. Samuel Langhorne Clemens to Orion Clemens, February 21, 1878 (*UCCL 01531*), *Mark Twain's Letters, 1876–80, Mark Twain Project Online.*

28. Ibid.

29. Orion Clemens to Samuel Langhorne Clemens, February 26, 1878, MTP.

30. Fanning, *Mark Twain and Orion Clemens*, 175.

31. Ibid., 176.

32. "Minutes of Session," 159.

33. Samuel Langhorne Clemens to Orion Clemens, May 29, 1879 (*UCCL 01662*), *Mark Twain's Letters, 1876–80, Mark Twain Project Online.*

34. Orion Clemens to Samuel Langhorne Clemens, March 17, 1878, MTP.

35. Ibid.

36. Samuel Langhorne Clemens to Orion Clemens, March 23, 1878 (*UCCL 01547*), *Mark Twain's Letters, 1876–80, Mark Twain Project Online.* A year later, Sam stated to Howells that Orion had "dropped [the Kingdom of Sir John Franklin] in the middle of the last chapter, last March." See Samuel Langhorne Clemens to William Dean Howells, February 9, 1879 (*UCCL 02529*), *Mark Twain's Letters, 1876–80, Mark Twain Project Online.*

37. Samuel Langhorne Clemens to Orion Clemens, March 23, 1878 (*UCCL 01547*), *Mark Twain's Letters, 1876–80, Mark Twain Project Online.*

38. Ibid.

39. Ibid.

40. See Cummings, *Mark Twain and Science*, 14–15. For more on the effect that his wife's formal tutoring in science had on Clemens, see Harris, *Courtship of Olivia Langdon*, 48. For information on Twain's anti-vivisectionist writings, see Fishkin, *Mark Twain's Book of Animals*, 26–33.

41. See Baetzhold, "Well, My Book Is Written," 43–44.

42. See Smith, *Mark Twain's Fable of Progress*, 43.

43. Paine, *Mark Twain's Notebook*, 171. See also Baetzhold, "Well, My Book Is Written," 44.

44. Qtd. in Stone, *The Innocent Eye*, 159.

45. Dime-novel fiction writers like Ellis also wrote sensationalized popular histories published by such libraries. See Pfitzer, *Popular History and the Literary Marketplace*, 228–81.

46. Qtd. in Stone, *The Innocent Eye*, 179.

47. For more on Cooper's influence on Western dime novels see Johannsen, *The House of Beadle*, 32; Pearson, *Dime Novels*, 4; and Brown, *Reading the West*, 3.

48. See Dodge, *Our Wild Indians*, 536, which states, "Cruelty is both an amusement and a study. So much pleasure is derived from it, that an Indian is constantly thinking out new devices of torture, and how to prolong to the utmost those already known. His anatomical knowledge of the most sensitive portions of the human frame is most accurate, and the amount of whipping, cutting, flaying, and burning that he will make a human body undergo, without seriously affecting the vital

power, is astonishing." While Jim says that he has learned of Indian cruelties from the Widow Douglas, Twain is careful to make his understanding more accurate, at least in terms of Twain's racist source material, than Tom's Cooperesque views.

49. Several scholars note that Twain abandoned the text at least partially because it would result in frankly addressing rape and its repercussions in a novel aimed at middle-class readers. Indeed, Dodge states, "I believe I am perfectly safe in the assertion that there is not a single wild tribe of Indians . . . which does not regard the person of the female captive as the inherent right of the captor" and the woman will "soon become a victim to the brutality of every member of the party of her captors" (33). See Gribben, *Mark Twain's Library*, 197; Stone, *The Innocent Eye*, 178–79; Armon and Blair, "Explanatory Notes," 272; and Pfitzer, "Iron Dudes," 43. It is worth noting that the first Frank Reade Jr. dime novel, *Frank Reade, Jr. and His Steam Wonder* (1882), fits Dodge's bigoted criticism precisely, as it features two abducted white heroines who are rescued from the Apache by Reade Jr. and his device. No harm appears to have come to them despite spending more than a year among their captors.

50. See Powers, *Mark Twain*, 560.

51. Qtd. in Gribben, *Mark Twain's Library*, 197.

52. Knoenagel, "Mark Twain's Further Use," 98.

53. Quirk, *Mark Twain and Human Nature*, 164.

54. For more on the distinction between the time-travel motif and technology in *A Connecticut Yankee*, see Ketterer, "Power Fantasy."

55. The motif of awing superstitious natives by predicting an eclipse is borrowed wholesale from the quintessential lost-race novel, H. Rider Haggard's *King Solomon's Mines* (1882). For more on Twain's imitation of Haggard, see Michelson, *Printer's Devil*, 172–73.

56. Howells, "Editor's Study," 320.

57. Martí, *On Art and Literature*, 194–95.

58. See Slotkin, *Fatal Environment*, 501–29; Rowe, *Literary Culture*, 133; Sewell, "Hank Morgan," 150.

59. Hsu, *Sitting in Darkness*, 115.

60. Rowe, "How the Boss Played," 186. For more on Morgan's failure to train his public, see Driscoll, "'Man Factories,'" 12.

61. For an overview of this debate, see Mitchell, "Lines, Circles, Time Loops," 232–33.

62. See Fulton, *The Reverend Mark Twain*, 23, 139. See also Fick, "Mark Twain's Machine Politics," 30–42; Durocher, "Mark Twain," 32–34; and Wilson, "Catholicism," 130–32.

63. Fessenden, "The Problem of the Postsecular," 154–55.

64. See Phipps, *Mark Twain's Religion*, 292.

65. See Baetzhold, "Well, My Book," 50–51; Carter, "The Meaning," 8, 440; Driscoll, "'Man Factories,'" 8; and Smith, *Mark Twain's Fable of Progress*, 55.

66. See Bush, *Mark Twain and the Spiritual Crisis*, 107–16, 213–15; and Messent, *Mark Twain and Male Friendship*, 70–72.

67. For more on Twain's continued perception of himself as a Presbyterian, see

Fulton, *The Reverend Mark Twain*, 15; and Bush, *Mark Twain and the Spiritual Crisis*, 26.

68. For more on Morgan's self-awareness of his own flaws and prejudices, see Quirk, *Mark Twain and Human Nature*, 184–89; and Cummings, *Mark Twain and Science*, 166–71.

69. See Tomes, *The Gospel of Germs*, 48, 62. For more on Twain's comments aligning cleanliness with conversion, particularly targeted at Native Americans of his era, see Driscoll, "'Man Factories,'" 11.

70. For more on Morgan's performativity, see Lerer, "Hello, Dude," 471–503.

71. See Zlatic, "Language Technologies," 468.

72. See Michelson, *Printer's Devil*, 176–78.

73. See Starr, *The Creation of the Media*, 251–52; and Folkerts and Teeter, *Voices of a Nation*, 45, 92.

74. Folkerts and Teeter, *Voices of a Nation*, 262–63.

75. See Kasson, *Civilizing the Machine*, 202.

76. For a general overview of Twain, technology, and Paige's compositor, see Cummings, *Mark Twain and Science*, 14–15; Kasson, *Civilizing the Machine*, 202–5; and Michelson, *Printer's Devil*, 10–15. See also Powers, *Mark Twain*, 521, who suggests parallels in Twain's mind between the "tinkerer-hero" Paige and Hank Morgan, and Rasmussen, *Mark Twain A to Z*, 350.

77. Qtd. in Powers, *Mark Twain*, 526.

78. Knoper, *Acting Naturally*, 160.

79. For more on technology and strong-arm politics in *A Connecticut Yankee*, see Pfitzer, "Iron Dudes," 53; and Sewell, "Hank Morgan," 141–42.

80. Samuel Langhorne Clemens to Howells, *Selected Mark Twain-Howells Letters*, 287. For an elderly Twain's reflection on imperialism and *A Connecticut Yankee*, see DeVoto, *Mark Twain in Eruption*, 211–13.

81. Anderson, "Introduction," xiii.

82. Stone, *The Innocent Eye*, 104.

83. See DeVoto, *Mark Twain's America*, 303; Stone, *The Innocent Eye*, 187; and Knoenagel, "Mark Twain's Further Use," 99.

84. Twain, *A Pen Warmed-Up in Hell*, 62.

85. Ibid.

86. For a detailed list of similarities and probable influence, see McKeithan, "Mark Twain's *Tom Sawyer Abroad*," 257–70. See also Stone, *The Innocent Eye*, 180–81; Knoenagel, "Mark Twain's Further Use," 98–99; and Gribben, *Mark Twain's Library*, 726.

87. For a persuasive close reading of the professor's disappearance, see McCoy, "Cultural Critique," 78, which suggests that, in fact, Jim throws the professor overboard to save Tom and Huck, but that Huck is "unable to bear that Jim might commit murder to save them" partly because he "believes in the mask, in the fiction that a former slave must love and respect whites."

88. See DeVoto, *Mark Twain's America*, 185; and McCoy, "Cultural Critique," 86, for more on the problematic portrayal of Jim in *Tom Sawyer Abroad*.

89. See Briden, "Twainian Epistemology," 43, which suggests that Twain had this

scene in mind when he told Fred J. Hall at Webster's publishing house that "nobody will suspect that a whole book has been written . . . merely to get that episode."

90. Budd, *Mark Twain: Social Philosopher*, 231. See also Briden, "Twainain Epistemology," 50.

91. "It Was a Bloody Fray," 1. At least one Edisonade dime novel incorporated the Valparaiso Incident into a plotline: *Tom Edison, Jr.'s Chilian Explorer; or, the Sea and Air Terror* in Street and Smith's *The Nugget Library* on March 17, 1892, mere months after the mob attack.

92. "Chile Must Make Reparation," 1.

93. "Chile Must Apologize," 1.

94. "Chile Pays Indemnity," 4.

95. Briden, "Twainian Epistemology," 47.

Chapter 6

1. Draper, *The Rocket; or, Adventures in the Air*, 3–30. For publication dates, see Bleiler, *Science-Fiction*, 208.

2. Bleiler, *Science-Fiction*, 559.

3. Ibid., 615.

4. See Nevins, *Fantastic Victoriana*, 282; and Bleiler, *Science-Fiction*, 743.

5. See Franklin, *Future Perfect*, 315.

6. Lane, *Mizora*, 103–4.

7. See Bleiler, *Science-Fiction*, 136–7, 501.

8. Astor, *A Journey in Other Worlds*, 310–86. The novel is illustrated by Dan Beard, whose work adorned original printings of Twain's *A Connecticut Yankee* and *Tom Sawyer Abroad*.

9. Granville, *The Fallen Race*, 132 (hereafter cited parenthetically).

10. Lewes, "Gynotopia," 40.

11. Adolph, *Arqtiq*, 3 (hereafter cited parenthetically).

12. Bleiler, *Science-Fiction*, 5.

13. See Kessler, "Notes toward a Bibliography," 67.

14. See Clareson, "Lost Lands, Lost Races," 121. For a later variant of this same satirical approach to lost-race novels, see H. G. Wells's "Country of the Blind" from 1904.

15. Paine, *The Great White Way*, 9 (hereafter cited parenthetically).

16. Bergman, "Oh the Poor Women," 193.

17. See Stokes, *Altar at Home*, 29, 163; and Elliott, *Angel Out of the House*, 22–26.

18. Ammerman, "Golden Rule Christianity," 196.

19. Clareson notes that "whatever else it might be, the 'lost race' novel was a love story." See Clareson, "Lost Lands, Lost Races," 123.

20. Paine, *Mark Twain: A Biography*, 631.

21. Ibid. For a contrasting view, see Bush, *Mark Twain and the Spiritual Crisis of his Age*, 7–12.

22. Ibid., 1353.

23. Campbell, "Garrett P. Serviss," 668.

24. Ibid., 670–71. See also Gunn, *Alternate Worlds*, 106–7.

25. Campbell, "Garrett P. Serviss," 668.

26. For a standard description of evolutionary theory in *War of the Worlds*, including T. H. Huxley's influence on Wells, see Gunn, *Alternate Worlds*, 91–94. See also Malia's "Public Imbecility," 82–84, for more on Wells's use of Darwin for satire in *War of the Worlds*.

27. Clute, "Edisonade," 369.

28. Serviss, *Edison's Conquest of Mars*, 12 (hereafter cited parenthetically).

29. Rieder, *Colonialism*, 136.

30. For information on Hopkins's editorial career at *Colored American Magazine* and the publication of *Of One Blood*, see Carby, "Introduction," xxix–xxxvii, xliii–xlviii.

31. For further consideration of utopian and proto-science fiction elements in Hopkins's treatment of race, see Fabi, *Passing*, 44–48, and Reid, "Utopia is in the Blood," 96–101.

32. For more on Hopkins's sense of audience and her adoption of popular literary style to appeal to them, see Carby, "Introduction," xxix; Gruesser, "Pauline Hopkins' *Of One Blood*," 80; Sundquist, *To Wake the Nations*, 570; and Bould, "Revolutionary African-American Sf," 61.

33. For more on Hopkins's use of William James, Alfred Binet, and other early psychologists, including her consideration of them in her *Colored American Magazine* columns, see Brown, *Pauline Elizabeth Hopkins*, 393–94.

34. James, "The Hidden Self," 361.

35. Ibid.

36. See Kucich, *Ghostly Communion*, 140–42, for more regarding Hopkins blending of the occult and science as a means to deal with race.

37. See Gillman, *Blood Talk*, 32–72, for a sustained analysis of the multiple interpretations of race and identity in *Of One Blood*, particularly in the context of America's fascination with Egyptology and psychology.

38. Hopkins, *Of One Blood*, 468–69 (hereafter cited parenthetically).

39. Winchell, *Adamites and Pre-Adamites*, 21–22.

40. See Khouri, "Lost Worlds," 170.

41. Brown, *Pauline Elizabeth Hopkins*, 388.

42. Japtok, "Pauline Hopkins's *Of One Blood*," 403.

43. Gaines, "Black Americans' Uplift," 450.

44. See ibid., 435, and Michaels, *Our America*, 23–24.

45. Michaels, *Our America*, 59.

46. Kassanoff, "Fate Has Linked Us Together," 167.

47. Ibid., 172.

48. Twain, *Letters from the Earth*, 12. For an overview of Twain's writing and the delayed publication process of *Letters from the Earth*, see Rasmussen, *Mark Twain A to Z*, 280–82.

49. Ibid., 21–22.

50. See Shelden, *Mark Twain, The Man in White*, 383–84.

51. Ibid., 36–37.

52. For more on Paine's oversight of Twain's legacy, see Smith, "Introduction," 2–4, and Powers, *Mark Twain: A Life*, 620–23. See also DeVoto, "Preface," vii–viii.

53. Shelden, *Mark Twain, The Man in White*, 367.

54. Ibid., 403–7; and Powers, *Mark Twain*, 626.

55. Ibid., 406.

56. See Bleiler, "From the Newark Steam Man," 110, and Dizer, "Authors," 82–84. For more on Stratemeyer's transition from writer to publisher of cloth book series, see Johnson, *Edward Stratemeyer*, 2–11. For contextualization of Stratemeyer in nineteenth-century dime novels and juvenile literature (including Twain), see Dizer, *Tom Swift and Company*, 15–29.

57. Stratemeyer Syndicate Records, New York Public Library.

58. Bleiler, "From the Newark Steam Man," 112.

59. Asimov, *In Memory Yet Green*, 107.

60. Appleton, *Tom Swift and His Motor-Cycle*, 56, 87.

61. Ibid., 131–32, 138.

62. Appleton, *Tom Swift and His Airship*, 157 (hereafter cited parenthetically).

63. For more about transitions in theme and content in the Swift series' publication history, see Johnson, *Edward Stratemeyer*, 51.

64. For a summary of the Scopes trial, see Ruse, *The Evolution-Creation Struggle*, 164–67, and Moran, *American Genesis*, 94–100.

Conclusion

1. Kittel, *The Scientific Study of the Old Testament*, 93, 255.

2. Ibid., 256–69.

3. Ibid., 5.

4. See Zimmer, "In Science," *New York Times*, April 8, 2016.

5. Moran, *American Genesis*, 104.

6. Zimmer, "In Science," *New York Times*, April 8, 2016.

7. Miller, "Can the Ussher Chronology Be Trusted?"

8. Moran, *American Genesis*, 112–15. The court found against the Board who adopted *Of Pandas and People*, at least in part because research found the book was simply a revision of a creationist textbook with the word "creator" replaced by "designer" throughout the text.

9. Davis and Kenyon, *Of Pandas and People*, 112.

10. Ibid., 133.

11. See Moran, *American Genesis*, 121.

12. *Bible Secrets Revealed*, season 1, episode 2, "The Promised Land," aired November 20, 2013 on the History Channel.

13. Ibid.

14. For an example of reviewers connecting the Indiana Jones series to Haggard, see Higgins, "Bestseller," 65; Baylen, "Review," 587; and Brantlinger, "Review," 218.

While many studies of Haggard do not mention the films, reviews of Haggard biographies often foreground Haggard's modern influence by acknowledging them.

15. *Decoding the Past*, "Mysteries of the Garden of Eden," History Channel, DVD, A&E Television, 2007.

16. Ibid.

17. Key works from the 1980s include Levine, *Highbrow/Lowbrow*; Reynolds, *Beneath the American Renaissance*; and Tompkins, *Sensational Designs*.

18. Newport, "In U.S, 42% Believe Creationist View," 2.

Bibliography

Abate, Michelle Ann. "'Bury My Heart in Recent History': Mark Twain's 'Hellfire Hotchkiss,' the Massacre at Wounded Knee, and the Dime Novel Western." *American Literary Realism* 42, no. 2 (Winter 2010): 114–28.

Adolph, Anna. *Arqtiq: A Story of the Marvels at the North Pole.* Hanford, CA: Author, 1899. Microform.

Akin, William E. *Technocracy and the American Dream: The Technocrat Movement, 1900–1941.* Berkeley: University of California Press, 1977.

Alden, Elizabeth. "A Writer of a Thousand Thrillers." *American Magazine,* 91, no. 4 (April 1921): 57.

Aldiss, Brian. *Trillion Year Spree.* London: Victor Gollancz Ltd., 1986.

Alemán, Jesse, and Shelley Streeby. *Empire and the Literature of Sensation: An Anthology of Nineteenth-Century Popular Fiction.* New Brunswick, NJ: Rutgers University Press, 2007.

"An American Jules Verne." *Amazing Stories* 3, no. 3 (June 1928): 270–72.

"An American Jules Verne." *Science and Invention* 8, no. 6 (October 1920): 622–23, 665.

"American Newspaper Man Liberated." *New York Times.* February 27, 1896: 5. *https://search.proquest.com/docview/1013626785?accountid=14505.*

Ammerman, Nancy T. "Golden Rule Christianity: Lived Religion in the American Mainstream." *Lived Religion in America: Toward a History of Practice.* Ed. David D. Hall, 196–216. Princeton, NJ: Princeton University Press, 1997.

Anderson, Benedict. *Imagined Communities: Reflections on the Origin and Spread of Nationalism.* London: Verso, 1991.

Anderson, Frederick. "Introduction." *A Pen Warmed-up in Hell: Mark Twain in Protest,* by Mark Twain, x–xviii. New York: Harper and Row, 1972.

"Answers to Correspondents." *Happy Days* 90 (July 4, 1896): 3.

"Answers to Correspondents." *Happy Days* 123 (February 20, 1897): 7.

Antelyes, Peter. *Tales of Adventurous Enterprise: Washington Irving and the Poetics of Western Expansion.* New York: Columbia University Press, 1990.

Appleton, Victor [Howard R. Garis]. *Tom Swift and His Airship, or, The Stirring Cruise of the Red Cloud.* Bedford, MA: Applewood, 1992.

———. *Tom Swift and His Motor Cycle, or, Fun and Adventures on the Road.* Bedford, MA: Applewood, 1992.

Armon, Dahlia, and Walter Blair. "Explanatory Notes." *Huck Finn and Tom Sawyer among the Indians*, by Mark Twain. Berkeley: University of California Press, 1989.

Asad, Talal. *Formations of the Secular: Christianity, Islam, Modernity.* Stanford, CA: Stanford University Press, 2003.

Ashley, Mike. *The Time Machines: The Story of the Science-Fiction Pulp Magazines from the Beginning to 1950.* Liverpool: Liverpool University Press, 2000.

Asimov, Isaac. *In Memory Yet Green.* New York: Doubleday, 1979.

Astor, John Jacob. *A Journey in Other Worlds: A Romance of the Future.* New York: D. Appleton, 1894. *Archive.org.* June 16, 2016. https://archive.org/details/ajourneyinother02astgoog.

Baetzhold, Howard G. "'Well, My Book Is Written—Let it Go. . . .'" *Biographies of Books: The Compositional Histories of Notable American Writings.* Ed. James Barbour and Tom Quirk. Columbia: University of Missouri Press, 1996.

Baker, Joseph O. "Public Perceptions of Incompatibility between 'Science and Religion.'" *Public Understanding of Science* 21, no. 1 (2012): 340–53.

Barber, Greg. "A Mysterious Manuscript." *Online News Hour.* PBS. June 25, 2001. http://www.pbs.org/newshour/updates/entertainment-jan-june01-twain_06–25/.

Baylen, J. O. Review of *Rider Haggard and the Lost Empire: A Biography*, by Tom Pocock. *English Literature in Translation* 37, no. 4 (1994): 587–91.

Beaver, Harold. "Introduction." *The Science Fiction of Edgar Allan Poe*, vii–xxi. New York: Penguin, 1976.

Beecher, Henry Ward. "Progress of Thought in the Church." *North American Review* 135, no. 309 (August 1882): 99–119. https://archive.org/details/jstor-25118195.

Behling, Laura L. "Replacing the Patient: The Fiction of Prosthetics in Medical Practice." *Journal of Medical Humanities* 26, no. 1 (Spring 2005): 53–66.

Bell, Alexander Graham. "From the Inventor of the Telephone." *Science and Invention* 8, no. 6 (October 1920): 609.

Benesch, Klaus. *Romantic Cyborgs: Authorship and Technology in the American Renaissance.* Amherst: University of Massachusetts Press, 2002.

Bergman, Jill. "'Oh the Poor Women': Elizabeth Stuart Phelps's Motherly Benevolence." *Our Sisters' Keepers: Nineteenth-Century Benevolence Literature by American Women.* Ed. Jill Bergman and Debra Bernardi, 190–212. Tuscaloosa: University of Alabama Press, 2005.

Berkove, Lawrence I., and Joseph Csicsila. *Heretical Fictions: Religion in the Literature of Mark Twain.* Iowa City: University of Iowa Press, 2010.

Berkley, James. "Post-Human Mimesis and the Debunked Machine: Reading Environmental Appropriation in Poe's 'Maelzel's Chess-Player' and 'The Man That Was Used Up.'" *Comparative Literature Studies* 41, no. 3 (2004): 356–76.

Berrey, Sara. "Frank Reade, Jr.'s Dirigibles and Speaking Trumpets: How Dime Novels Dream Technology." *Dime Novel Roundup* 74, no. 4 (2005): 115–32.

Beuka, Robert. "The Jacksonian Man of Parts: Dismemberment, Manhood, and Race in 'The Man That Was Used Up.'" *Edgar Allan Poe Review* 3, no. 1 (2002): 27–44.

Bible Secrets Revealed. "The Promised Land." Season 1, episode 2. Aired November 20, 2013, on History Channel. http://www.history.com/shows/bible-secrets-revealed/. Accessed May 9, 2016.

"Biography of Lu Senarens." *Dime Novel Round-Up* 114 (March 1942): 10–11.

Bleiler, Everett F. "A Chronological Note for the Reader." *The Frank Reade Library*. Vol 1, xv. New York: Garland, 1979.

———. "Dime-Novel SF." *The Encyclopedia of Science Fiction*. Ed. John Clute and Peter Nicholls, 334–36. New York: St. Martin's Press, 1993.

———. "From the Newark Steam Man to Tom Swift." *Extrapolation* 30, no. 2 (1989): 101–16.

———. "Introduction." *The Frank Reade Library*, 1: vii–xiv. New York: Garland, 1979.

———. *Science-Fiction: The Early Years*. Kent, OH: Kent State University Press, 1990.

Blount, Roy Jr. "Afterword." *A Murder, A Mystery, and A Marriage* by Mark Twain, 67–105. New York: W.W. Norton, 2001.

Blum, Edward J. *Reforging the White Republic: Race, Religion, and American Nationalism, 1865–1898*. Baton Rouge: Louisiana State University Press, 2005.

Bould, Mark. "Revolutionary African-American Sf before Black Power Sf." *Extrapolation* 51, no. 1 (Spring 2010): 53–81.

Brantlinger, Patrick. Review of *Rider Haggard and the Fiction of Empire: A Critical Study of British Imperial Fiction*, by Wendy R. Katz. *English Literature in Translation* 32, no. 2 (1988): 217–20.

Briden, Earl F. "Twainian Epistemology and the Satiric Design of *Tom Sawyer Abroad*." *American Literary Realism* 22, no. 1 (Fall 1989): 43–52.

Brown, Bill, ed. *Reading the West: An Anthology of Dime Westerns*. Boston: Bedford/St. Martin's, 1997.

———. "Science Fiction, the World's Fair, and the Prosthetics of Empire, 1910–1915." *Cultures of United States Imperialism*. Ed. Amy Kaplan and Donald E. Pease, 129–63. Durham, NC: Duke University Press, 1993.

Brown, Lois. *Pauline Elizabeth Hopkins: Black Daughter of the Revolution*. Chapel Hill: University of North Carolina Press, 2008.

Bruce, Robert V. *The Launching of Modern American Science, 1846–1876*. New York: Alfred A. Knopf, 1987.

Budd, Louis J. *Mark Twain: Social Philosopher*. Bloomington: Indiana University Press, 1952.

Bucchi, Massimiano. *Beyond Technocracy: Science, Politics and Citizens*. Trans. Adrian Belton. New York: Springer, 2009.

Bush, Harold K., Jr. *Mark Twain and the Spiritual Crisis of His Age*. Tuscaloosa: University of Alabama Press, 2007.

Butcher, William. "Journey Without End: On Translating Verne." *Zvi Har'El's Jules Verne Collection*. http://jv.gilead.org.il/butcher/jwe.html.

Butler, Jon, Grant Wacker, and Randall Balmer. *Religion in American Life: A Short History*. Oxford: Oxford University Press, 2000.

Campbell, James L. Sr. "Garrett P. Serviss." *Science Fiction Writers*. 2nd ed. Ed. Richard Bleiler, 667–72. New York: Scribner's, 1999.

Carby, Hazel V. "Introduction." *The Magazine Novels of Pauline Hopkins*, by Pauline Hopkins, xxix–l. New York: Oxford University Press, 1988.

Carter, Everett. "The Meaning of *A Connecticut Yankee*." *American Literature* 50, no. 3 (November 1978): 418–40.

"Chile Must Apologize." *Chicago Daily Tribune*. October 25, 1891: 1. https://search .proquest.com/docview/174572967?accountid=14505.

"Chile Must Make Reparation." *New York Times*. October 25, 1891: 1. https://search .proquest.com/docview/94876578?accountid=14505.

"Chile Pays Indemnity." *New York Times*. July 20, 1892: 4. *https://search.proquest.com/ docview/94939431?accountid=14505.*

Clareson, Thomas D. "Lost Lands, Lost Races: A Pagan Princess of Their Very Own." *Many Futures, Many Worlds*. Ed. Thomas D. Clareson, 117–39. Kent, OH: Kent State University Press, 1977.

———. *Science Fiction in America. 1870s-1930s: An Annotated Bibliography of Primary Sources*. Westport, CT: Greenwood Press, 1984.

Clute, John. "Edisonade." *The Encyclopedia of Science Fiction*. Ed. John Clute and Peter Nicholls. New York: St. Martin's Press, 1993.

Coleman, Dawn. *Preaching and the Rise of the American Novel*. Columbus: Ohio State University Press, 2013.

Comstock, Anthony. *Traps for the Young*. 1883. Ed. Robert Bremner. Cambridge, MA: Belknap Press of Harvard University Press, 1967.

Constant, Edward W. II. "Communities and Hierarchies: Structure in the Practice of Science and Technology." *The Nature of Technological Knowledge: Are Models of Social Change Relevant?* Ed. Rachel Laudan, 27–46. Dordrecht: D. Reidel, 1984.

Cox, J. Randolph. *The Dime Novel Companion*. Westport, CT: Greenwood Press, 2000.

Croce, Paul Jerome. *Science and Religion in the Era of William James, Volume 1*. Chapel Hill: University of North Carolina Press, 1995.

Cummings, Sherwood. *Mark Twain and Science: Adventures of a Mind*. Baton Rouge: Louisiana State University Press, 1988.

Dana, A. H. "New Version Analyzed." *Brooklyn Daily Eagle*. January 23, 1887: 12. Brooklyn Public Library. https://bklyn.newspapers.com/image/60773710/.

Davis, Percival, and Dean H. Kenyon. *Of Pandas and People: The Central Question of Biological Origins*. 2nd ed. Dallas: Haughton Publishing, 1993.

Decoding the Past. "Mysteries of the Garden of Eden." Produced by Gary Tarpinian and Paninee Theeranuntawat. DVD. A&E Television, 2007.

Denning, Michael. *Mechanic Accents: Dime Novels and Working-Class Culture in America*. London: Verso, 1987.

De Solla Prince, Derek. *Little Science, Big Science*. New York: Columbia University Press, 1963.

DeVoto, Bernard. *Mark Twain in Eruption*. New York: Harper and Brothers, 1922.

———. *Mark Twain's America*. Boston: Little, Brown, 1935.

———. "Preface." *Letters from the Earth* by Mark Twain, vii–viii. New York: Crest, 1963.

Dighe, Ranjit S., ed. *The Historian's Wizard of Oz: Reading L. Frank Baum's Classic as a Political and Monetary Allegory*. Westport, CT: Praeger, 2002.

"A Dime Novelist." *New York Times*, December 29, 1939: 14. *https://search.proquest .com/docview/102908270?accountid=14505*.

Dizer, John T. "Authors Who Wrote Dime Novels and Series Books, 1890–1914." *Pioneers, Passionate Ladies, and Private Eyes: Dime Novels, Series Books, and Paperbacks*. Edited by Larry E. Sullivan and Lydia Cushman Schurman, 73–85. New York: Haworth Press, 1996.

———. *Tom Swift and Company*. Jefferson, NC: McFarland, 1982.

Dobkin, J. B. "Treatment of Blacks in Dime Novels." *Dime Novel Round-Up* 55 (August 1986): 50–56.

Dodel, Arnold. *Moses or Darwin? A School Problem for All Friends of Truth and Progress*. Trans. Frederick W. Dodel. New York: The Truth Seeker Company, 1891.

Dodge, Richard Irving. *Our Wild Indians: Thirty-Three Years' Personal Experience among the Red Men of the Great West*. 1883.

Draper, Allyn. *The Rocket; or, Adventures in the Air. Pluck and Luck* 76 (November 15, 1899).

Drinnon, Richard. *Facing West: The Metaphysics of Indian-Hating and Empire-Building*. Minneapolis: University of Minnesota Press, 1980.

Driscoll, Kerry. "'Man Factories' and the 'White Indians' of Camelot: Re-reading the Native Subtext of *A Connecticut Yankee in King Arthur's Court*." *Mark Twain Annual* 2 (2004): 7–23.

Durocher, Aurele A. "Mark Twain and the Roman Catholic Church." *Journal of the Central Mississippi Valley American Studies Association* 1, no. 2 (Fall 1960): 32–43.

"Editorial." *New York Times*. April 2, 1896: 4. *https://search.proquest.com/docview/1013633905 ?accountid=14505*.

Elliott, Dorice Williams. *The Angel out of the House: Philanthropy and Gender in Nineteenth-Century England*. Charlottesville: University Press of Virginia, 2002.

Ellis, Edward S. *The Huge Hunter; or, The Steam Man of the Prairies*. 1868. New York: Beadle and Adams, 1870. http://dimenovels.lib.niu.edu/.

Ellison, Ralph. *Shadow and Act*. New York: Vintage, 1953.

Elmer, Jonathan. *Reading at the Social Limit: Affect, Mass Culture, and Edgar Allan Poe*. Stanford, CA: Stanford University Press, 1995.

Etter, William. "Teaching Poe in the Disability Studies Classroom: 'The Man That Was Used Up.'" *Approaches to Teaching Poe's Prose and Poetry*. Ed. Jeffrey Andrew Weinstock and Tony Magistrale, 177–85. New York: Modern Language Association, 2008.

Evans, Arthur B. "Jules Verne's English Translations." *Science Fiction Studies* 32, no. 1 (March 2005): 80–104.

Fabi, Giulia. *Passing and the Rise of the African American Novel.* Urbana: University of Illinois Press, 2001.

Fanning, Philip Ashley. *Mark Twain and Orion Clemens: Brothers, Partners, Strangers.* Tuscaloosa: University of Alabama Press, 2003.

Ferrer, Ada. *Insurgent Cuba: Race, Nation, and Revolution, 1868–1898.* Chapel Hill: University of North Carolina Press, 1999.

Fessenden, Tracy. *Culture and Redemption: Religion, the Secular, and American Literature.* Princeton, NJ: Princeton University Press, 2007.

———. "The Problem of the Postsecular." *American Literary History* 26, no. 1 (Spring 2014): 154–67.

Fick, Thomas H. "Mark Twain's Machine Politics: Unmetaphoring in *A Connecticut Yankee in King Arthur's Court.*" *American Literary Realism* 20, no. 2 (Winter 1988): 30–42.

Fishkin, Shelley Fisher, ed. *Mark Twain's Book of Animals.* Berkeley: University of California Press, 2010.

Fitting, Peter. *Subterranean Worlds: A Critical Anthology.* Middletown, CT: Wesleyan University Press, 2004.

Folkerts, Jean, and Dwight L. Teeter Jr. *Voices of a Nation: A History of Media in the United States.* New York: Macmillan, 1989.

Frank, Frederick S., and Diane Hoeveler, eds. *The Narrative of Arthur Gordon Pym,* by Edgar Allan Poe. 1838. Peterborough, ON: Broadview, 2010.

Franklin, H. Bruce. *Future Perfect: American Science Fiction of the Nineteenth Century.* Rev. ed. New Brunswick, NJ: Rutgers University Press, 1995.

Fulton, Joe B. *The Reverend Mark Twain: Theological Burlesque, Form, and Content.* Columbus: Ohio State University Press, 2006.

Gaines, Kevin. "Black Americans' Uplift Ideology as 'Civilizing Mission': Pauline E. Hopkins on Race and Imperialism." *Cultures of United States Imperialism.* Ed. Amy Kaplan and Donald E. Pease, 433–55. Durham, NC: Duke University Press, 1993.

Garne, Gaston. *Maceo's Boy Guerillas; or, Fighting to Free Cuba.* In *Happy Days* 4, no. 80 (April 25, 1896): 2–3.

———. *Maceo's Boys, or Young America in the Cuban War.* In *Happy Days* 5, no. 123 (February 20, 1897): 12–13.

Gauchat, Gordon. "Politicization of Science in the Public Sphere: A Study of Public Trust in the United States, 1974 to 2010." *American Sociological Review* 77, no. 2: 167–87.

Gernsback, Hugo. "A New Kind of Magazine." *Amazing Stories* 1 (July 1926): 3.

Gillman, Susan. *Blood Talk: American Race Melodrama and the Culture of the Occult.* Chicago: University Press of Chicago, 2003.

———. "*Ramona* in 'Our America.'" *José Martí's "Our America."* Ed. Jeffrey Belnap and Raúl Fernández, 91–111. Durham, NC: Duke University Press, 1998.

Godin, Benoit. "The Linear Model of Innovation: The Historical Construction of an Analytical Framework." *Science, Technology & Human Values* 31, no. 6 (November 2006): 639–67.

Granville, Austyn W. *The Fallen Race*. New York: F. T. Neely, 1892. Microform.

Gribben, Alan. *Mark Twain's Library: A Reconstruction*. 2 vols. Boston: G. K. Hall and Company, 1980.

Gruesser, John. "Pauline Hopkins' *Of One Blood*: Creating an Afrocentric Fantasy for a Black Middle Class Audience." *Modes of the Fantastic: Selected Essays from the Twelfth International Conference on the Fantastic in the Arts*. Ed. Robert A. Latham and Robert A. Collins, 74–83. Westport, CT: Greenwood Press, 1991.

Gunn, James. *Alternate Worlds*. Englewood Cliffs, NJ: Prentice-Hall, 1975.

———. *The Road to Science Fiction, Volume 1: From Gilgamesh to Wells*. Lanham, MD: Scarecrow Press, 2002.

———. *The Road to Science Fiction, Volume 2: From Wells to Heinlein*. Lanham, MD: Scarecrow Press, 2002.

Haggard, H. Rider. *King Solomon's Mines*. Ed. Gerald Monsman. Peterborough, ON: Broadview, 2002.

Hajdu, David. *The Ten-Cent Plague: The Great Comic Book Scare and How It Changed America*. New York: Farrar, Strauss, Giroux, 2008.

Hamlin, Kimberly A. "Sexual Selection and the Economics of Marriage: 'Female Choice' in the Writings of Edward Bellamy and Charlotte Perkins Gillman." *America's Darwin: Darwinian Theory and US Literary Culture*. Ed. Tina Gianquitto and Lydia Fisher, 151–80. Athens: University of Georgia Press, 2014.

Hanson, Carter F. "Lost among White Others: Late-Victorian Lost Race Novels for Boys." *Nineteenth-Century Contexts* 23, no. 4 (2002): 497–527.

Haraway, Donna. "A Cyborg Manifesto." *The Cultural Studies Reader*. 2nd ed. Ed. Simon During, 271–91. New York: Routledge, 1999.

Harris, Susan K. *The Courtship of Olivia Langdon and Mark Twain*. Cambridge: Cambridge University Press, 1996.

———. *God's Arbiters: Americans and the Philippines, 1898–1902*. New York: Oxford University Press, 2011.

Hemyng, Bracebridge. "Young Jack Harkaway among the Cuban Insurgents." *The Five Cent Wide Awake Library* 2, no. 1302 (January 15, 1897).

Heilbroner, Robert L. "Do Machines Make History?" *Does Technology Drive History?: The Dilemma of Technological Determinism*. Ed. Merritt Row Smith and Leo Marx, 53–65. Cambridge, MA: MIT Press, 1994.

Hendel, Ronald S. "Of Demigods and the Deluge: Toward an Interpretation of Genesis 6:1–4." *Journal of Biblical Literature* 106, no. 1 (March 1987): 13–26.

Higgins, Sydney. "Bestseller: Rider Haggard and the Cinema." *Sight and Sound* 56, no. 1 (Winter 1986): 64–65.

Hobsbawm, E. J. *The Age of Capital, 1848–1875*. London: Weidenfeld and Nicolson, 1975.

Hodge, Charles. *What Is Darwinism?* New York: Scribner, Armstrong, and Company, 1874. http://www.gutenberg.org/files/19192/19192-h/19192-h.htm.

Hoffman, Daniel. *Poe Poe Poe Poe Poe Poe Poe*. Garden City: Doubleday, 1972.

Hopkins, Pauline. *Of One Blood; or, The Hidden Self*. In *The Magazine Novels of Pauline Hopkins*, 441–621. New York: Oxford University Press, 1988.

Howells, W. D. "Editor's Study." *Harper's New Monthly Magazine* 80, no. 476 (January 1890): 318–23. https://hdl.handle.net/2027/uc1.31175023709952.

Hsu, Hsuan. *Sitting in Darkness: Mark Twain's Asia and Comparative Racialization.* New York: New York University Press, 2015.

Hutchisson, James M. *Poe.* Jackson: University Press of Mississippi, 2005.

Iglesias Utset, Marial. "A Sunken Ship, a Bronze Eagle, and the Politics of Memory: The 'Social Life' of the USS *Maine* in Cuba (1898–1961)." *State of Ambiguity: Civic Life and Culture in Cuba's First Republic.* Ed. Steven Palver, José Antonio Piqueras, and Amparo Sánchez Cobos, 22–53. Durham, NC: Duke University Press, 2014.

Irving, Washington. *A History of New York.* 1820. In *History, Tales and Sketches*, 362–729. New York: Library of America, 1983.

"It Was a Bloody Fray." *Chicago Daily Tribune.* October 18, 1891: 1. *https://search.proquest.com/docview/174605208?accountid=14505.*

James, William. "The Hidden Self." *Scribner's Magazine* 7, no. 3 (March 1890): 361–74. http://www.unz.org/Pub/Scribners-1890mar-00361.

Japtok, Martin. "Pauline Hopkins's *Of One Blood*, Africa, and the 'Darwinist Trap.'" *African American Review* 36, no. 3 (Autumn 2002): 403–15.

Johannsen, Albert. *The House of Beadle and Adams and Its Dime and Nickel Novels: The Story of a Vanished Literature, Vol. 1.* Norman: University of Oklahoma Press, 1950.

Johnson, Deidre. *Edward Stratemeyer and the Stratemeyer Syndicate.* New York: Twayne, 1993.

Jones, Brian Jay. *Washington Irving: An American Original.* New York: Arcade, 2008.

Kassanoff, Jennie A. "'Fate Has Linked Us Together': Blood, Gender, and the Politics of Representation in Pauline Hopkins's *Of One Blood*." *The Unruly Voice: Rediscovering Pauline Elizabeth Hopkins.* Ed. John Cullen Gruesser, 158–81. Urbana: University of Illinois Press, 1999.

Kasson, John F. *Civilizing the Machine: Technology and Republican Values in America 1776–1900.* New York: Grossman, 1976.

Kelly, Alfred, ed. *The German Worker: Working-Class Autobiographies from the Age of Industrialization.* Berkeley: University of California Press, 1987.

Kessler, Carol Fairley. "Notes Toward a Bibliography: Women's Utopian Writing, 1836–1899." *Legacy* 2, no. 2 (Fall 1985): 67–71.

Ketterer, David. "Introduction." *Tales of Wonder*, by Mark Twain. Edited by David Ketterer, xiii–xxxiii. 1984. Lincoln: University of Nebraska Press, 2003.

———. "Power Fantasy in the 'Science Fiction' of Mark Twain." *Bridges to Fantasy.* Ed. George E. Slusser, Eric S. Rabkin, and Robert Scholes, 130–41. Carbondale: Southern Illinois University Press, 1982.

Khouri, Nadia. "Lost Worlds and the Revenge of Realism." *Science-Fiction Studies* 10, no. 2 (July 1983): 170–90.

Kittel, Rudolf. *The Scientific Study of the Old Testament: Its Principal Results, and their Bearing upon Religious Instruction.* Trans. J. Caleb Hughes. London: Williams and Norgate, 1910.

Knight, Damon. "The Early History of Science Fiction." *The Literature of Science Fiction Film Series.* Dir. James Gunn. DMZ, 2002.

Knoenagel, Axel. "Mark Twain's Further Use of Huck and Tom." *International Fiction Review* 19, no. 2 (1992): 96–102.

Knoper, Randall. *Acting Naturally: Mark Twain in the Culture of Performance*. Berkeley: University of California Press, 1995.

Kobre, Sidney. *The Yellow Press and Gilded Age Journalism*. Tallahassee: Florida State University Press, 1964.

Kucich, John J. *Ghostly Communion: Cross-Cultural Spiritualism in Nineteenth-Century American Literature*. Hanover, NH: Dartmouth University Press, 2004.

Landon, Brooks. "Dime Novels and the Cultural Work of Early SF." *Science Fiction Studies* 36, no. 2 (July 2009): 198.

———. *Science Fiction after 1900: From the Steam Man to the Stars*. New York: Twayne, 1997.

Lane, Mary E. Bradley. *Mizora: A Prophecy*. 1890. Boston: Gregg Press, 1975.

Latour, Bruno. *Reassembling the Social: An Introduction to Actor-Network-Theory*. Oxford: Oxford University Press, 2005.

———. *Science in Action: How to Follow Scientists and Engineers through Society*. Stony Stratford: Open University Press, 1987.

Lears, Jackson. *Rebirth of a Nation: The Making of Modern America, 1877–1920*. New York: HarperCollins, 2009.

LeBlanc, Edward T. *Bibliographic Listing of the Boys of New York*. Fall River, MA: Edward T. LeBlanc, 1965.

———. *Bibliographic Listing of Wide Awake Library*. Fall River, MA: Edward T. LeBlanc, 1964.

Lee, Maurice S. "Probably Poe." *American Literature* 81, no. 2 (June 2009): 225–52.

Lerer, Seth. "Hello, Dude: Philology, Performance, and Technology in Mark Twain's *Connecticut Yankee.*" *American Literary History* 15, no. 3 (Fall 2003): 471–503.

Levine, Lawrence W. *Highbrow/Lowbrow: The Emergence of Cultural Hierarchy in America*. Cambridge, MA: Harvard University Press, 1988.

Levine, Stuart, and Susan Levine, eds. *The Short Fiction of Edgar Allan Poe, an Annotated Edition*. Urbana: University of Illinois Press, 1990.

Lévi-Strauss, Claude. "The Structural Study of Myth." *Literary Theory: An Anthology*. Rev. ed. Ed. Julie Rivkin and Michael Ryan, 101–15. 1998. Malden, MA: Blackwell, 2002.

Levy, Andrew. *Huck Finn's America*. New York: Simon and Schuster, 2015.

Lewes, Darby. "Gynotopia: A Checklist of Nineteenth-Century Utopias by American Women." *Legacy* 6, no. 2 (Fall 1989): 29–41.

Lindey, Sara. "Boys Write Back: Self-Education and Periodical Authorship in Late-Nineteenth-Century Story Papers." *American Periodicals* 21, no. 1 (2011): 72–88.

"Literary Notices." *Popular Science Monthly* 44, no. 12 (December 1893): 270–78. http://www.popsci.com/archive-viewer.

Lofficier, Jean-Marc, and Randy Lofficier. *French Science Fiction, Fantasy, Horror and Pulp Fiction*. Jefferson, NC: McFarland and Company, 2000.

Lomas, Laura. *Translating Empire: José Martí, Migrant Latin Subjects, and American Modernities*. Durham, NC: Duke University Press, 2008.

Love, Eric T. L. *Race over Empire: Racism and US Imperialism, 1865–1900*. Chapel Hill: University of North Carolina Press, 2004.

"L. P. Senarens Dies; Dime Novel Author." *New York Times*, December 28, 1939: 21. *https://search.proquest.com/docview/102911873?accountid=14505*.

MacLeod, Christine. "Concepts of Invention and the Patent Controversy in Victorian Britain." *Technological Change: Methods and Themes in the History of Technology*. Ed. Robert Fox, 137–53. Amsterdam: Harwood Academic Press, 1996.

Mailloux, Steven. *Rhetorical Power*. Ithaca, NY: Cornell University Press, 1989.

Malia, Jennifer. "'Public Imbecility and Journalistic Enterprise': The Satire on Mars Mania in H. G. Wells's *The War of the Worlds*." *Extrapolation* 50, no. 1 (Spring 2009): 80–101.

Mark Twain Papers. Bancroft Library, University of California, Berkeley.

Martin, Brian. "Strategies for Alternative Science." *The New Political Sociology of Science: Institutions, Networks and Power*. Ed. Scott Frickel and Kelly Moore, 272–98. Madison: University of Wisconsin Press, 2006.

Marsden, George. *Fundamentalism and American Culture*. New York: Oxford University Press, 1980.

Marsh, Clayton. "Stealing Time: Poe's Confidence Men and the 'Rush of the Age.'" *American Literature* 77, no. 2 (June 2005): 259–89.

Martí, José. *On Art and Literature*. Ed. Philip S. Foner. Trans. Elinor Randall. New York: Monthly Review Press, 1982.

———. *Selected Writings*. Ed. and trans. Esther Allen. New York: Penguin, 2002.

Marx, Leo. *The Machine in the Garden*. Oxford: Oxford University Press, 2000.

McCoy, Sharon. "Cultural Critique in *Tom Sawyer Abroad*: Behind Jim's Minstrel Mask." *Mark Twain Annual* 4 (2006): 71–90.

McGann, Jerome. "Washington Irving, *A History of New York*, and American History." *Early American Literature* 47, no. 2 (2012): 349–76.

McKeithan, D. M. "Mark Twain's *Tom Sawyer Abroad* and Jules Verne's *Five Weeks in a Balloon*." *University of Texas Studies in English* 28 (1949): 257–70.

Mead, Joan Tyler. "Poe's 'The Man That Was Used Up': Another Bugaboo Campaign." *Studies in Short Fiction* 23 (1986): 281–86.

Messent, Peter. *Mark Twain and Male Friendship: The Twichell, Howells, & Rogers Friendships*. Oxford: Oxford University Press, 2009.

Michaels, Walter Benn. *Our America*. Durham, NC: Duke University Press, 1995.

Michelson, Bruce. *Printer's Devil: Mark Twain and the American Publishing Revolution*. Berkeley: University of California Press, 2006.

Mielke, Laura L. *Moving Encounters: Sympathy and the Indian Question in Antebellum Literature*. Amherst: University of Massachusetts Press, 2008.

Mieszkowski, Jan. "Exhaustible Humanity: Using Up Language, Using Up Man." *Differences: A Journal of Feminist Cultural Studies* 14, no. 2 (Summer 2003): 106–33.

Miller, John D. "Can the Ussher Chronology Be Trusted?" *Institute for Creation Research*. http://www.icr.org/article/can-ussher-chronology-be-trusted.

Miller, Walter James. "Afterword." *20,000 Leagues under the Sea* by Jules Verne, 448–61. Trans. Mendor T. Brunetti. New York: Signet, 2001.

"Minutes of Session." *National Archives of the PC(USA)*. Presbyterian Historical Society. April 29, 1879.

Mitchell, Lee Clark. "Lines, Circles, Time Loops, and Mark Twain's *A Connecticut Yankee in King Arthur's Court*." *Nineteenth-Century Literature* 54, no. 2 (1999): 230–48.

Moody, Dwight Lyman. *Moody's Latest Sermons*. Chicago: The Bible Institute Colportage Association, 1900. *The Sermon Depository*. http://www.sermondepository .com/Books/dlmoodybooks/ Moody_s_Latest_Sermons.pdf.

Moran, Jeffrey P. *American Genesis: The Evolution Controversies from Scopes to Creation Science*. New York: Oxford University Press, 2012.

Moretti, Franco. "Conjectures on World Literature." *New Left Review*. January-February 2000, 54–68. https://newleftreview.org/II/1/franco-moretti-conjectures -on-world-literature.

———. *Graphs, Maps, Trees: Abstract Models for a Literary History*. London: Verso, 2005.

Moskowitz, Sam. *Explorers of the Infinite*. Cleveland: World Publishing Company, 1963.

"Must Tell Why Dygatt Is Held." *Chicago Daily Tribune*. March 26, 1896: 2. *ProQuest Historical Newspapers*. February 5, 2009.

Nevins, Jess. *Encyclopedia of Fantastic Victoriana*. Austin, TX: Monkeybrain Books, 2005.

Newport, Frank. "In US, 42% Believe Creationist View of Human Origins." *Gallup*. June 2, 2014. http://www.gallup.com/poll/170822/believe-creationist-view-human -origins.aspx.

Noname [Lu Senarens]. *Across the Continent on Wings; or, Frank Reade, Jr.'s Greatest Flight*. In *The Frank Reade Library* 34 (May 13, 1893). University of South Florida Libraries. http://digital.lib.usf.edu/SFS0000002/00038/1x—.

———. *The Flying Avenger; or, Jack Wright Fighting for Cuba*. In *The Boys' Star Library* 376 (April 10, 1896).

———. *Frank Reade, Jr., and His Adventures with His Latest Invention*. In *The Frank Reade Library*. Vol. 2. Ed. E. F. Bleiler. New York: Garland, 1980.

———. *Frank Reade, Jr., and His Air-Ship*. In *The Frank Reade Library*. Vol. 2. Ed. E. F. Bleiler. New York: Garland, 1980.

———. *Frank Reade, Jr., and His Electric Boat*. In *The Frank Reade Library*. Vol. 2. Ed. E. F. Bleiler. New York: Garland, 1980.

———. *Frank Reade, Jr., and His Electric Coach; or, The Search for the Isle of Diamonds, Part I*. In *The Frank Reade Library*. Vol. 4. Ed. E. F. Bleiler. New York: Garland, 1985.

———. *Frank Reade, Jr., and His Electric Coach; or, The Search for the Isle of Diamonds, Part II*. In *The Frank Reade Library*. Vol. 4. Ed. E. F. Bleiler. New York: Garland, 1985.

———. *Frank Reade, Jr., and His Steam Wonder*. In *The Frank Reade Library*. Vol. 2. Ed. E. F. Bleiler. New York: Garland, 1980.

———. *Frank Reade, Jr., Exploring a Submarine Mountain; or, Lost at the Bottom of the Sea*. In *The Frank Reade Library*. Vol. 5. Ed. E. F. Bleiler. New York: Garland, 1985.

———. *Frank Reade, Jr., in Cuba; or, Helping the Patriots with His Latest Air-Ship*. In *The Frank Reade Library*. Vol. 9, no. 159. Ed. E. F. Bleiler. New York: Garland, 1979.

———. *Frank Reade, Jr., in the Sea of Sand; and His Discovery of a Lost People*. In *The Frank Reade Library*. Vol. 3. Ed. E. F. Bleiler. New York: Garland, 1985.

———. *Frank Reade's Search for the Isle of Diamonds*. London: Aldine Publishing Company, n.d.

———. *The Mysterious Mirage; or, Frank Reade, Jr.'s Desert Search for a Secret City with His New Overland Chaise*. In *The Frank Reade Library*. Vol. 7. Ed. E. F. Bleiler. New York: Garland, 1985.

———. *Over the Andes with Frank Reade, Jr., in His New Air-Ship; or, Wild Adventures in Peru*. In *Dashing Diamond Dick and Other Classic Dime Novels*. Ed. J. Randolph Cox, 70–137. New York: Penguin, 2007.

———. *Running the Blockade; or, Jack Wright Helping the Cuban Filibusters*. In *The Boys' Star Library* 374 (March 13, 1896).

———. *Six Days under Havana Harbor; or, Frank Reade, Jr.'s Secret Service Work for Uncle Sam*. In *The Frank Reade Library* 183 (April 15, 1898). *Nickels and Dimes from the Collections of Johannsen and LeBlanc*. Northern Illinois University Libraries. http://dimenovels.lib.niu.edu.

Nugent, Walter. *Habits of Empire: A History of American Expansion*. New York: Alfred A. Knopf, 2008.

Numbers, Ronald L. *Creation by Natural Law: Laplace's Nebular Hypothesis in American Thought*. Seattle: University of Washington Press, 1977.

———. *Darwinism Comes to America*. Cambridge, MA: Harvard University Press, 1998.

O'Brien, Timothy L., and Shiri Noy. "Traditional, Modern, and Post-Secular Perspectives on Science and Religion in the United States." *American Sociological Review* 80, no. 1: 92–115.

Paine, Albert Bigelow. *The Great White Way*. 1901. New York: Arno Press, 1975.

———. *Mark Twain: A Biography*. 3 vols. New York: Harper and Brothers, 1912.

———. *Mark Twain's Notebook*. New York: Harper and Brothers, 1935.

Pearson, Edmund. *Dime Novels; or, Following an Old Trail in Popular Literature*. Boston: Little, Brown, 1929.

Peréz, Louis A. Jr. *The War of 1898: The United States and Cuba in History and Historiography*. Chapel Hill: University of North Carolina Press, 1998.

Pfitzer, Gregory M. "'Iron Dudes and White Savages in Camelot': The Influence of Dime-Novel Sensationalism on Twain's *A Connecticut Yankee in King Arthur's Court*." *American Literary Realism* 27, no. 1 (Fall 1994): 42–58.

———. *Popular History and the Literary Marketplace, 1840–1920*. Amherst: University of Massachusetts Press, 2008.

Pizer, Donald. "Evolution and American Fiction: Three Paradigmatic Novels." *American Literary Realism* 43, no. 3 (Spring 2011): 204–22.

Poe, Edgar Allan. *The Collected Works of Edgar Allan Poe*. Ed. Thomas Ollive Mabbott. 3 vols. Cambridge, MA: Belknap Press of Harvard University Press, 1978.

———. *Eureka*. Ed. Stuart Levine and Susan F. Levine. Urbana: University of Illinois Press, 2004.

Phipps, William E. *Mark Twain's Religion.* Macon, GA: Mercer University Press, 2003.

Powers, Ron. *Mark Twain: A Life.* New York: Free Press, 2005.

Quirk, Tom. *Mark Twain and Human Nature.* Columbia: University of Missouri Press, 2007.

Rabkin, Eric S. "Science Fiction and the Future of Criticism." *PMLA* 114, no. 3 (May 2004): 457–73.

Rasmussen, R. Kent. *Mark Twain A to Z: The Essential Reference to His Life and Writings.* New York: Facts on File, 1995.

Raymond, P. T. *Two Yankee Boys in Cuba; or, Fighting with the Patriots.* In *Happy Days* 2, no. 44 (August 17, 1895): 2–3.

———. *Two Yankee Boys in Cuba; or, Fighting with the Patriots.* In *Happy Days* 2, no. 47 (September 7, 1895): 2–3.

Reid, Mandy A. "Utopia is in the Blood: The Bodily Utopias of Martin R. Delany and Pauline Hopkins." *Utopian Studies* 22:2 (2011) 91–103.

"Review of Knickerbocker's History of New York." *Boston Review* 8 (February 1810): 123–28 In *Critical Essays on Washington Irving.* Ed. Ralph M. Alderman. Boston: G. K. Hall, 1990.

"The Revised New Testament." *Boston Daily Advertiser* 137:117 (May 17, 1881): n.p. http://find.galegroup.com/ncnp/infomark.do?.

Reynolds, David S. *Beneath the American Renaissance.* Cambridge, MA: Harvard University Press, 1988.

Rieder, John. *Colonialism and the Emergence of Science Fiction.* Middletown, CT: Wesleyan University Press, 2008.

Roberts, Jon H. *Darwinism and the Divine in America: Protestant Intellectuals and Organic Evolution, 1859–1900.* Madison: University of Wisconsin Press, 1988.

Rosenberg, Nathan. *Exploring the Black Box: Technology, Economics, and History.* Cambridge: Cambridge University Press, 1994.

Rossi, William. "Emerson, Nature and Natural Science." *A Historical Guide to Ralph Waldo Emerson.* Ed. Joel Myerson, 101–50. New York: Oxford University Press, 2000.

Rowe, John Carlos. "How the Boss Played the Game: Twain's Critique of Imperialism in *A Connecticut Yankee in King Arthur's Court.*" *The Cambridge Companion to Mark Twain.* Ed. Forrest G. Robinson, 175–92. Cambridge: Cambridge University Press, 1995.

———. *Literary Culture and US Imperialism.* Oxford: Oxford University Press, 2000.

"Rumor That W. G. Dygert Is Dead." *Daily Inter-Ocean.* March 26, 1896: 1. http://find.galegroup.com/ncnp/infomark.do?.

Ruse, Michael. *The Evolution-Creation Struggle.* Cambridge, MA: Harvard University Press, 2005.

Rust, Richard D. "Irving Rediscovers the Frontier." *Washington Irving: The Critical Reaction.* Ed. James W. Tuttleton, 156–63. New York: AMS Press, 1993.

Sarfati, Jonathan. "Archbishop's Achievement: James Ussher's Great Work Annals of the World is Now Available in English." *Creation* 26, no. 1 (December 2003): 24–27. http://creation.com/archbishops-achievement.

Said, Edward W. *Culture and Imperialism.* New York: Vintage, 1993.

Schirmer, Daniel B., and Stephen Rosskamm Shalom. *The Philippines Reader: A History of Colonialism, Neocolonialism, Dictatorship, and Resistance.* Boston: South End Press, 1987.

Schlereth, Thomas J. *Victorian America: Transformations in Everyday Life, 1876–1915.* New York: Harper Perennial, 1991.

Schurman, Lydia Cushman. "Nineteenth-Century Reprint Libraries: When a Book was not a Book." *The Oxford History of Popular Print Culture, Vol 6. US Popular Print Culture 1860–1920.* Edited by Christine Bold, 81–96. Oxford: Oxford University Press, 2012.

Senarnes, Lu [Senarens, Lu]. *Ralph, the Rover; or, The Cuban Patriots.* Chicago: Pictorial Printing Company, 1879.

Serviss, Garrett P. *Edison's Conquest of Mars.* 1898. Burlington, ON: Apogee, 2005.

Sewell, David R. "Hank Morgan and the Colonization of Utopia." *Mark Twain: A Collection of Critical Essays.* Edited by Eric J. Sundquist, 140–53. Englewood Cliffs, NJ: Prentice-Hall, 1994.

Shelden, Michael. *Mark Twain: The Man in White.* New York: Random House, 2010.

Silverman, Kenneth. *Edgar A. Poe: Mournful and Never-ending Remembrance.* New York: HarperCollins, 1991.

Sismondo, Sergio. *An Introduction to Science and Technology Studies.* 2nd ed. Chichester: Wiley-Blackwell, 2010.

Slotkin, Richard. *The Fatal Environment: The Myth of the Frontier in the Age of Industrialization, 1800–1890.* Norman: University of Oklahoma Press, 1985.

Smith, Harriet Elinor. "Introduction." *The Autobiography of Mark Twain, Volume 1.* Ed. Harriet Elinor Smith et al., 1–58. Berkeley: University of California Press, 2010.

Smith, Henry Nash. *Mark Twain's Fable of Progress: Political and Economic Ideas in "A Connecticut Yankee."* New Brunswick, NJ: Rutgers University Press, 1964.

Spencer, David R. *The Yellow Journalism: The Press and America's Emergence as a World Power.* Evanston, IL: Northwestern University Press, 2007.

Starr, Paul. *The Creation of the Media: Political Origins of Modern Communications.* New York: Basic Books, 2004.

Stokes, Claudia. *The Altar at Home: Sentimental Literature and Nineteenth-Century American Religion.* Philadelphia: University of Pennsylvania Press, 2014.

Stone, Albert E. Jr. *The Innocent Eye: Childhood in Mark Twain's Imagination.* Hamden, CT: Archon, 1970.

Stratemeyer Syndicate Records. Manuscripts and Archives Division. The New York Public Library. Astor, Lenox, and Tilden Foundations.

Stross, Randall. *The Wizard of Menlo Park.* New York: Three Rivers Press, 2007.

Sundquist, Eric J. *To Wake the Nations.* Cambridge, MA: Belknap Press of Harvard University Press, 1993.

Suvin, Darko. *Metamorphoses of Science Fiction: On the Poetics and History of a Literary Genre.* New Haven, CT: Yale University Press, 1979.

———. *Victorian Science Fiction in the UK: The Discourses of Knowledge and of Power.* Boston: G. K. Hall, 1983.

Thomas, Brooks. "Frederick Jackson Turner, José Martí, and Finding a Home on the Range." *José Martí's "Our America."* Edited by Jeffrey Belnap and Raúl Fernández, 275–92. Durham, NC: Duke University Press, 1998.

Tomes, Nancy. *The Gospel of Germs: Men, Women, and the Microbe in American Life.* Cambridge, MA: Harvard University Press, 1998.

Tompkins, Jane. *Sensational Designs: The Cultural Work of American Fiction, 1790–1860.* New York: Oxford University Press, 1985.

Tone, John Lawrence. *War and Genocide in Cuba, 1895–1898.* Chapel Hill: University of North Carolina Press, 2006.

Tresch, John. "Extra! Extra! Poe Invents Science Fiction!" *The Cambridge Companion to Edgar Allan Poe.* Ed. Kevin J. Hayes, 133–47. Cambridge: Cambridge University Press, 2002.

Twain, Mark [Samuel Langhorne Clemens]. *Adventures of Huckleberry Finn.* 1885. Ed. Susan K. Harris. Boston: Houghton Mifflin, 2000.

———. *A Connecticut Yankee in King Arthur's Court.* 1889. Ed. Bernard L. Stein. Berkeley: University of California Press, 1979.

———. *Huck Finn and Tom Sawyer among the Indians, and Other Unfinished Stories.* Berkeley: University of California Press, 1989.

———. *Letters from the Earth.* Ed. Bernard DeVoto. 1962. New York: Crest, 1963.

———. *Mark Twain's Letters, 1876–80.* Ed. Michael B. Frank and Harriet Elinor Smith. Mark Twain Project Online. Berkeley: University of California Press, 2002, 2007. www.marktwainproject.org.

———. *Mark Twain's Letters to his Publishers, 1867–1894.* Ed. Hamlin Hill. Berkeley: University of California Press, 1967.

———. *Mark Twain's Notebooks and Journals, Volume II (1877–1883).* Ed. Frederick Anderson, Lin Salamo, and Bernard L. Stein. Berkeley: University of California Press, 1975.

———. *A Murder, a Mystery, and a Marriage.* New York: W.W. Norton, 2001.

———. *A Pen Warmed-up in Hell: Mark Twain in Protest.* Ed. Frederick Anderson. New York: Harper and Row, 1972.

———. *Selected Mark Twain-Howells Letters: 1872–1910.* Ed. Frederick Anderson, Williams, M. Gibson, and Henry Nash Smith. Cambridge, MA: Belknap Press of Harvard University Press, 1967.

———. *Tom Sawyer Abroad.* 1894. The Oxford Mark Twain Series. Ed. Shelley Fisher Fishkin. New York: Oxford University Press, 1996.

Verne, Jules. *From the Earth to the Moon.* Trans. Lowell Bair. New York: Bantam, 1993.

———. *A Journey to the Interior of the Earth.* Trans. Frederick Malleson. London: Ward, Lock, and Company. 1877. http://www.gutenberg.org/cache/epub/3748/pg3748-images.html.

———. *A Journey to the Centre of the Earth.* Griffith and Farran, 1871.

———. *20,000 Leagues under the Sea.* Trans. Mendor T. Brunetti. 1969. New York: Signet, 2001.

———. *Voyage au Centre de la Terre.* 1864. http://www.gutenberg.org/cache/epub/4791/pg4791-images.html.

Warne, Vanessa. "'If You Should Ever Want an Arm': Disability and Dependence in Edgar Allan Poe's 'The Man That Was Used Up.'" *Atenea* 25, no. 1 (June 2005): 95–105.

Warrick, Patricia S., Charles G. Waugh, and Martin H. Greenberg. *Science Fiction: The Science Fiction Research Association Anthology*. New York: Longman, 1988.

Webb, George E. *The Evolution Controversy in America*. Lexington: University Press of Kentucky, 1994.

Weldon, Fred. "Ned Buntline." *The Mark Twain Encyclopedia*. Ed. J. R. LeMaster and James D. Wilson, 105. New York: Garland Press, 1993.

"Weyler Rules Like a Despot." *New York Times*. February 24, 1896: 1. *https://search .proquest.com/docview/1013619655?accountid=14505.*

"Weyler's Draconian Laws." *New York Times*. February 18, 1896: 5. *https://search .proquest.com/docview/95433787?accountid=14505.*

Whalen, Terence. *Edgar Allan Poe and the Masses: The Political Economy of Literature in Antebellum America*. Princeton, NJ: Princeton University Press, 1999.

"What Caused the Great Flood?" *Science and Invention* 8, no. 6 (October 1920): 606, 667–68.

White, Trumbull. *Our War with Spain for Cuba's Freedom*. Chicago: The Chas. B. Ayer Company, 1898.

Whitson, John H. *Fighting for Cuba's Freedom: A Story of the Struggle for Cuban Independence. New York Ledger* 52, no. 16 (April 25, 1896): 1–3.

Williams, Raymond. "Utopia and Science Fiction." *Science Fiction: A Critical Guide*. Ed. Patrick Parrinder, 52–65. London: Longman, 1979.

Willis, Martin. *Mesmerists, Monsters, & Machines: Science Fiction and the Cultures of Science in the Nineteenth Century*. Kent, OH: Kent State University Press, 2006.

Wilson, James D. "Catholicism." *Mark Twain Encyclopedia*. Ed. J. R. LeMaster and James D. Wilson, 130–32. New York: Garland, 1993.

Winchell, Alexander. *Adamites and Preadamites: or A Popular Discussion Concerning the Remote Representatives of the Human Species and their Relation to the Biblical Adam*. Syracuse: John T. Roberts, 1878.

Wisan, Joseph E. *The Cuban Crisis as Reflected in the New York Press (1895–1898)*. New York: Columbia University Press, 1934.

Wyatt, Sally. "Technological Determinism Is Dead; Long Live Technological Determinism." *The Handbook of Science and Technology Studies*. 3rd ed. Ed. Edward J. Hackett et al., 165–80. Cambridge, MA: MIT Press, 2008.

Zimmer, Carl. "In Science, It's Never 'Just a Theory.'" *New York Times*, April 8, 2016.

Zlatic, Thomas D., "Language Technologies in *A Connecticut Yankee*." *Nineteenth-Century Literature* 45, no. 4Fn (March 1991): 453–77.

Index